PRINCIPLES
OF
COMPARATIVE PSYCHOLOGY

PRINCIPLES OF COMPARATIVE PSYCHOLOGY

NICKY HAYES

A volume in the series
Principles of Psychology

Series Editors
Michael W. Eysenck
Simon Green
Nicky Hayes

LEA LAWRENCE ERLBAUM ASSOCIATES, PUBLISHERS LEA
Hove (UK)   Hillsdale (USA)

Lawrence Erlbaum Associates Ltd., Publishers
27 Palmeira Mansions
Church Road
Hove
East Sussex, BN3 2FA
UK

British Library Cataloguing in Publication Data

A catalogue record for this book is available from the British Library

ISBN 0-86377-292-7 (hbk)
ISBN 0-86377-293-5 (pbk)
ISSN 0965-9706

Cartoons by Sanz
Illustrations by Kevan Burke
Subject index compiled by Sue Ramsey
Cover design by Stuart Walden and Joyce Chester
Printed and bound by BPC Wheatons Ltd, Exeter

Contents

To my niece Olivia, with my love

Acknowledgements

This book is the outcome of some 20 years' interest in comparative psychology, and I would like to thank Jim Wright of Leeds University for his encouragement throughout that time. I am also deeply appreciative of the help I have received from Simon Green in the preparation of the final manuscript. My thanks, too, are due to John Rogers of Leeds University, to Pete Sanders, to Steven Rose, and to many A level psychology teachers, for their assistance, feedback, and encouragement.

Nicky Hayes

Comparative psychology and evolution

1

Comparative psychology is concerned with the systematic study of animal behaviour. Psychologists have been interested in animals throughout the history of psychology: partly because learning about animals may help to inform us about ourselves; but also because animals are intrinsically interesting as subjects of study in their own right. In this book, we will be looking at some of the basic findings and theories of comparative psychology, as well as at some of the ways that comparative theories have been applied to our understanding of human beings.

Animals and human beings

The relationship between human beings and animals is a very ancient one. Animals have lived with human beings, worked for human beings, been kept by human beings, been hunted by human beings, and have been observed by them. The legends and traditions of every non-technological society provide accounts of the relationships between people and animals, and of the animals themselves, providing explanations for how their distinctive behaviours have come to be, or why they are like they are. This interest in the other creatures that share this planet persists even in technological societies: television documentaries about animal behaviour abound, people keep pets of various kinds, and go to see animals in reserves and zoos.

Interest in animals, then, is a very long-standing human tradition. Partnership with animals, in hunting, tracking, or seeking out foodstuffs, seems to be almost equally old. Human beings have used dogs, pigs, cassowaries, and many other species in day to day living, in a relationship in which the animal expresses its own behavioural inclinations in such a way that the human being can also benefit from them; and people have also observed the behaviour of other, wild species in order to identify the appropriate time to seek out sources of food.

With the development of agriculture came a change in the nature of the relationship between animal and human being. Gatherer-hunter societies depended on finding, and knowing about, plants that had grown randomly—or at least, according to evolved systems of dispersal and ecology. That isn't to say that such people were passive: for example, the Native Australians have used fire to regenerate areas of bush in a regular and periodic manner for over 30,000 years; and the Native Americans managed their plains and forests in such a way as to encourage as much growth and life as possible. But, ultimately, these societies encouraged whole systems, and left matters such as what plants would grow where to nature.

Agricultural societies, as they emerged, took such matters literally into their own hands. They decided what should grow where, and when. This produced a new type of relationship with the natural world: human beings were taking charge more, and the relationship was becoming less of a partnership. A similar change can be seen in the systematic use of animals in more structured ways, like the use of horses and cattle in farming, which appeared as agricultural societies developed. The vagaries of climate ensured that total control was never possible, and human beings learned to work within the constraints offered by their environment; but the relationship was nonetheless qualitatively different.

As technological societies emerged from agricultural ones, attitudes became even more exploitative: plants, land, and water were seen as "resources", there to be used, and animals, too, became perceived as a resource to be used. While people have continued to keep animals as companions, and even as partners, these new approaches have become the social norm. It is only recently that human beings have begun to question the nature of our relationship with the rest of the world.

The Western philosophical tradition

Cartesian dualism

The Western philosophical tradition, beginning with the Greek philosophers, established a conceptual framework for this new relationship. The Greek philosopher Heraclitus put forward the argument that human beings are qualitatively different from, and superior to, animals because they have souls, whereas animals do not. The concept became a significant strand in Western thought, eventually becoming part of the influential distinction made by Descartes. In essence, Descartes not only reiterated this view, but also proposed that animals, unlike human beings, do not think, and that their behaviour is entirely determined by physiological mechanisms and instincts. Descartes acknowledged that human beings, too, possess physiological mechanisms—his account of the structure and functioning of the eye is often considered to be one of the very first psychological studies. But he then went on to propose that the human mind is entirely separate from, and independent of, the body anyway.

This distinction had many far-reaching effects, such as legitimising the introduction of the factory system to industry (if peoples' minds and souls are separate and distinct, then it doesn't matter what you do with their bodies), as well as having effects on medicine, and on comparative psychology. For comparative psychology, it established a framework which stated that, on the one hand, animals were entirely different from human beings as far as feelings and thoughts were concerned, so it was not necessary to worry about causing pain or distress; whereas, on the other hand, it was a good idea to study animals because their physiological mechanisms could be expected to operate on similar principles to those of humans.

It must be remembered, of course, that it wasn't specifically Descartes himself who was drawing out these implications. Rather, his theory, influential as it was, established the set of assumptions in society which made these conclusions possible. In many non-technological societies, a different set of social assumptions—for example, that animals could feel, sense, and work things out in a similar way to humans, although not as well—had produced different outcomes.

With the advent of the theory of evolution, proposed by Charles Darwin in 1859, the assumed qualitative distinction between human beings and animals was seriously challenged, and the social furore that resulted was enormous. By proposing a direct developmental link between animals and human beings, Darwin's theory laid open to question the whole idea of human superiority to animals, which by then had become such a central tenet of Western industrial society that to challenge it was unthinkable. As evolutionary theory took hold in society, it was quickly redefined in terms of "progress", and various steps were taken to "show" that human beings were at the top of the evolutionary scale, and therefore still superior to other animals. Similarly, a number of "popular" versions of evolutionary theory came to be used in political debates. Although these were sometimes linked only loosely with the theory that Darwin had proposed, they exerted their influence, not just on the socio-political ideas of their society but also on comparative psychology. Because evolution is such a fundamental concept in comparative psychology—one that is effectively taken for granted as underlying the discipline—we will be looking at it in more detail later in this chapter.

Empiricism

Descartes was not alone in providing a framework of assumptions that helped to set the groundwork for Western technological society. Other empiricist philosophers of the 16th and 17th centuries had also produced ideas which became established as part of social knowledge. In part, these were based on the idea that human beings only had access to five types of information, provided by the external five senses of vision, hearing, taste, smell, and touch. This led towards assumptions about the nature of objective reality, and the idea that it is possible somehow to stand apart from that world—to know about it without being affected by it. This assumption exerted a powerful influence over methodology and theories in psychology.

But psychologists and physiologists now know that there are also internal, kinaesthetic senses, which provide internal information about internal states and reactions in the body. We don't just experience outside things, we also respond to them, and we receive information (however unconsciously) about our responses. Moreover, we perceive actively: we select what we will pay attention to, and shape the information that we receive in terms of our own prior assumptions and ideas. So it is not really possible for human beings to be detached from the world: our own responses are part of our experience too, and therefore we are involved with the world, not separate from it. Although this might seem like a digression, the idea of objectivity and detachment, and the idea that humans are somehow separate from, and above, the world around them has formed a powerful influence in the development of psychological knowledge, as well as in society.

Associationism

The empiricist philosopher John Locke argued that when the human being was first born, the mind was simply a blank slate—a *tabula rasa*—waiting to be written on by experience. Locke believed that our experience shapes who we are and who we become—and therefore he also believed that, given different experiences, human beings would have different characters. The influence of these ideas was profound, particularly for the new colonies in America, for example, because these were conscious attempts to make a new start and to form a new society. The new society was to operate on a different basis from that of European culture, which was based on the feudal system in which people's place in society was almost entirely determined by birth, and which therefore tended to emphasise innate characteristics. Locke's emphasis on the importance of experience in forming the human being provided an optimistic framework for those trying to form a different society.

Locke believed that the way that experience built up to have these large-scale effects was through association. An external stimulus (such as a cup) would produce a response from the person (such as drinking), and the two would become linked. That would be a learned association. This type of learning formed the basis for human experiences because one small bit of learning would link up with another small bit, and this in turn would link with a third, and so on until long chains of learning were built up. Eventually, through chains of associations, the person would be able to have quite complex experiences, like, say, being able to recognise someone at a glance from their picture.

Behaviourism

Locke's associationism formed the underlying approach of the school of thought known as *behaviourism*, proposed by the American psychologist J.B. Watson in 1913. Watson argued that the understanding of both human beings and animals needed to take place through the study of their behaviour, because trying to infer what was going on in the mind was unscientific and not open to objective scrutiny. Behaviour, Watson argued, should be studied in terms of the associations between the external stimulus and the behavioural response, and the way that chains of stimulus and response could be combined into complex sequences of behaviour and action.

To Watson, the stimulus-response unit was the "atom" of psychology. Following the physicists' model of the atom, or the biological model of the simple cell, Watson argued that psychology should begin by studying the simplest form of stimulus-response link. Animal learning, he argued, would be relatively uncontaminated by other kinds of factors; and so would be a suitable area of study to form the foundation of the new science. If stimulus-response links were the basic foundation of behaviour, then all stimulus-response links would be similar in essence, in the same way that different atoms in physics, or cells in biology were then considered to be similar in essence.

Behaviourism has been a fundamental concept in comparative psychology. It dominated American and British (though not European) psychology for much of the 20th century, only becoming seriously challenged when technological developments made a more objective study of the mind possible, and cognitive psychology came to the fore. As such, behaviourism also brought the study of animals into prominence in "mainstream" psychology: the use of the term "organism" to describe the individual became common throughout the discipline, and emphasised the assumption that human and animal psychologies were essentially the same thing. Although psychology as a whole has moved on from this point, the influence of this type of comparative psychology can still be identified in the methodologies and practices of many areas of research.

Themes and traditions in comparative psychology

The American comparative tradition

The perspectives and philosophies that have just been outlined exerted a strong influence over the way that comparative psychology emerged and developed. In terms of its own more recent history, this branch of psychology developed from two very different traditions of academic thought. One of these comes from the behaviourist tradition which has just been described. This meant that, in America in particular, the study of animal behaviour tended to concentrate on laboratory studies, looking at various types of stimulus-response learning, and at behavioural aspects of motivation, such as curiosity and exploration. The idea of the stimulus-response link as the "pure" form of learning led to the idea that studying this type of learning under laboratory conditions would result in identifying the essential features of learning that were common to all organisms.

Because the idea was to conduct these studies in research conditions that were as "uncontaminated" as possible, so that only the causal features of the behaviour could be identified, standard laboratory animals, such as pigeons and small rodents—particularly the albino rat —were used extensively in these experiments, although some studies also extended to monkeys and apes. The principles of classical and operant conditioning, which we will be looking at in Chapter 2, were two fundamental psychological concepts established during this period.

The European ethological tradition

The second tradition in modern comparative psychology is the European *ethological* approach. This developed through the 18th and 19th centuries with the work of amateur naturalists, who would engage in the meticulous documentation of animal behaviour, often submitting papers to learned societies, and reporting their observations to journals. Around the beginning of the 20th century, this approach became systematised into a more formal discipline, which gradually came to centre on the work of the European ethologists Konrad Lorenz and Niko Tinbergen.

As an approach, ethology emphasises the study of behaviour in its natural environment. Rather than studying animals in the laboratory, ethologists are concerned that the behaviour should be seen in respect to the animal's own habitat, so that the way the animal, its environment, and its peers interact can be taken into account. Although ethologists do sometimes perform simple experiments to clarify the relationship between a behaviour and its apparent functions, for the most part, ethological studies are observational, and are concerned with observing, recording, and correlating different features of behaviour, as they occur in context.

As can be seen, the comparative and ethological traditions are quite different; but from about the 1950s or so they began to come together, as researchers in the different fields began to learn from each other. Modern comparative psychology now draws from both of these traditions, and in this book we will be looking at research from both, as each has made important contributions to our understanding of animal behaviour.

Levels of explanation

The process of describing behaviour itself isn't always as simple as it might appear to be. Whenever we make any observations, we are interpreting what we see—that's an unavoidable feature of the process of perception itself. As a result, it is very easy for those interpretations to influence our judgement, so comparative psychologists have tended to try to be very explicit about exactly what kind of behaviour they are describing at any given moment. Hinde (1970) argued that, in terms of scientific description of behaviour, it is necessary to distinguish between two different *levels of description*. The first level, and perhaps the most fundamental one for the comparative psychologist, is concerned with simply describing actions. For example, Lorenz (1958) performed a series of observations of the stereotyped nature of duck courtship displays, showing that the same actions were performed every time. These observations involved the meticulous description of the physical movements that the duck actually made: the movements that resulted as its muscles contracted. So this level of description includes words like "running", "swallowing", or "bobbing the head".

The second level of description is to do with descriptions which focus on the effect that the animal has on its environment. Terms like "drinking", "pressing a lever" or "running away" are all externally focused—they emphasise the context of the action, and are not just a simple description of muscle actions. This is an important distinction to make, because it is very easy to confuse the two levels, but doing so can colour what we are actually saying to the point of even changing its meaning. Describing the duck as "bobbing its head to its mate" does not assume that the purpose of the duck's behaviour is already known. If we are investigating what the purpose of a particular behaviour is, it is generally better to avoid jumping to conclusions about what it is for. At the same time, the second type of description is useful when we are trying to take a broad, contextual view of what is going on—and that is as important for comparative psychology as the detailed observations.

This idea of *levels of explanation* is another important concept in modern comparative psychology—indeed, in psychology as a whole. This is the idea that behaviour can be looked at in a number of different ways, ranging from minute description to wide contexts, and that each of these ways may be useful depending on what the focus of interest is. If we are interested in, say, the mechanisms by which animals communicate, then minute behavioural descriptions of, say, the actions that a dog makes when it encounters another dog are useful to us. But if we are trying to look at general tendencies of behaviour, like territoriality or dominance, then we might be more interested in a general description of the outcome of the behaviour of the two dogs, rather than the minute specific accounts of exactly what they do. Both levels of description are useful, and at some point they could be combined to aid our understanding of the whole thing. It isn't the case that only one level of explanation is right and the others are wrong; but it is the case that we need to be clear about which level of explanation we are using, and what we are using it for.

The principle of parsimony

When we are choosing appropriate levels of explanation for describing behaviour, there are two basic principles that we need to keep in mind. One of these is the *principle of parsimony*, which is also sometimes known as Occam's razor, after the medieval bishop William of Occam. Essentially, this principle is about the scientific way of choosing between two alternative explanations. If you have two possible explanations for something, but one of them is reasonably straightforward whereas the other is elaborate and complex, it is more scientific, or at least economical, to choose the simpler explanation. The simpler explanation is viewed as being inherently more plausible, simply because it invokes fewer necessary conditions.

A related, and very influential idea in comparative psychology derives from one of the very first comparative textbooks, written by Lloyd Morgan in 1894. It is generally referred to as *Lloyd Morgan's canon*. Morgan proposed that, when we are looking for explanations for animal behaviour, we should always go for the explanation that is "lower in the phylogenetic scale" of behavioural mechanisms. In other words, if it is possible to explain an act or sequence of actions as having developed through learning or habit, then it is more appropriate to do so than to use "higher-order" ideas like "understanding" or "belief", to explain how the animal has developed the behaviour.

Morgan was warning against the error known as *anthropomorphism*: the attribution of human traits or characteristics to animals. At the time that he was writing, accounts of animal behaviour were often extremely anecdotal, and tended to anthropomorphise badly; so as a warning it was very necessary. But some modern researchers, particularly those exploring animal cognition or animal language, feel that this principle may have been carried too far in modern cognitive psychology. The idea that animals operate entirely either through genetically controlled behaviour or by learned stimulus-response associations—which are pretty well the lowest levels of explanation—became so dominant in comparative psychology, that it became almost automatic for comparative psychologists to argue that animals never did any thinking whatsoever—that they were entirely unable to process information mentally. Some researchers feel that this viewpoint seriously held back the study of animal cognition—a research area that is only now beginning to develop more fully.

"HOW *DO* THESE POOR, MINDLESS CREATURES SURVIVE...?.... QUIT SHOVING ME, BENSON!..YOU'LL GIVE US AWAY...."

Areas of research in comparative psychology

In 1963, Niko Tinbergen identified four main areas of comparative research into animal behaviour: development, mechanisms, function, and evolution. Traditional comparative psychology used to be mainly concerned with development—how an individual grows and matures—and with the mechanisms by which behaviour occurs within the individual. But with the merging of ethology and comparative psychology, the discipline became broader, so that more recent trends have resulted in comparative psychologists looking more closely at the functions of behaviour—what purpose it serves in the animal's life—and also at the evolutionary contexts and implications of both animal behaviour and animal cognition.

In this book, we will be looking at examples of each of these four areas. We will look at how some forms of behaviour develop within the individual, such as birdsong, or attachment and mothering behaviour in primates. We will also look at some of the neurological research underpinning these behaviours: research into the process of imprinting, for example, has revealed complex interactions between neurology and behaviour. This brings together the two different levels of ethological and neurophysiological research into what has recently become known as neuroethology, and allows us to look at some of the basic mechanisms that underpin the behaviour.

When we look at aspects of animal behaviour such as territoriality, aggression, and peacemaking, we will be looking at some of the theories and models that have been proposed to explain the functions of such forms of animal behaviour; and throughout this book, whether explicitly or implicitly, we will be looking to see how, and what, research evidence contributes to our knowledge of evolution and its processes.

The theory of evolution

Because the theory of evolution forms such a very basic assumption within the whole of comparative psychology—it is, after all, the reason why we make comparisons between species in the first place—it is worth spending some time looking at the theory. Evolutionary theory itself, as put forward by Charles Darwin, was a general framework describing how things happen. Since it was first published, scientists and others have been interpreting and developing the theory. Some of these interpretations have been scientific attempts to come to terms with how things work. Others have been popular versions of the idea, going way beyond the scientific data. For the rest of this chapter, we will look at evolutionary theory and at some of the variations on it which have been developed since it was first put forward.

In 1859, Charles Darwin put forward a theory which essentially proposed that the huge diversity of different species of animals and plants could ultimately be seen as having arisen as a result of a developmental process, occurring over many generations, in which species had gradually changed to adapt better to their environment. These changes occurred as a result of the ordinary process of genetic variability, and this in turn was possible because random changes occurred within the genetic stock of the species. Genetic mutations would occur from time to time, and these would make an individual who possessed them slightly different from other members of its species.

Darwin proposed that, if this difference proved beneficial, then there would be a good chance that the individual would be stronger and healthier than the others. This meant that (a) it would be more likely to find a mate and reproduce; and (b) it would be more likely to survive in difficult conditions—for example, if it were stronger it would be more able to endure a severe winter than others. So it would be more likely to breed, and to pass on its beneficial gene to its offspring; so both it and its offspring would be more likely to survive hard times. As the weaker ones died out and the stronger ones survived, the population would come to contain a greater proportion of those sharing the beneficial characteristic, and fewer of those without it, until eventually, many generations later, virtually all the members of that particular population would have the characteristic.

One of the experiences that helped Darwin to formulate this theory was his observation of the different species of finch on the various islands of the Galapagos, off the coast of South America, which he had seen while travelling as naturalist on the HMS *Beagle*, collecting information about the various plants and animals. It was clear to Darwin that the finches had at some time or other developed from the same species—common ancestors, which might perhaps have found their way to the islands by accident. But each group of finches on each island was subtly different, and better adapted to the diet that was available to it on the islands. On one island, where the main diet was hard-shelled seeds, the finches had developed thick, heavy beaks; on another, where their food was insects hiding under rocks, the beaks had become elongated; and there was even one species of finch that had become a "vampire", drinking the blood of the other animals on the island.

The important theme which was apparent, Darwin noticed, was that the finches had adapted to their environments. Each island offered slightly different opportunities for survival, and the finch species had changed until it fitted into the island's ecology. This raised the idea of an *ecological niche*: a place in the total ecology which offers opportunities for survival. The most important factor that will make an animal stronger or more robust than others is likely to be a good, dependable food source. If an animal uses a source of food which is freely available, because there is a lot of it, because other species do not use it, or because it is better at getting it than members of another species, then it is more likely to be well fed. So it will be fitter and well adapted to its place in the total ecology of that environment.

The implication, then, was that the reason why a genetic change would prove beneficial to a species would be because it would adapt the individual to its environment better: it would help it to exploit a particular ecological niche. But it's important to remember that this is only the case as long as the environment doesn't change. If the environment changes, then there will be new demands on the species, and different characteristics will prove beneficial. If an animal is too closely adapted to one single environment, it may not be able to survive at all if that environment changes.

Darwin stated, in his theory, that evolutionary change would be gradual and systematic, and he kept to this view although he was warned against it by his friend and defender T. H. Huxley. Huxley saw no reason why evolution should not vary in its pace, with periods of environmental change producing a rapid rate of evolutionary change while periods of environmental stability would produce a much slower rate of change. Huxley's views were echoed by Eldredge and Gould (1972), who argued that the fossil record of evolutionary change suggested a process of *punctuated equilibrium*—that evolutionary changes would tend to produce periods of relative stability, or equilibrium, which were interrupted from time to time by periods of rapid change.

Phylogeny

Darwin's theory doesn't just talk about how a particular species changes to adapt to its environment. It is wider than that, because Darwin was proposing that the survival of the fittest might be the basic mechanism which had produced the whole of life on Earth. Not just individual species, but whole groups of species—*phyla*—could be considered to have evolved, very gradually, as a result of this mechanism. Darwin argued that it is possible to detect relationships between different species, and that these relationships are actually manifestations of their common evolutionary history. For example, although wolves and dogs are now different species, at one time in the past they will have shared a common ancestor species, which gradually differentiated into the two different types—in the same way that the several different species on the Galapagos had all evolved from one group of finches which had somehow arrived on the islands.

The idea of *phylogeny*—that groups of species had developed through evolutionary mechanisms, rather than being created by God—was really the one that caused such a stir in 19th-century Western society. The idea that a species itself could be changed gradually was well-established: farmers and dog-breeders had been breeding different animals by mating certain individuals together for centuries. But the accepted orthodox idea was that it was God who had created the different species, and huge debates occurred when Darwin's theory was finally published. He had held it back for many years, fearing just such a furore, and in the end it was Huxley (who became nicknamed "Darwin's bulldog") who championed the cause, and argued the case with the religious and orthodox establishment, while Darwin himself stayed in semi-retirement in the country. There are still some religious fundamentalists who do not accept the idea, in much the same way as there are still people who believe that the Earth is flat. But in science as a whole, and in biology and comparative psychology in particular, the concept of phylogeny is both established and accepted.

The evolutionary tree

The evolution of species is often portrayed in terms of a *phylogenetic tree.* This is intended to provide a broad description of which different groups of species evolved from one another, and also of roughly when they did so. An example of such a phylogenetic tree is given on the next page. The more recently evolved species are shown near the top of the tree, those which evolved a long time ago are shown near the bottom. The branches represent "families" of species, or phyla.

Inevitably, however, a diagram like this is a little deceptive, because it only really shows those species that are still alive, or that we know about from the fossil record. Species have been evolving throughout the history of life on Earth, and they have also been dying out as the world has changed and the particular environments to which they were fitted have disappeared. Many of them have disappeared without trace. Although the recent catastrophic impact of human beings on the world's ecology has speeded up that process dramatically, and has changed environments in ways that may be irreversible, the process of species evolution and species extinction has been happening in a less dramatic form throughout the history of organic life.

A phylogenetic tree

The phylogenetic tree that is illustrated here is one that is based on the idea of genetic similarities. Species are grouped together because they share a large proportion of their genes: for example, something like 99% of genetic material is the same in human beings and chimpanzees. It's the one that has been chosen here, because it maps most closely on to general evolutionary theory. But there are other ways of devising phylogenetic trees: for example, the biological approach known as *cladistics* groups species together on the basis of the observable characteristics that they share, like similarity in the shapes of fins or wings.

The phylogenetic scale

Another concept that derives from the idea of phylogeny, and which can sometimes be useful, is that of the *phylogenetic scale*. This is an idea that we need to treat very cautiously: it's very easy to come to very misleading conclusions if we try to use this scale for anything other than very general comparisons. Effectively, a phylogenetic scale takes one particular characteristic—usually quite a vague one, like "learning ability"—and ranks different species according to how well they measure up on that characteristic. In reality, of course, as Hodos and Campbell (1969) argued, a phylogenetic scale places human beings at the top, and ranks other animals in terms of how "close" they are to human beings.

There are a lot of rather questionable assumptions underlying the idea of the phylogenetic scale, not least of which is the idea that human beings represent the highest achievement of evolution. The same could be claimed for almost any species alive today, if we took different criteria. On a scale based on jumping distance relative to body size, for instance, the flea would represent the most highly evolved species, and human beings would come very close to the bottom. So the phylogenetic scale as it is generally used is a highly *anthropocentric* concept—it assumes that everything centres around human beings, and that they are more important than anything else.

Nonetheless, even though it isn't an accurate representation of evolutionary processes, many researchers, particularly comparative psychologists, have found that it can be useful when we are trying to look at things like, say, the evolution of the brain, or the control of behaviour, as long as we take it as just a broad generalisation and nothing more. Looking at how different species might fall along a phylogenetic continuum can help us to see how different parts of the brain may have evolved from more primitive ones, or to see how individual learning and adaptation have become more important for some species. We will be looking at some of these ideas in Chapter 6, when we look at comparative research within a general framework.

Models of evolution

One of the reasons why it is important to have a good understanding of evolutionary theory is because it isn't just an academic theory. Popular versions of evolutionary theory have been used politically to justify social and economic policies since the theory was first articulated; and evidence drawn from the study of animal behaviour has often been quoted in support of these ideas. Comparative psychology has contributed a great deal to social debates, and it is a two-way relationship: social contexts and debates have also coloured theories in comparative psychology itself. We will be looking at some of these issues as they arise throughout this book; but here, we will begin by looking at some of the more scientific versions of evolutionary theory, before going on to consider some of the more political versions of evolutionary theory which have been so influential.

Lamarckian genetics

When Darwin was first developing his theory of evolution, he was working with the knowledge of his time. That knowledge included the theory of inheritance proposed by Lamarck (1809), who saw inherited characteristics as having largely developed as a result of the effort that individual animals had expended during their lifetimes. In one well-known example, Lamarck (1809, p.122) wrote:

> …the giraffe … is obliged to browse on the leaves of the trees and to make constant efforts to reach them. From this habit long maintained in all its race, it has resulted that the animal's fore-legs have become longer than its hind legs, and that its neck is lengthened.

The idea that acquired characteristics could be inherited is one that is now no longer particularly acceptable to the scientific community in general. However, in Darwin's time it was generally accepted that this was probably how species acquired their characteristics, and so it is included as a possible mechanism in Darwin's writings. Although he discussed how random variations in the proportions of body parts would favour survival—the accepted modern explanation for evolutionary change—Darwin also talked about combining these with the inherited effect of increased use of bodily parts.

The Lamarckian view of evolution—that characteristics which had been acquired through effort and exercise could be passed on to the next generation—proved to be a popular one in some quarters, with its implicit message that striving for perfection could bring results. It was particularly popular in Soviet Russia, as it fitted well with the official ideology of trying to build the new society, and the New Soviet Man, who would be concerned primarily with communal responsibility rather than bourgeois individualism. In fact, Larmarckian genetics was so much a part of the official establishment view in Russia that it was retained as the "official" belief long after it had been discredited in the West, and scientists who challenged it were in danger of being ostracised from the scientific community.

Mendelian genetics

A more recent approach to inheritance in evolutionary theory—and the one that is generally accepted by the scientific establishment—draws on the genetic theory put forward by the monk Gregor Mendel (1866). This model makes an important distinction between *genotype* and *phenotype*. The idea is that the genes contained in each cell within the body carry instructions for the development of the physical organism: this is the *genotype*. But these instructions only really become manifest through interacting with the individual's environment, and so the resulting organism which actually develops—the *phenotype*—is a product of both environmental and genetic influences.

According to Mendelian genetics, only genes can be passed from one generation to another, because the experiences that an individual has in life do not alter the geneotype, and it is only the genotype that is carried by reproductive cells. Mendel proposed that units of heredity—"genes"— were organised in pairs, known as *alleles*. During sexual reproduction, the chromosomes which carry the genes in the nucleus of the cell divide, in such a way that they form new cells, each with only one gene from each pair. These form the reproductive cells, which are *haploid*—they only have half the usual number of chromosomes. When the reproductive cell combines with another one—also haploid—the two half-sets combine, producing a new combination, half of which has come from one parent and half from the other. This is known as the process of *meiosis*. We will be looking at this process again in Chapter 2.

The Mendelian model is now the one that is generally accepted in scientific thinking. With the discovery of DNA (deoxyribonucleic acid), which forms the basic material from which genes appear to be composed, and the later discovery of how the strands of DNA are organised into a double helix shape, this acceptance became even more firmly established. Electron microscopy showed how pairs of chromosomes split during meiosis, such that only one set of alleles from each pair is transferred to the reproductive cell; sexual reproduction then produces new combinations of DNA as these haploid cells fuse with others.

In evolutionary terms, Mendelian genetics implies that new characteristics will only be passed on if they are contained within the genetic structure of the individual. So new characteristics which could prove an evolutionary advantage to a species come from new combinations of genes. These arise from one of two sources: either from recessive characteristics which were already in the gene pool but were previously overshadowed by the actions of dominant alleles; or from random genetic mutations (there are always imperfect copies). Learning or experience does not exert an influence on species evolution as such, although, as we shall see in the next chapter and in Chapter 6, the capacity to learn has its own evolutionary role to play.

Recapitulation and neoteny

One of the many ideas about evolution which were prevalent in the first half of this century was the idea of recapitulation—to put it in full, the idea that *ontogeny recapitulates phylogeny*. Put into more everyday English, this was the idea that the development of the single individual (ontogeny) goes back over (recapitulates) the development of the species (phylogeny). According to this view, the various stages of foetus development mimic—or rather, re-play—the various stages of evolution. At one point in its development, for example, the human foetus has external gill-like structures, and these were thought to be a genetic throwback to an evolutionary phase of fishes.

Although recapitulation theory has long since been discredited in biology, it exerted a considerable influence in its time, some of which still remains. One of the best-known and most influential theories of cognitive development, for example, is that of Jean Piaget, who argued that the child proceeds through distinct mental stages as it develops adult-style intellectual capabilities. These stages, Piaget believed, occurred because the child's mental development recapitulated the evolutionary development of the capacity for abstract thought.

An alternative view, but one that, unlike recapitulation theory, has not been invalidated by more recent knowledge, is the idea of *neoteny*. This is the idea that the human infant is born prematurely: in terms of its stage of development, it is still a foetus, albeit a very large one. Most animals give birth at a distinct time in development, when the bones of the infant are beginning to harden, when brain and skull growth is more or less complete, and so on. But in humans, these processes continue for some months after birth. Gould (1978) argued that this enables the human brain to develop far more than would otherwise be possible, and that the extended period of dependency allowed far more learning to take place.

The theory of neoteny was first proposed by Bolk (1926) who suggested that human beings were essentially underdeveloped apes. Many of the distinctive characteristics of human beings are very similar to juvenile characteristics of chimpanzees or gorillas: young chimpanzees, for instance, have flatter faces and small jaws, like human beings, but as they grow older the muzzle becomes more pronounced and the face becomes quite different. They also have a rounded cranium, as human beings do, and the foramen magnum—the hole in the base of the skull from which the spinal cord protrudes—points downwards, as does ours. In the adult chimpanzee, these characteristics are all different: the cranium of the chimpanzee has become lower and relatively smaller, as other parts of the body and face have grown and it has remained the same; and the foramen magnum has migrated to a position behind the skull—a position that is more suitable for a quadruped.

There are many other characteristics which Bolk identified as being similarities between human beings and juvenile apes. Although Bolk's ideas were rejected at the time, there are many modern biologists who consider that they may have some validity. Gould (1978) suggests that this retarded development became adaptive for human beings because of the potential it allows for continuing to learn. The human being, Gould argues, is essentially a learning animal. By retaining the characteristics of juvenile apes—also rapidly learning animals—while at the same time allowing the brain to continue to grow after birth and sexual maturity to be delayed, neoteny allows us to increase our potential and to continue learning throughout life.

Evolution through group selection

Wynne-Edwards (1962) proposed that natural selection operates at the group level, as well as at the individual one. According to this model, a group that has favourable characteristics is more likely to survive than one that has less favourable ones, and this will gradually mean that all members of that species, as a group, will come to share the favourable characteristics. The way in which this happened was through population control.

The density of an animal population, Wynne-Edwards observed, reflects the environmental opportunities that they have. Dense populations come about as a result of living in an environment full of rich natural resources; at times when natural resources are depleted, or in impoverished environments, populations are thinner. Environments that changed from being enriched to being impoverished exerted an evolutionary pressure on the animal population at the level of the group, which resulted in the group's composition changing to fit the new circumstances by adjusting its population. The weak would die off, and the strong survive.

Wynne-Edwards argued that the various forms of social organisation, particularly social structures such as dominance hierarchies, had evolved because they helped to ensure the survival of the group. If food was scarce, an even distribution would simply mean that all the animals were underfed. This could, potentially, leave them too weak to survive a lengthy period of difficulty, and so meant that, in extreme conditions, there was a risk that the group, and even the species, could become extinct. But under a hierarchical dominance system, some animals (those with high positions in the dominance hierarchy) would be adequately fed and remain healthy, despite the shortages. The population would be thinned, as the weaker members died off, but the group as a whole would survive.

Another of the examples given in this theory was that of territoriality. There is considerable evidence that the average size of an animal's territory varies from season to season, according to the amount of food available. Wynne-Edwards argued that natural selection had favoured those species in which territorial behaviour had become adjusted to ensure an adequate distribution of food to those holding territories, because those holding territories would be stronger and more likely to survive. A species in which territorial competition was so extreme that each animal held a territory which was too small to provide sufficient food would produce weaker individuals, who were less likely to survive and reproduce.

Because fewer individuals in a social group could hold territories or obtain food in times of scarcity, this would also mean that fewer of them would reproduce successfully. In this way, the reproductive rate of the species would be adjusted to the new circumstances. Times of abundance would result in a high birthrate and a higher level of survival of offspring, so the population would grow to match the new circumstances.

This group selection model of evolution became very popular, and was used as the basis for a number of other theories during the 1960s and early 1970s. For example, Lorenz (1966) proposed that species develop inherited mechanisms for inhibiting aggressive behaviour towards other members of their own species. This was a way of maximising the chances of survival of the group as a whole, by making sure that intraspecies aggression did not build up to the extent that members of the same species would kill one another and so weaken the group and reduce its chances of survival.

One of the weaknesses of this theory, however, was its emphasis on group selection, in that it is hard to comprehend mechanisms by which it could happen. Natural selection, and survival of the fittest, as outlined by Darwin, are mechanisms acting on the individual, not on the group. They may exert an influence on the group indirectly, because of the way that they act on the individual, but that does not mean that the evolutionary pressure is operating on the group itself. Lack (1943) showed that birds which lay more eggs than other birds in a given year may end up rearing fewer young, because the available food will have to be spread more thinly between them. In that sense, fewer birds will survive, but it is the individual's reproductive rate that is affected, not the group as a whole.

Sociobiology

Although the idea of group selection became largely discredited, it had nonetheless served to focus attention on animal social organisation. Crook and Gartlan (1966), and later Crook (1970), argued that the relationship between social organisation within animal groups and the relevant ecology was a significant factor in natural selection; and that a new approach of "socioecology" would be worth pursuing. These ideas led to a number of studies exploring the relationship between animal social organisation and evolutionary mechanisms.

The new interest in social organisation raised another issue. One of the problems for a theory of natural selection which acts purely on the individual has always been the question of altruism. Among social animals, altruistic acts are reasonably common; but if animals are inherently in competition to survive, as an individual view of natural selection suggests they may be, altruistic acts appear to be counter-productive. Why should we have evolved to be able to help someone else if it is of no evolutionary benefit to us personally?

Trivers (1971) proposed that there was an argument for the evolution of altruism. The case for this is all to do with time and individual recognition. Altruistic acts, Trivers argued, could benefit the actor, as long as the receiving animal was capable of recognising individual members of its species and remembering events or emotional responses. If it was, then helping it could result in it repaying the favour, or some similar one, at some time in the future. *Reciprocal altruism,* as it was called by Trivers, represents a mechanism by which altruistic behaviour may become evolutionarily advantageous.

Another argument for altruism dated back to a paper by Hamilton (1964), who argued that there was a case for altruistic behaviour, and even individual self-sacrifice, as long as this behaviour had been directed towards aiding the survival of relatives. Hamilton pointed out that natural selection wasn't so much about the survival of individuals, as about the survival of genotypes. So although the individual concerned might not survive, if their death allowed relatives sharing the same genes to survive, then the genotype was likely to be perpetuated. This idea came to be referred to as the idea of *inclusive fitness*: it wasn't the fitness of the individual that was essential, but the fitness of the genotype.

Wilson (1975) applied these concepts to detailed studies of the behaviour of Hymenoptera—bees, ants, and wasps. The social behaviour of these insects has always represented an evolutionary puzzle, because most members of the colony are sterile, and devote their lives to supporting and guarding the colony, and caring for the eggs and larvae produced by the "queen". An individual-survival model of evolution cannot explain this behaviour, because on the surface there is no advantage to an individual to be sterile and raise the offspring of others. But Wilson showed that, if the evolution of mechanisms of *kin selection* were taken into account, the behaviour made evolutionary sense, in that it aided the inclusive fitness of the individual. As this concept is fundamental to sociobiology, it is worth exploring it in some detail.

Most animals that reproduce by sexual reproduction are diploid—that is, they possess two sets of chromosomes, one from each parent. This means that parents on average share 50% of their genes with each child, and each sibling, on average, shares 50% of its genes with its brothers and sisters. It is reported that the great biologist J.B.S. Haldane, during an argument in the pub about altruism, did some quick calculations on the back of an envelope before remarking "I will lay down my life for two brothers or eight cousins" (Gould, 1978). This represents the "break-even" sum—two brothers would each share 50% of his genes, making 100% in total (as long as they had different halves). But cousins only have 12.5% of their genes in common, so an altruistic action would need to save far more cousins than siblings to get to the "break-even" point.

Hymenoptera, though, are what is known as haplodiploid: the females are diploid, but the males are haploid, having only one set of chromosomes, from the queen. So the mathematics are different in such a case. What this means is that hymenopteran sisters are more closely related to one another than, say, human sisters would be, because they share 75% of their genes. Each has inherited a set of genes from the mother, and on average, 50% of the time these will be the same—as with humans or other diploid animals. But each sister has also inherited a set of genes from their father—and their father only had one set. So that set is 100% identical. Adding the two means that, on average, each female hymenopteran will share 75% of her genes with her other sisters. Any offspring she has herself, of course, would only be 50% similar. The result of all this is that it becomes much more advantageous, in terms of inclusive fitness, for an individual ant, bee, or wasp to be sterile but help her mother to raise more offspring, as that way, especially if they are sisters, she will maximise her own genes' chances of surviving.

The mathematics are less good for raising brothers, because a brother and sister will only share 25% of their genes. But if there were no brothers raised at all, there would be no mates for the sisters and therefore no survival. Based on this calculation, Trivers and Hare (1976) predicted that workers are likely to nurture the eggs selectively, investing more energy in raising sisters. Trivers and Hare measured the weight of fertile offspring in 21 different ant species, and found that the females were heavier than the males by a ratio of 3:1—exactly as the theory would have predicted.

It was possible, of course, that these differences had come from some other biological factors: perhaps females were just naturally heavier than males, and the differences didn't represent the energy invested by the workers at all. But studies of slave-making ants, which capture members of other ant species to work in their nest, showed that the degree of relationship did indeed seem to be the important factor. Members of the captive species also showed a 3:1 ratio in the weight of females to males when they were in their own nest. But when they were raising young in the slave-maker ant's nest, and had no relationship with the offspring that they were rearing, the ratio was a simple 1:1—males and females were equally heavy.

The implication, then, is that inclusive fitness and kin selection are real biological mechanisms, at work in the process of evolution. But these mechanisms were not simply added to the known repertoire of possible sources of variation in animal behaviour. Instead, Wilson (1975) produced a detailed analysis of social organisation across animal societies, presenting almost all forms of social organisation—including human social organisation—as the outcome of the action of these mechanisms. The application of these specific mechanisms into an entire theory of evolutionary processes became known as *sociobiology*.

Shortly after the publication of his book on sociobiology in animals, in which human behaviour was only discussed in the final chapter, Wilson produced a second book, *On human nature* (Wilson, 1978), which was a detailed application of sociobiological theory to the understanding of human behaviour and culture. There was also a paperback version of the theory produced by Dawkins (1976), which we will look at when we examine popularised versions of evolutionary theories later in this chapter. Effectively, this theory of sociobiology rested on two concepts: first, that the details of both past and present social arrangements are manifestations of genetic action; and second, that the genes which produce such results have been selected during evolution because they maximise inclusive fitness.

The theory of sociobiology put forward by Wilson attracted a number of criticisms. Some of these were concerned with the popularised versions of sociobiology, and these will be addressed later in this chapter. But others were concerned with the scientific nature of the theory itself.

One set of criticisms was particularly concerned with the method of sociobiological enquiry, as detailed by Wilson (1975). This was a retrospective method, which boiled down to three significant steps. The first was to identify the subject under study—some kind of "universal" form of behaviour, which was a likely candidate as a manifestation of genetic action. The second was to identify a "gene" (defined as a "unit of heredity") by which such a universal might be coded and transmitted. And the third was to apply the concepts of inclusive fitness and direct natural selection in such a way as to show how such a gene might have been selected by evolutionary pressure.

There are problems with just about every stage of this methodology, particularly where it was applied to human behaviour, but also in its application to animal behaviour. The more we study animal behaviour, the more we find diversity: "universals" are hard to discover. In many sociobiological accounts, the supposed "universals" are anecdotal or speculative: for example, Dawkins (1976) constructs an elaborate argument on an anedotal account of a male lion joining a pride and killing the existing cubs—assuming that this will represent standard behaviour for most mammals. As we will see later in this book, animal behaviour is not even consistent within one species, but can vary from one group to another. The evidence for human "universals" is even less—little attempt is made to examine anthropological or other cross-cultural evidence, but the examples are usually taken from general beliefs common in Western industrial society. This too is a highly questionable practice, in scientific terms.

The question of the gene as the "unit of heredity", and the action of the genes, is also used in a rather unscientific fashion. Sociobiological accounts make it clear that the term "gene" is not being used to represent the same biological phenomenon as is studied by geneticists, and it has been argued that it is used in sociobiology as a magical concept, rather than a scientific one (Hayes, 1986). Moreover, sociobiological accounts of human behaviour are often extremely unclear about the mechanisms whereby, or the degree to which, the "gene" influences the behaviour concerned.

The phase of the sociobiological method that involves the development of a plausible evolutionary account elevates speculation and imagination into supposedly scientific method. Although nobody would dispute that a study of evolution inevitably involves some degree of reconstruction, the important feature is that such historical reconstructions should be firmly based on the evidence available. Regrettably, this has rarely been evident in sociobiological theorising: such evidence as has been used has tended to consist of single exemplars or anecdotes from animal or human societies.

There are internal contradictions, too, within the theory as conventionally applied to animal studies, particularly in the question of what is "beneficial". Sociobiology explicitly rejects arguments that such and such a behaviour has evolved because is beneficial for the individual, group, or species, arguing that it is only the mechanical consequences of differential reproduction of genotype that count in natural selection. The individual is seen as simply a vehicle for its genes. However, many empirical investigations of sociobiological concepts have rested on identifying behaviours or strategies that are beneficial to the individual—either because they optimise "fitness" through maximising the individual's access to a resource, like food; or because they establish what is seen mathematically as an "evolutionarily stable strategy", or ESS (we will be looking at both of these ideas in more detail later in this book). The inherent contradiction here is ignored, as the benefit is seen simply as representing genetic adaptation—but this is a circular argument. Such behaviours, particularly in human societies but also possibly in animal ones, may have developed quite differently. If it is concluded that the only possible way for them to be manifest is as expressions of specific geno-types, then they cannot be taken as scientific investigations of the theory, as no other explanation is possible within that framework.

A third source of criticism concerns the level of explanation used in sociobiological argument and investigation. The method of trying to "explain" single behaviours or instances of behaviour means that it is too easy to end up asking entirely the wrong questions. Rather than trying to look for single advantageous behaviours, or to argue, as Dawkins does, that a behaviour "must" have evolved because it is genetically advanta-geous to do so, Gould (1981) argued that we need to look for the underpinning principles and mechanisms which can generate such behav-ioural flexibility. We will be coming back to this point in Chapter 6, where we discuss models of interpreting animal behaviour and evolutionary mechanisms in terms of biological potential rather than biological deter-minism.

The tendency towards biological determinism in its arguments leads to another methodological weakness of sociobiology—the way that it tends to look only for confirmatory instances of animal behaviour, and to ignore those examples that don't seem to "fit". For example, Faaberg and Patterson (1981) described how unrelated groups of male Galapagos hawks will often share a mate, and mate equally often; and Packer and Pusey (1983) showed how Tanzanian lions often form co-operative coali-tions in hunting behaviour, including large numbers of non-relatives. We will come across several other such examples in this book; but as a general rule this type of behaviour is ignored in orthodox sociobiology.

Some evolutionary biologists have taken an extremely broad definition of sociobiology, arguing that it represents something very like the original concept proposed by Crook (1970)—a recognition of the way that social behaviour can also be a factor in evolution. These researchers tend to distance themselves from the specific claims of Wilson and the "hard-core" sociobiologists, and to see sociobiology as little more than a version of evolutionary theory which includes the possibilities of kin selection and inclusive fitness. But Gould (1981) argues that this is broadening the concept of sociobiology to the extent where the term becomes meaning-less. Moreover, this view of sociobiology, he argues, is very different from the specific theory put forward by Wilson in 1975. Very few biologists or comparative psychologists would deny that kin selection and inclusive fitness represent evolutionary mechanisms; but that is quite different from adopting the full theory of sociobiology. There are other ways of working within an evolutionary framework, which allow for the question of biological potential rather than adopting the arguments of biological determinism. We will look at one of these in Chapter 6.

Coevolution

The theory of coevolution also looks at the relationship between the individual and its environment, but in a very different way. Put very briefly, this view argues that evolution is not simply a one-way process, with the environment exerting demands which the individual has to conform to or risk extinction. Rather, coevolution takes the view that there is a dialectical relationship between organisms and their environment. In other words, organisms are not simply acted upon by their environments, they act on their environments too, and in the process both are changed.

Rose (1983) pointed out that even an amoeba changes the water in which it swims, as it consumes nutrients in the fluid and emits waste products. As a result of this process, the water itself is changed, so the amoeba is then interacting with a different environment than before. Evolutionary forces come about because of the synthesis resulting from the interaction between these two: the organism and the environment. So, for example, the horse did not simply evolve as an adaptation to the existence of grass in the environment providing an ecological niche into which it could fit. Rather, the grazer and the grassland coevolved: the grasses themselves became modified in an adaptation to the ecological demands of the grazer (Bateson, 1973).

A striking example of this relationship was described by Trevor (1992), in a television documentary of the ecological effects of the elephant population in Tsavo National Park, in Kenya. In most African wildlife parks, the elephant population is systematically culled in order to ensure that the population does not grow too large and damage the environment. The administrators of Tsavo National Park, however, took a policy decision that they would allow nature to take its course, without human interference. The outcome was dramatic.

At the beginning of the 1960s, the elephant population numbered roughly 5,000 elephants, in a dense bushland environment. By 1965, the population had grown to 15,000 elephants, and experts warned that if they were not culled they would destroy all the vegetation, resulting in desertification. By the end of the 1960s, it looked as though their predictions were coming true: the elephant population had risen to some 45,000 animals, the area's vegetation had become extremely sparse, and many places were almost barren of plants. But other changes were taking place as well: the deep-rooted grasses, which were the only ones that could survive, had broken through the subsoil, and several new springs had welled up; and the ground itself was also becoming enriched from the elephant population: it was estimated that dung beetles were burying something like 1,500 tons of protein-rich elephant dung each day.

Serious droughts in the early 1970s resulted in thousands of elephants dying. But their death also provided nutrients for the other animals in the ecosystem, and the living elephants sought out shallow waterholes and kept them open—even deepening them by the action of their feet and by carrying away mud on their backs after wallowing. When the rains eventually returned and the system gradually began to regenerate, it became apparent that the activities of the elephants had brought about a greatly enriched environment. By the end of the 1980s, Tsavo was a verdant, diverse ecosystem—not only far removed from the desert that had been predicted, but also with a much higher level of ground cover and species diversity than in other areas, in which the elephants' full interactions with their environments had been restricted. Although it had been very hard for the Tsavo administrators to stand back and watch the starvation and death of many of the elephants, by allowing the process to continue they became aware that the interaction of the animals and their environment was not only beneficial to the elephant species itself, but in the long run was also beneficial to the other species—plant and animal—in the ecosystem.

The coevolution approach, then, makes a case for a much greater consideration of multidimensionality in interpreting the evolution of animal behaviour. Although individual evolutionary mechanisms such as natural selection and inclusive fitness are undoubtedly at work, to interpret evolution as simply the actions of those mechanisms ignores the effects of interaction between the species and its environment. As we look at animal behaviour—or at almost any other manifestation of evolutionary processes—we become aware of enormous diversity. The potential for interactive relationships between organisms and their environments is vast. The concept of coevolution is a reminder that behavioural evolution cannot simply be accounted for by invoking simplistic one-way mechanisms: there are many more complex factors at work.

Popularised versions of evolutionary theory

Since the very first publication of *The origin of species,* popular versions of evolutionary theory have abounded. Some of these theories have been serious attempts to use the popular media to speculate about possible ways in which evolutionary mechanisms might have affected human society. Others have been little more than thinly disguised political propaganda, designed to produce a "scientific" justification for a particular social belief or economic policy. Although such theories are often disregarded by the scientists working in this area, they have nonetheless had powerful social effects, and they therefore raise a number of questions about the social responsibility of science. For the rest of this chapter, we will look briefly at some of these theories, and at some of the problems inherent in their arguments, before going on to look at how models of evolution may be seen in their social contexts.

Social Darwinism

One of the first ways that evolutionary theory was used politically was in what became known as "Social Darwinism". This idea was particularly developed by the philosopher Herbert Spencer (1820–1903), and placed a strong emphasis on the idea of a struggle for survival, in which evolution was largely seen in terms of species competing with each other for ecological resources. The "survival of the fittest" was seen as the survival of those species that were most ruthless, and therefore most able to take advantage of others: the image portrayed was of "Nature red in tooth and claw".

Spencer's Social Darwinism appealed to a number of sectors in Victorian society, particularly as it was used to support the idea of laissez-faire capitalism, as opposed to a system in which the State would provide help to industry in terms of support and training. According to Spencer's philosophy, capitalism should be allowed to develop as it wished: it didn't matter how cut-throat or vicious the competition became, because ultimately that would be good for the economy. And safety networks, like social welfare programmes, would ultimately interfere with the "survival of the fittest".

Although these ideas do have some superficial resemblance to evolutionary theory—they use the same terms, and appear to be talking about similar mechanisms—they are really quite different. They rest entirely on metaphors: the idea that an organisation, like an industrial firm, is somehow "like" a species. But there are many very real differences between species and industrial firms. For one thing, every member of a species forms part of the gene pool, and so may produce offspring that show the survival traits; whereas access to privileged positions in industrial firms is restricted to very few of the individuals working in them.

The talk about "survival of the fittest" used in Social Darwinism was really an argument used to justify exploitation: it implied, for example, that weaker people who couldn't survive the intolerable conditions of the Victorian factory system should just be allowed to die off; and that this would "strengthen" the species, and therefore would be better than social reforms like limiting the number of hours someone worked, giving them weekends off, or pensions, or any of the other practices which we now consider to be basic and necessary.

A similar version of Social Darwinism talked in terms of different races of human beings, ranking them in order of "evolutionary progress" with whites at the top of the tree and blacks at the very bottom. It also assumed that the strong would always dominate the weak, because aggression was an innate capacity and therefore biologically inevitable. As you might expect, this model, which had no basis at all in any scientific sense, was used to justify colonial exploitation, by portraying members of non-white cultures as "inferior", and thereby justifying the idea of cultural dominance and exploitation of the weak.

Ultimately, of course, this view of racial evolution contributed to the rise of the Nazi party in Germany, and the atrocities that it committed. The attempted genocide of the Jews and Poles, and the annihilation of the European Gypsies, was based on the idea that, because these "races" were closest to white Aryans (according to this supposed evolutionary ranking), but inferior to them, interbreeding between the two could set back evolutionary progress, which was, it was claimed, ultimately destined to produce a super-race. As well as the concentration camps, the Nazis set up breeding centres, where young men of "pure" Aryan stock were encouraged to get as many women and girls as possible pregnant. The women were also "pure" Aryans, and the Nazi's aim was to strengthen the racial group, and ultimately to breed the "*Supermensch*"—the super-human who would be the pinnacle of evolution.

Of course, like the other versions of Social Darwinism, these ideas have no scientific basis, but as the Nazis showed, an idea doesn't have to be based on scientific fact to do a great deal of harm. By taking the vocabulary and descriptions of evolutionary theory and applying them to social categories, they made it appear as though they were describing some basic biological principle—a principle, moreover, which was already widely known and discussed. As Arendt (1966) pointed out: the Nazis failed to comprehend how the outside world regarded what they were doing, because they assumed that most other people shared the same views. When they were faced with outright opposition from those they assumed thought the same way—for example, when they asked the Danes to make their Jews wear the identifying yellow star, and were met with a blank refusal—they backed down, because they hadn't imagined that they would meet with any opposition at all.

The idea of *eugenics*—the political theory that is concerned with trying to "improve" the human race by preventing those who have undesirable physical characteristics from breeding—has unfortunately still not died out, although eugenic theorists are not as outspoken as they used to be. In America, compulsory sterilisation laws for those who are subnormal in intelligence still exist in some states, and these are based on the same principles. But the concept of evolution that underlies these ideas bears little relationship to the concept of evolution that is held by biologists and comparative psychologists.

The "naked ape" theory

In 1967, Desmond Morris published a paperback proposing that human beings were really nothing more than "naked apes"—that all people were really doing in society was expressing the animal side of their natures, but in a disguised form. Morris rested this argument on parallels that he drew between accounts of animal behaviour and human social practices. He compared the erecting of fences around gardens, for instance, to the territorial behaviour of sticklebacks; the ventures of artists and musicians were seen as simply manifestations of a "biological" exploratory drive; and religion as an expression of a biological urge to submit to a dominant animal.

There were two particular themes that permeated the naked ape theory. One of these concerned aggression, and the other sex. Drawing heavily on Lorenz's ideas, Morris argued that human beings were innately aggressive, and that as this was an inevitable part of our biology it was pointless to try to stop it. Instead, it needed to be channelled into safe outlets for society, through competitive sports and other forms of demanding competition. Moreover, Morris argued, aggression and territoriality were part of human "biological" nature, and therefore wars and boundary disputes were inevitable. Thinning the population was, he argued, the only really effective way of preventing this: "To sum up, then, the best solution for ensuring world peace is the widespread promotion of contraception or abortion." (Morris, 1967, p. 156).

Morris also argued that human beings were the most sexually active of all the animals, as their sexual activities were not restricted to an oestrus cycle. A great many of the facets of the female body, he argued, had evolved in order to attract the male. The fatty, hemispherical breasts of human females, for instance, were supposed to be imitations of the buttocks, and to derive their sexual attractiveness from animal rear-mounting behaviour. (This example alone illustrates very clearly how ethnocentric Morris's account was: in societies where women don't wear bras, as was presumably the case during human evolution, breasts are not at all hemispherical— if anything, they are pendulous and sometimes almost tubular.) Numerous other physical characteristics of the human being were deemed to have evolved for sexual attraction, including bodily hairlessness, long hair on the head, and subcutaneous fat.

Naturally enough, Morris's theory attracted a considerable amount of criticism. He had drawn very heavily on Lorenz's work, and, like Lorenz, had ignored examples of animal behaviour that didn't "fit" the explanations. For example, in Chapter 4 we will see how several studies of primate social organisation presented very different pictures of baboons and how they interact with one another, but both Lorenz and Morris drew heavily on the Washburn and deVore studies, which presented baboons as highly aggressive and hierarchical, and ignored other primate research, including the studies of chimpanzees by Reynolds and Goodall, which suggested that primate social interaction was mostly co-operative.

One of the most powerful critics of Morris's theory was Morgan (1973), who showed how many of the flaws in his arguments had come from the use of the term "he" to stand for all human beings, women included. As a result of this, Morgan argued, the role of women in evolution had been completely overlooked. Many of the arguments in Morris's theory were overly elaborate attempts to explain things purely from the male point of view, like the sexual attractiveness argument. Morgan argued that if a more rounded view of evolution was taken, which took into account the practices and roles of both sexes, a very different picture emerged. In particular, considering child-rearing demands meant that several of the physical characteristics that Morris had attributed to "sexual attraction" could be perceived quite differently.

The "aquatic ape" theory

Morgan's approach to human evolution involved looking at the picture of human evolution that emerged when the demands of food-gathering and child-rearing were also taken into account, rather than simply the needs of the hunter. As there is some indication that something like 90% of primaeval diets consisted of vegetable matter, generally thought to be gathered by the women, Morgan suggested that such societies should be described as "gatherer-hunter" rather than "hunter-gatherer". Several of the evolutionary adaptations of the human being which require complex explanation in terms of hunting can be re-interpreted more simply, Morgan argued, when these aspects of life are taken into account. The use of the generic pronoun "he" had distorted the thinking of evolutionary theorists: both men and women are human, and the survival and adaptation of each contributed to evolutionary fitness; so the "standard"

"WHY ARGUE M'DEAR?.....MAN NEEDS HIS MATE...AND WHAT COULD BE MORE DESIRABLE TO YOU, THAN ME...MMM?"

version of evolutionary theory which emphasised only the contribution of the male was scientifically inadequate.

As part of this argument, Morgan (1973) drew on several different accounts of evolutionary origins, and focused particularly on one, which argued that at some time in their evolutionary history, human beings had spent some time living in and around water. Living on the shoreline of perhaps a lake or the sea, they would retreat into the water if threatened from the land, and on to the land if threatened by the sea. Consequently, like other aquatic mammals, they had evolved a number of physical characteristics such as subcutaneous fat and vestigial webbing between the fingers. Long hair on the top of the head gave protection from the sun, and also something for a small baby to hold on to: hair on the rest of the body was superfluous. In 1982, Morgan identified many other characteristics of human beings, both behavioural and physical, which make sense in the context of the aquatic ape theory.

The aquatic ape theory, however, despite being at least as well argued as that put forward by Morris, did not receive the same degree of publicity or acceptance. Feminist theoreticians argue that this reflects the implicitly patriarchal bias of evolutionary theorists; other evolutionary theorists argue that there is little evidence for the theory. There wasn't much evidence for Morris's theory either, but Morris reflected the conventional assumptions of contemporary society, and Morgan didn't.

The "selfish gene" theory

Another popularisation of evolutionary theory that received considerable publicity yet rested on very little evidence was put forward in 1976, by Richard Dawkins. Called *The selfish gene*, Dawkins' book provided an account of the sociobiological approach, which had been proposed by Wilson in 1975. In his original book, Wilson had presented a detailed biological account of a version of evolutionary theory which brought together recent ideas about evolutionary mechanisms such as inclusive fitness and kin selection. Although he made wild speculations in the final chapter of the book concerning the applications of this model to human beings, for the most part Wilson's book was a thorough academic treatment of a scientific approach to evolutionary theory.

In *The selfish gene*, however, Dawkins presented a version of sociobiology that rested heavily on metaphors drawn from animal behaviour, and extrapolated these, with the occasional caveat, to human society. Dawkins argued that human beings were really simply "survival machines" for genes which aimed to replicate themselves. Genes, he argued, "exert ultimate power over behaviour" (Dawkins, 1976, p. 64), and the purpose of all life was to ensure that their genes could be replicated.

Dawkins then went on to discuss a number of examples of human behaviour, and to argue that these could be "explained" simply as the actions of the "selfish genes". So step-parents, for example, would inevitably tend to be hostile to their step-children; language inevitably would be used to lie and deceive; and people would always be aggressive and hostile towards strangers because these were all strategies that maximised the gene's survival.

We saw earlier in this chapter how one of the weaknesses of the sociobiological approach is that it tends only to seek confirmatory examples from among the huge diversity of animal behaviour. Dawkins did not deviate from this tradition. In common with other biological determinists, he selected only the negative aspects of human behaviour like aggression and cheating, and portrayed them as inevitable biological consequences. More positive aspects of human behaviour, like co-operation, friendliness, and honesty could equally well have been selected and identified as "inevitable" using the same structure of argument. But they were not.

Dawkins' arguments are also strikingly lacking in supporting evidence to support the claims that he makes about biological inevitability. For example, he claims that step-parents tend to be hostile to step-children, but cites no research on the issue. (In fact, there is no evidence to support this assertion, apart from it being a common situation in fairy-tales.) On this assertion, Dawkins builds an elaborate case to show that such hostility is biologically inevitable, drawing from two examples of animal behaviour to "prove" it—and, of course, completely ignoring the many documented examples of animal behaviour that belie it.

There are numerous other weaknesses in Dawkin's arguments, many of which were addressed by Hayes (1986). Among others, these included the way that the sociobiological use of the term "gene" (a unit of natural selection) differed considerably from what geneticists meant by the term "gene" (a chromosomal structure initiating protein synthesis), and Hayes concluded that the term was invoked as a "magical" concept, rather than as a scientific one. The pseudo-scientific vocabulary, however, gave the theory some apparent credibility. In Dawkins' version of sociobiology, as in the earlier versions of "pop" ethology, an attempt to formulate an evolutionary account of behaviour was used to portray human society as "inevitably" vicious and competitive.

Biological determinism

Although there are differences between sociobiology and Lorenzian approaches, there are some very striking similarities. Both sets of theories— the popular theories of Morris and Dawkins, and their scientific counterparts from Lorenz and Wilson—are clear examples of biological determinist theories about human nature. Rose, Kamin, and Lewontin (1984) argued that one of the biggest problems with biological determinism is the way that it ignores other levels of analysis. To come to an understanding of human behaviour, we need to be able to consider many different levels of explanation: sociocultural, social, interpersonal, cognitive, behavioural, and physiological. To focus on just one of these and ignore all the others is to distort, very seriously, the picture of human society.

In addition, the biological determinist writers have tended to look for universals in behaviour: to assume that if a behaviour proved advantageous for one type of organism, it was therefore inevitably advantageous for others. But animal behaviour is more complex than that. Evolutionary processes and adaptational demands interlink with phenotypic development and learning capacity to produce a wide range of possibilities: whether a given type of animal shows a particular form of behaviour depends on much more than some single genetic imperative. Whether a particular form of behaviour is an evolutionary advantage for an animal will depend on the particular circumstances of that particular species. As Gould (1981) pointed out, to argue that one particular behaviour is inevitable because it is "biological" is nonsense: there is always a range of possible biological behaviours. Such arguments rest on a highly misleading view of the nature of biological influence, which allows for possibilities, alternatives, and diversity, not just single solutions.

Metaphor and analogy in evolutionary accounts

One of the problems of evaluating the quality of models of evolution is the prevalence of metaphors. We seem to draw parallels between human and animal society almost inevitably, and we use metaphors to help us to symbolise or encapsulate a set of ideas. But the problem is that these metaphors can be extremely misleading. We will see in Chapter 4 how the use of the word "harem" to describe a group of female deer and their relationship to a single male has distorted our understanding of territoriality in that species, and there are numerous other examples which we will come across through this book.

The issue here is the distinction between analogy and homology. Analogy is all about identifying resemblances—we say something "looks like" or "sounds like" something else, but we don't actually mean that it is identical. For example, we would use the term "singing like a bird" to mean that someone was singing particularly sweetly and tunefully—but we wouldn't literally mean that they were producing chirrups and trills as a bird does. By using analogies and metaphors in this way, we can often give ourselves a starting point for understanding what is going on.

But, far too often, the fact that a comparison was actually an analogy is forgotten. Instead, it is taken as if it were homology—as if it were genetically exactly the same thing. In biology, for example, we would say that there is a homologous relationship between a bat's wing and a human hand, in the sense that they involve the same bones of the skeleton, and, back in the dim and distant past, they both evolved from the forelimb of a common ancestor. Genetically speaking, there is a homology between the bat's wing and the human hand, even though they actually look entirely different.

So, for example, writers like Desmond Morris notice that it is possible to draw an analogy between, say, the way that people put fences around their homes, and the way that a stickleback patrols the boundaries of a defined area during the mating season, and they come to the conclusion that these two actions are homologous—that in evolutionary terms, they represent the same phenomenon. But analogy is not homology: there is no reason at all to suppose that this seasonal courtship behaviour of the male stickleback has any genetic relationship with a cultural practice which, in any case, is manifested by only a relatively small section of the human species. The word we use to describe them is the same—territori-ality—but that is because it is a metaphor. The behaviours are actually quite different in origin. In this way, the fact that we use the same word leads to all sorts of conceptual problems.

In 1987, Hinde listed four sources of difficulty for those attempting to draw inferences from ethological observation to human social behaviour. The first of these concerns differences in cognitive ability between animals and human beings, and we will come back to look at this question more carefully in Chapter 6. The second is the human capacity for language and culture, which means that we are able to transmit, not just learned behav-iour, but entire styles of interactions, assumptions, perspectives, and frameworks across generations. The third is the diversity of behaviour in animal species—which, as we will see over the next few chapters, is extremely large—and the fourth is the difficulty of drawing comparisons at an appropriate level of analysis. Human behaviour needs to be exam-ined using a number of levels of analysis: just focusing on one level and drawing parallels, no matter how plausible, is inevitably going to be inadequate in explaining what is going on in human social behaviour.

Comparative theories and the Zeitgeist

Theories of animal behaviour have always tended to mirror their times. One of the reasons for this concerns the unconscious attitudes of those who are researching into animal social behaviour. Scientists are members of their society, and tend to adopt the social assumptions of their times. In addition, many scientific theories are put forward in the scientific literature, but not all of them are taken up by other scientists or by the media: many are simply ignored or forgotten. As a result of both of these processes, scientific theories show a powerful tendency to reflect their Zeitgeist—the spirit of their times. And this is particularly true of comparative research—perhaps more so than in any other single field.

Sometimes we can see these influences most clearly by taking a histori-cal perspective. One example we can take concerns studies of chimpanzee social organisation. From the painstaking evidence of researchers such as Reynolds (1963) and Goodall (1968), we know that chimpanzees in the wild live in large, loose-knit groups, often of 30 or so individuals. Mobile groups seem to show little evidence of dominance structures, and females mate freely when they come into season. But because chimpanzees are so close to human beings in so many ways, it is very easy for us to see human society or human behaviour mirrored in the ways that they act, and reports of chimpanzee social life have reflected this.

The very first Western observations of chimpanzee behaviour were by the explorer Livingstone, in his *Last diaries*, who wrote that chimpanzees lived in groups of between 15 or 30 individuals, with each male having his own female, and that if one male should "take the female of another, he is resoundly beaten and his ears are boxed by the whole group". It is not hard to see the projection of Victorian morality in this account.

It wasn't just the Victorian researchers who projected their own social values onto chimpanzee behaviour. Reflecting the values of his own culture, the American primatologist Robert Yerkes (1925) argued that chimpanzees in the wild lived in loosely organised large groups, which were led by an individual who was chosen for his qualities of initiative, daring, courage, and responsibility.

Other comparative theories, too, have been influenced by their culture and context. Lorenz's ideas of genetically determined behaviour, and of aggression, were conceived in the context of the rise of National Socialism in Germany and Austria. Genetic determinism was widely accepted at that time, and formed the basis for the murder of six million Jews, the European Gypsies, and others in the concentration camps (Müller-Hill, 1988). The idea that it was basic to human nature to be competitive and aggressive, and that the strong would inevitably dominate the weak, was also a part of the ideological basis of Nazi expansionism. Lorenz's own associations with the Nazi party are well known, and it is not hard to detect in his theory of aggression a model of the nature of the human being that fits very closely with Nazi ideology.

In a similar way, the emphasis on sexuality of Morris's "naked ape" theory reflects the "sexual revolution" period of the 1960s, in which a high level of interest in sexuality was generated by the media, and conventional assumptions of morality and fidelity were increasingly challenged. By presenting a theory which stated explicitly that a high level of sexuality was a biological fundamental in the human species—particularly the male—Morris attracted a great deal of media attention. His later popular-isation of Lorenz's ideas of aggression in the context of football crowds similarly reflected the concerns of its time. Presenting football violence as an "inevitable" consequence of evolution, provided a "biological" theory that generated substantial public interest (Morris, 1981).

More serious theories of evolution and animal behaviour have also reflected their times. It is possible to see the "group selection" theories of Wynne-Edwards as reflecting the expanding economy and increased social concerns of the 1960s, and the opposing kin selection approach in sociobiology as reflecting the "each to their own" Thatcherite/Reaganite philosophies of the 1980s. It is a little early to predict which comparative theories will emerge in the 1990s, but there does seem to be a detectable growth of interest in the ways that environmental factors influence how animals interact with one another and their surroundings, and it is possible that this reflects the growth of ecological awareness in society as a whole.

To try to separate a theory from its social context would be a fruitless task. And simply to state that a theory "fits" its social context isn't necessarily a damning criticism. All science takes place within a social context and social concerns will always trigger the interest of scientists. We should be aware of this, of course; but the important criteria when we are evaluating any theory concern the quality of the evidence on which it rests. Does it depend purely on analogy and metaphor, or is it based on rigorous and systematic observation? Does it take account of diversity and levels of interaction, or does it just select a few examples and ignore the rest? Does it take account of the many different levels of explanation, or does it just focus on one biological process and claim that everything else is caused by that? These are the kinds of criteria that we need to apply when we are evaluating theories of animal behaviour.

In the next chapter, we will look at the two basic mechanisms of animal behaviour: genetics and learning, exploring how each of these operates, and also looking at how they work together, within an evolutionary context, to aid the individual's chances of survival. In the following three chapters, we will be looking at some specific areas of research in comparative psychology: at courtship, mating, and reproduction in Chapter 3; territoriality, social organisation, and aggression in Chapter 4; and research into the reception of sensory information and communication in Chapter 5. In Chapter 6, we will look at some of the research into animal cognition, and at how we may integrate our awareness of the diversity of human and animal behaviour into an evolutionary framework.

When we are looking at real animals, of course, we find that the different mechanisms and processes that ethologists and comparative psychologists have studied all merge together. But when we are studying comparative psychology, we often need to separate them in order to see them more clearly. So the chapters in this book reflect some of the major distinctions and groupings which can be made when we look at comparative psychology—but it is important to remember that they are all interlinked. If we were looking at how a single species of bird produces its next generation, we might need to consider not just the genetics of reproduction (Chapter 2) but also that species' courtship, mating, and parenting behaviour (Chapter 3), questions of seasonal territoriality and aggression (Chapter 4), and at how birdsong functions and develops (Chapter 5). Like most other areas in psychology, the different areas are closely linked when we look at them in real life.

Summary: Comparative psychology and evolution

- Comparative psychology arose within the Western philosophical tradition, and included concepts such as Cartesian dualism, empiricism, associationism, and behaviourism.
- Modern comparative psychology comes from two historical roots: the American experimental tradition, and the European ethological tradition.
- Animal behaviour can be studied on a number of levels. Comparative psychology is concerned with four main aspects of animal behaviour: development, mechanisms, function, and evolution.
- Darwin's theory of evolution showed how species could develop as a result of incremental genetic changes which help individuals to adapt to their environment.
- There have been many versions of evolution, encompassing the genetic theories of Lamarck and Mendel, ideas of recapitulation and neoteny, group selection, sociobiology, and coevolution. Sociobiological theories can be useful, but many of their more sweeping claims have been heavily criticised.
- Popularised versions of evolutionary theory include Social Darwinism, the "naked ape" theory, the "aquatic ape" theory, and the "selfish gene" theory. There have often been concealed sociopolitical dimensions to these arguments.
- Both scientific and popular comparative theories have tended to reflect the Zeitgeist—the spirit of the times.

2 The basis of behaviour

In this chapter, we will be looking at the some of the mechanisms that underlie behaviour. When we are looking at a particular behaviour shown by an animal, one of the first things we tend to ask is: where does this behaviour come from? How did it come to be like it is?

Comparative psychology has addressed this question from a number of levels, ranging from that of the neurological factors controlling behaviour, to the influence of contexts and timing on whether the behaviour shows itself or not. Effectively, the origins of behaviour can be seen as coming from one of two sources, genetic transmission or learning—although it is important to remember that any behaviour that we actually observe an animal doing, at least in its natural environment, will almost always have been influenced by both factors. We will look first at how these different mechanisms work, before going on to see how they may combine together to influence what animals actually do.

Genetic transmission

Genetic transmission is the way that characteristics are passed on from one generation to another through inheritance. The way that it takes place is through a special kind of cell division. Each cell nucleus in the body contains long double strands of deoxyribonucleic acid, or DNA for short. These strands contain coded sequences of amino acids which form what we know as genes—units of heredity. Each gene has a pair, called an *allele*, on the opposite strand of DNA, and cross-links between the strands ensure that the two stay in place with respect to one another.

A gene, when it becomes active, effectively issues an instruction to a particular cell that, at a given time, it should synthesise a particular protein. But the combined effects of millions of genes working together in a complex and ordered fashion, are such that this process can result in the development and growth of a whole living creature. The "genetic blueprint" in the coded strands of DNA contains the codes that will produce the individual, given the right environmental conditions and resources.

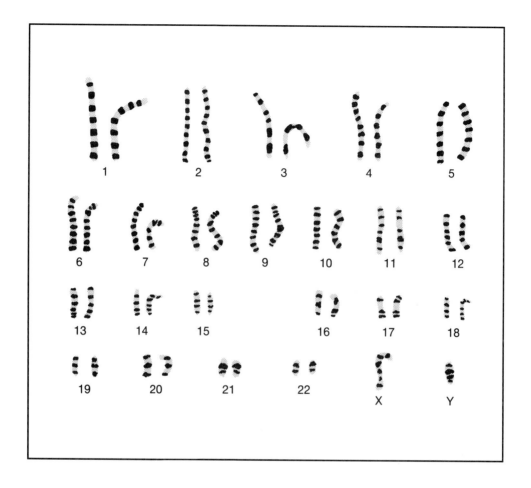

Much recent research has concentrated on identifying the functions of different sequences of DNA. There is even a huge research project going on at the moment designed to map the human genome—to identify and categorise the millions of genes involved in human heredity. This might be of some value in medical terms, for example, in identifying the genetic sources of illnesses such as cystic fibrosis, and in time it may lead to better medical treatments as a result. In psychological terms, though, there is considerable dispute over whether the type of knowledge obtained from the human genome project is likely to be useful to us. There is some anxiety that, by emphasising genetics so strongly, it may actually blind the medical profession to the importance of environmental and psychological influences in both physical illness and mental disorders.

The process of genetic engineering, in which sequences of DNA are removed from a cell nucleus of one creature and inserted into the DNA of another, has already proved to have commercial application, as species are modified to make them more disease-resistant or more productive. This research also has its critics, mainly among those who are worried that the ecological implications of many of these changes have not been explored. There is also a debate about the issue of patents: the large American research agencies which have funded this research have taken out patents on specific sequences of DNA, but some scientists argue that living matter should not be patentable. It seems likely, however, that commerce rather than ethics will win this debate in the long run.

The long sequences of genetic codes are reproduced in the DNA of each cell in the body, organised into groups known as chromosomes. When cells multiply, as they do with growth, the chromosomes contract until they appear as X-shaped threads, and then they replicate themselves through a process known as *mitosis* (see below). As the nucleus divides into two, each half receives a complete new set of chromosomes, identical to the previous set. Then the whole cell divides into two, so each new cell

Mitosis

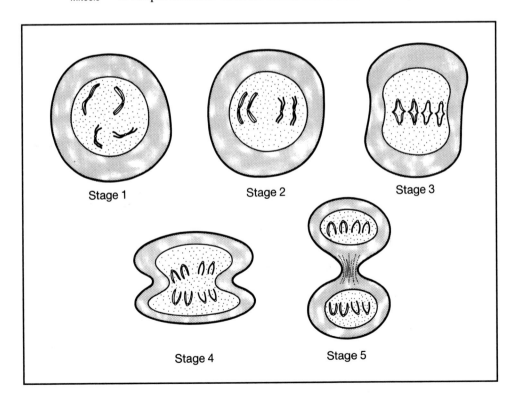

Stage 1   Stage 2   Stage 3

Stage 4   Stage 5

has a nucleus containing a full complement of DNA, with the "blueprint" for development of a whole individual.

Mitosis is the process that is used in growth, and in asexual reproduction, where a species reproduces itself by budding, or some other mechanism which just involves making exact copies. It is also the process that is involved in cloning. By providing the right environmental conditions to encourage cells to multiply (not a simple business), scientists have been able to clone frogs and small mammals, as well as many varieties of plants. There are, of course, large commercial applications for cloning: for example, all the Kiwi fruit on sale commercially have been cloned, which is why they tend to be so similar in shape and appearance.

The problem, though, is that cloned fruits or vegetables are also very vulnerable to disease, because a disease is likely to run rampant through a population so easily. As we saw in the last chapter, having each member of a species differ slightly increases the probability that some will have characteristics that will help them to survive in difficult times, but as clones are genetically identical, and have usually been reared in identical conditions as well, each individual is equally susceptible.

Mitosis, then, doesn't produce variation between different individuals—or at least only random differences which occur through faulty copying of the DNA sequences. But, as we saw in Chapter 1, individual variations are important for survival and adaptation, and ultimately are the source of the evolution of species as a whole. Individual genetic differences occur through sexual reproduction.

In sexual reproduction, cells divide to form new reproductive cells, but the chromosomes do not divide themselves by mitosis. Instead, they separate by a process known as *meiosis*. In this process the new cell has only half the full number of chromosomes—a condition known as *haploid*—and must join up with another similar cell before it can develop into a complete organism. Just before division, the DNA organises itself into thick thread-like chromosomes, arranged in pairs; and one chromosome from each pair goes to form the new cells (see overleaf). The result of the sex act is the fusing of two haploid cells, one from each parent, so the new individual inherits genetic material from each parent. The result is that each new organism is different from its parents, but at the same time resembles them in various ways. So there is continuity within the species while at the same time there is individual variation.

Most of the characteristics that interest psychologists are *polygenic*— that is, they arise from the action of several genes rather than just from a single one. But sometimes the influence of a single gene can make a lot of difference—although the baseline rule is that if someone inherits a gene for a typical characteristic and a matching allele for an unusual one, it is

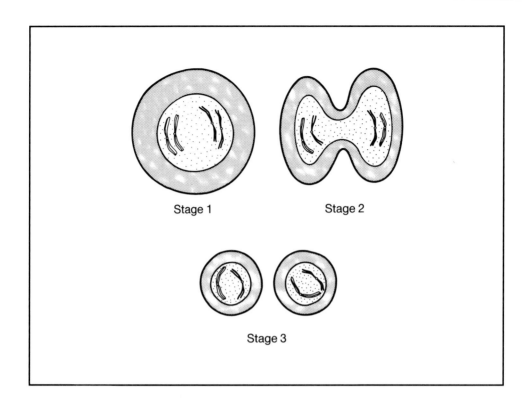

Stage 1   Stage 2

Stage 3

Meiosis the typical one that is dominant, and will be expressed in development. If you think about it, you'll see that this would pretty well have to be the case. Otherwise, it would be the other characteristic that would become typical.

For example, one of the genes available in the human gene pool, though not all that common, is for six-fingeredness. Most people who have this gene have five fingers, as normal, because they also have another matching gene—an allele—for five-fingeredness, and that is the dominant one. But if two people who each carry that gene produce children, then it is quite likely that one of their children will inherit a matching pair of six-fingered genes, and be born with six fingers on each hand. So a gene can be in the gene pool for a given species, but only show up occasionally.

This leads us to a very important distinction, and one that is often misunderstood, by psychologists as well as by other people. It concerns the distinction between the genotype and the phenotype. The *genotype* is the "genetic blueprint"—the set of potential instructions coded in the DNA of the cell nucleus. The genotype is effectively fixed at conception: when the two haploid cells fuse, they make the new pattern which is then replicated through the new individual's body as it grows, through mitosis. (Some recent research suggests that it may not actually be as fixed as all that, because a substance known as messenger RNA appears to "transport" bits of DNA between cell nuclei, but at the moment the evidence is very tentative—watch this space!)

But in reality, the genotype is a potential that is never actually seen; because from the moment that conception has taken place, the organism is interacting with its environment. It's not a one-way process: Rose (1983) argued that cells affect their immediate environments, by releasing chemicals into them, in addition to the environments affecting the cells. So what we find in a developing or developed organism is an interaction of environmental and genetic influences, producing the organism that actually develops in the real world—the *phenotype*. This is important, because we need to remember that, whenever we are looking at an inherited characteristic, or an inherited behaviour, we are looking at the outcome of a number of influences and not just the outcome of one single one.

So how do genes affect behaviour? I mentioned earlier that a gene is an instruction for protein synthesis, and it is quite a long gap between a protein synthesis and an inherited action. We are still not very sure about how it happens, but researchers into neuroethology are beginning to identify some of the links between the two. Before we look at this, however, it would be a good idea to identify what comparative psychologists mean when they talk of genetically determined behaviour.

Genetically determined behaviour

In the very earliest days of comparative psychology, it was generally assumed that most of the behaviour shown by animals in their natural environments was innate, or inherited. This idea arose mainly from the assumptions of Cartesian dualism, which we looked at in Chapter 1: if animal behaviour was entirely mechanistic, as Descartes argued, then the mechanisms that drove it were likely to have been inherited.

Lorenz and Tinbergen (1938) argued that there were four main criteria that should be applied if one was trying to determine whether a particular behaviour was genetically controlled or not. These criteria were:

1. *The behaviour must be stereotyped, always appearing in the same form.* The idea here is that if the behaviour is learned, then it would be likely to differ from time to time, but if it is controlled by the genes, because they

don't change the behaviour shouldn't either. In 1958, the ethologist Konrad Lorenz reported a set of observational studies of duck courtship behaviour. When they are trying to attract a mate, mallard ducks engage in an elaborate ritual of bobbing the head, ducking, and dipping the beak into the water. By meticulously observing and timing the stages, sequences, and actions in each part of the courtship display, Lorenz was able to show that, in any one duck, these always took a constant form and didn't vary from one occasion to the next.

2. *The behaviour should be species-specific.*
In other words, the behaviour should be typical of, and shared by, members of that species, and not shown by members of other species. Tinbergen (1959) showed how different gulls went through different greeting rituals when they landed in the colony. These were specific to the particular species of gull. Although there were sometimes some general similarities between the actions in the various rituals, the actual sequence of actions and responses was different for each species. Since gulls nest in closely packed colonies, these mechanisms would help to ensure that mating would only take place between members of that particular species of gull, and not between gulls of different species.

3. *The behaviour should appear in animals that have been isolated from others of their kind, and so haven't had a chance to learn it.*
In 1964, Marler and Tamura performed a study of the American white-crowned sparrow. These birds have a distinctive song which is shared by all members of the species right across America. But, in addition, there are slight variations to the song, which appear to be regional in nature: birds from one district will add a distinctive set of additional trills or warbles to the basic song, whereas those reared in another district will add a different set. Marler and Tamura reared young birds in isolation, such that they never had a chance to hear any other members of their species, and found that they still produced the basic song when they became adult. They didn't produce any of the regional variations, though: these seemed to be learned from other sparrows.

4. *The behaviour should appear fully developed in animals that have been prevented from practising it.*
This argument centres around the idea of maturation—the idea that if a behaviour is genetically determined, then it will show when the organism is mature enough, regardless of whether the organism has had a chance to practise it or not. So preventing opportunities for practice while animals were being reared may be one way of identifying genetically controlled

behaviour. Carmichael (1956) reared tadpoles in an anaesthetic solution, so that they were unable to contract their muscles. A control group was used to judge when the tadpoles were mature enough to swim normally. At that point the tadpoles were transferred to clear water. They swam freely, implying that they hadn't needed to practise the behaviour at all.

There were several similar studies carried out on different species. For example, Grohmann (1939) showed that pigeons who had been reared in tubes, and thereby prevented from flapping their wings, could fly almost as soon as they were released. (Again, a control group indicated when the appropriate maturational stage had been reached.) Eibl-Eiblesfeldt (1970) showed how squirrels' nut-burying behaviour appeared even if they had been raised entirely on liquid food, and Nice (1943) described how newly hatched song sparrows would crouch down in the nest even on the very first occasion that they heard their parent's alarm call.

The general conclusion, then, was that genetically controlled behaviour was fixed and unchanging, shared by members of that species but not others, and would be shown in the appropriate context regardless of whether the animal had had a chance to learn it or not, as long as the animal was old enough. These types of behaviour came to be referred to as *fixed action patterns*, or FAPs, and very quickly the attention of etholo- gists came to be centred on how they occurred, and how they were set in motion.

Sign stimuli and innate releasing mechanisms

Tinbergen (1951) investigated how innate actions were triggered by environmental stimuli. The story is that he was investigating the aggressive behaviour of male sticklebacks towards one another during the courtship season, when one male, in a tank on his own, suddenly began to produce a frantic aggressive display. Normally, such displays would be set off by the presence of another male, with its distinctive red belly, but in this case there was nothing else in the tank. But the fishtank was by the window, and Tinbergen realised that the fish had been reacting to the bright red of a post-office van going past. Intrigued, Tinbergen began to observe the stickleback's reactions to other red stimuli, noting the strength of the response, and the kinds of stimulus that would bring it out. He found that some reactions would be produced simply by red objects, but that the strongest reactions were aroused with a stimulus that was roughly fish-shaped, and which moved in a fish-like way.

Tinbergen proposed that each inherited behaviour has an innate releasing mechanism (IRM), which will release it when the appropriate external signal is present. The external signal itself—the sign stimulus—is pretty minimal: as we have seen, almost anything red can set off aggressive reactions in a male stickleback during the courtship period—although it does have a kind of "ideal form". But it acts as a kind of "on-off" switch: when the sign stimulus is present, the animal shows the behaviour; when it isn't, it doesn't.

Contrast and colour

Tinbergen and Perdeck (1950) investigated the begging response that herring gull chicks make when a parent gull returns to the nest. They began by presenting the chicks with a minimal stimulus—a cardboard cut-out model, with just an eye and a beak—and found that it was just as effective as a realistic three-dimensional model in eliciting the response. Adult herring gulls have white heads, yellow beaks, and a red spot on the lower part of the beak. By varying the beak and spot colours, and also the contrast between the spot and the beak, Tinbergen and Perdeck showed that the chicks were responding to two dimensions of the stimulus: "redness", and spot contrast.

These two dimensions seem to be independent in terms of their ability to elicit the response, even though in nature they go together. But the chicks in the study responded to "redness" regardless of whether it actually related to the spot—they even responded more to models with entirely red beaks than they did to naturalistic models with yellow beaks. They also responded most to models in which there was a sharp contrast between the spot and the beak, regardless of colour: white models with black spots on the beak elicited a strong begging response, but grey beaks with spots of a different shade of grey produced much weaker reactions.

Movement

Movement may also be part of the way that a sign-stimulus is identified. In one study, Lorenz and Tinbergen reported on the behaviour of some young turkey chicks when they were exposed to a bird's silhouette moving overhead on a wire. When it moved in one direction, the shape resembled a goose, flying with its long neck stretched out; and at such times the young chicks ignored it. But when it moved in the other direction, it resembled a hawk, with a short neck and long tail, and the young chicks would cower and freeze until it had passed over. Although the shape was the same in both cases, as shown on the page opposite, it was the direction of movement that determined whether it had acted as a sign stimulus or not.

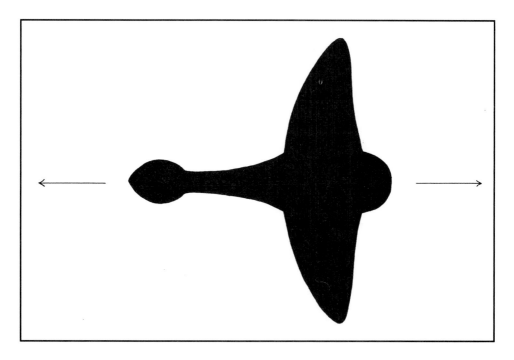

←————————   ————————→

The hawk-goose shape

Schneirla (1965) criticised the conclusions drawn by Lorenz and Tinbergen in this study, pointing out that it is a basic response in most animals with predators to freeze in response to sudden changes of light and dark. When the hawk-goose was moving with the long tail forward, Schneirla argued, the darkness of the shape would only approach the chicks gradually; but when it moved in the other direction the full shadow of the shape would appear suddenly, producing the response. A purely triangular shape, Schneirla argued, would have just the same effect: it was nothing to do with the resemblance of the figure to a predatory bird.

In this debate, Schneirla was applying Lloyd Morgan's canon—arguing that Lorenz and Tinbergen's explanation was unnecessarily complex, and that a simpler mechanism would do. But the argument produced some debate between researchers, as there does seem to be some evidence that movement is involved in some releasing mechanisms, and also that some kinds of pattern templates may be "wired-in" to the brain. We will find some similar mechanisms when we look at imprinting in Chapter 3.

Super-releasers

Tinbergen (1948) also showed that it was possible to create a sort of "super-releaser"—a stimulus that had all of the important characteristics of the sign stimulus, only more so. When the animal was exposed to this type of exaggerated stimulus, it would show an equally exaggerated response—performing the behaviour even more frantically. For example, when a herring gull's egg was placed near the nest of an oystercatcher, the bird chose to brood the gull egg in preference to its own. Herring gulls' eggs have almost identical markings to those of an oystercatcher, but they are roughly twice the size, so the egg may have acted as a super-releaser. It has been suggested, too, that the super-releaser mechanism has been exploited by some species. One possibility, for example, is that the reason why small birds will work so hard to feed a cuckoo chick is because the large gaping mouth of the cuckoo chick acts as a kind of super-releaser for their feeding behaviour.

It's not clear what role super-releasers serve in nature, or even if they serve any function at all. It is possible that the power of super-releasers is a side-effect of the neurological preparedness which gives the stimulus its power to release the behaviour in the first place. A young herring gull chick, for instance, clearly inherits some mental readiness to respond to the stimulus, but, as Tinbergen and Perdeck showed, the dimensions of that stimulus to which it actually responds are relatively simple, and of the sort that could be "programmed" neurologically. So a particularly powerful stimulus might trigger those brain cells to produce a particularly powerful response.

In 1984, Lea produced a modified list of characteristics of inherited behaviour. This list resembled that produced earlier by Lorenz, but also incorporated the idea of sign stimuli. Lea identified six characteristics of inherited behaviour, which are listed in the panel below.

Ritualisation and displacement

In a study of the mating behaviour of great crested grebes, Huxley (1942) showed how they act out an elaborate ritual, in which each member of the pair takes turns to perform actions, or to participate in sequences of

Characteristics of inherited behaviour, from Lea, 1984		
Stereotypy	The behaviour should always occur in the same form
Universality	The behaviour occurs in all members of a species
Independence of experience	The behaviour should appear regardless of the individual's past history
Ballisticness	The behaviour is unchanging once it has been triggered off, regardless of circumstances
Singleness of purpose	The action is not shown in other contexts, even if it might be useful
Triggering stimuli	The behaviour can be reliably triggered by a known stimulus

actions. In one part of the ritual, for instance, the male great crested grebe presents water-weed to the female, as if it were food; and the female accepts it and makes motions as if she is eating it. The total ritual always follows the same sequence, and always involves turn-taking on the part of the individuals concerned.

Interestingly, Huxley's observations showed how parts of the ritual clearly derived from everyday actions, but were not the same. For example, when the female accepts water-weed from the male, although her actions resemble eating, she doesn't actually consume it. Instead, the behaviour is undertaken in a stylised, ritual manner and is not a normal everyday action.

One observation which intrigued many researchers was the phenomenon that came to be called *displacement*. From time to time, observers had noticed that, if an animal was engaged in a ritual sequence, sometimes it would suddenly stop what it was doing and start doing something entirely different instead. For example, a gull engaged in a aggressive behaviour—like, say, a ritual of threat and counter-threat with another gull—might suddenly break off and begin preening its feathers. This new, sudden action seemed to be completely irrelevant to what had gone before, and to appear just randomly, for no reason.

Other researchers identified different kinds of *rituals*. Lorenz (1950; 1966) argued that most animals defend territories and social position by a series of ritualised gestures, designed to display the natural weaponry of the aggressor. So traditional threat gestures made by animals—a cat arching its back and spitting; a dog baring its teeth with the hair on its back standing on end—are designed to make the animal appear as fearsome as possible.

Such *threat displays* occur in many species. A male gorilla intent on scaring intruders from its territory stands up, roars and beats its chest, before charging at the intruder and coming up short only a metre or so away. Most animals, faced with such a display, will turn tail and run: in such cases, the gorilla rarely pursues, but instead returns quietly to its troop, grunting occasionally (Schaller, 1964). In a chimpanzee threat display, the animal's fur stands out all over its body, making it appear bigger than it really is, and it jumps up and down, building up staccato hoots into a crescendo of shrieks, and baring its teeth widely at the intruder. Another chimpanzee, faced with such a display, may respond with a similar display of its own, or may keep its distance and turn away.

Some animals, Lorenz argued, have developed exaggerated forms of natural weaponry which enhance the threat of their displays. The extremely enlarged claw of the male fiddler crab is more or less useless for feeding purposes, but it is used often for defence of territory: an occupying crab waves its claw at an intruder, and two antagonists will use their claws in battle. Similarly, Gould (1978) argued that the excessively large horns of the Irish elk—often cited as a classic example of evolution's absurdities—made sense if viewed as ritual weapons, designed to intimidate the opposition.

As a general rule, Lorenz argued, such threat displays would end in one animal backing down by running away or withdrawing from the territory. However, sometimes the other would respond by a similar display. Lorenz argued that in such cases, the nature of the fighting which the animals engaged in would be such as to limit the possibility of serious injury to the animals concerned. A study of mountain sheep by Geist (1966) showed that conflicts between these animals did seem to occur in such a way as to avoid serious damage. Instead of a free-for-all, animals engaging in fights with members of their own species would generally go for non-vital parts of the body. They would use their natural weaponry—in the case of mountain sheep, their curly horns—in such a way that the apparent threat was maximised while the real damage was minimised.

Lorenz took the view that such ritualisation of combat had evolved so as to ensure that members of a species did not kill one another—such mechanisms meant that the group as a whole was more likely to survive.

RODNEY HAD HIS OWN IDEAS ABOUT 'NATURAL' WEAPONRY.

He also believed that animals had an automatic system for stopping such conflicts, if one animal was obviously losing. This was achieved by the use of *appeasement gestures*—submissive postures designed to present the animal in a inoffensive light. Appeasement gestures often involve the exposure of vulnerable body parts, like the soft belly of a dog as it rolls on its back, or behaviour which resembles that of a young member of the species. Lorenz argued that these acted as automatic, innate brakes on aggressive behaviour—as sign stimuli signalling the end of the fighting. When faced with an appeasement gesture of this kind, Lorenz argued, virtually all species with the exception of rats and human beings would instantly refrain from further aggression.

According to Lorenz, the display of natural weaponry meant that the outcome of most conflicts could be predicted, in the sense that one contender was generally obviously stronger than the other, so most conflicts between members of the same species would not actually come to a fight. Even if that were not the case, and the two animals did end up fighting, the interplay of ritual threat gestures and ritual appeasement gestures meant that intraspecific antagonistic encounters (antagonistic encounters between members of the same species) would rarely result in serious injury.

As we shall see in Chapter 4, there have been many challenges to Lorenz's theory. Among other problems, Lorenz made the very Cartesian assumption that behaviour was essentially genetically controlled, and therefore mechanistic, no matter what the species of animal was. As we shall see later, there are grounds for thinking that the control of behaviour shifts gradually from genetic to learned social controls as we move up the phylogenetic scale. When we are talking about aggression in dogs or rats, although it is clear that the general types of actions have probably been inherited (dogs rarely fight by boxing one another with their forepaws, for instance!), we are certainly not talking about the same kind of formal, elaborate ritual that is found in some species of birds. As any owner of a pugnacious dog will tell you, dogs adopt different tactics on different occasions, and will change their behaviour during the course of a fight if it seems appropriate. So their actions don't exactly measure up to the characteristics of genetically controlled behaviour identified by Lorenz and Tinbergen (1938) which we looked at earlier.

The question remains, therefore, just how far a particular kind of behaviour can really be considered to be "purely" genetic, and independent of environmental factors. Although early work by Lorenz and Tinbergen tended to be based on the assumption that the behaviour was produced almost mechanically, as a result of inherited mechanisms, later researchers showed that the interaction of inherited mechanisms and environmental factors was very much more complicated. These issues will be coming up again as we look at specific areas of comparative research in later chapters; but it is worth exploring the general debate here.

Lorenz's hydraulic model

In 1950, Lorenz proposed that the mechanisms of sign stimuli, innate releasing mechanisms, and fixed action patterns might be visualised as operating like a hydraulic system. The idea was that if a certain form of behaviour was innate, then, given the right circumstances, the animal would experience a powerful inherited drive to perform that behaviour. This drive would be motivated by what Lorenz referred to as *action-specific energy*—energy that was directed towards performing that inherited behaviour and nothing else.

In Lorenz's model, below, the action-specific energy relating to a specific drive would be continually building up, rather in the way that a tank will fill with liquid from a continuously dripping tap. If an appropriate sign stimulus appears in the environment, it will operate the innate

Lorenz's model of action-specific energy

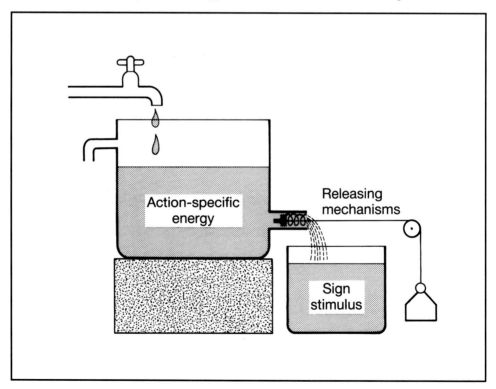

releasing mechanism (IRM) associated with that drive, and that will open a channel, allowing the action-specific energy to gush out, producing the behaviour. If the sign stimulus happens to be particularly powerful, it acts as a super-releaser, opening the channel very wide so that even more energy is released. But if no appropriate sign stimulus appears in the environment at all, then the tank will gradually fill up, until the action-specific energy overflows, randomly, producing displaced activities drawn from other innate behaviour patterns.

Tinbergen (1951) extended this idea into an hierarchical model of how action-specific energy develops and is applied (see below). At the top of the hierarchy in Tinbergen's model is the main drive centre, which is powerfully affected by the influence of hormones, seasonal cycles, and other such factors. This is where the action-specific energy builds up, but only in the right environmental conditions (for example, action-specific energy concerning aggression in male deer only builds up at the rutting time of year—the rest of the time they are quiescent and non-aggressive).

The action-specific energy then flows down to the next level in the form of motivational impulses. These produce what Tinbergen referred to as *appetitive behaviour* in the animal—behaviour that makes the occurrence of sign stimuli and the action of IRMs more likely. So, for example, a male

Tinbergen's adaptation of Lorenz's model

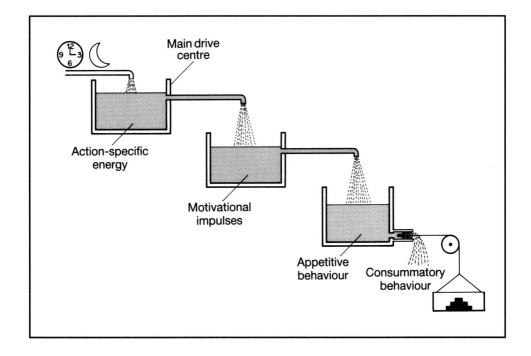

stickleback will patrol the boundaries of his territory, on the alert for any sign of a rival, rather than swimming about in the centre of the area. The patrolling behaviour makes it more likely that a rival male will be spotted, and so makes the release of aggressive behaviour more likely as well.

The next level is the one described in Lorenz's hydraulic model. If a sign stimulus actually appears in the environment, the action-specific energy becomes channelled into *consummatory behaviour*—the fixed action pattern that the action-specific energy is geared to produce. As this behaviour is performed, the action-specific energy drains away. Tinbergen had observed that a male stickleback which had just been involved in an aggressive display to a rival was much less likely to respond to another one immediately afterwards, or if it did respond, it did so less energetically. So the idea of the action-specific energy having been used up, and of the reservoir needing to refill itself, seemed to be a plausible model.

Tinbergen explained displacement as the outcome of the animal finding itself caught between two equally powerful drives, so that there were two sets of action-specific energy building up, but the animal could only consummate one. The most common of these, Tinbergen proposed, was the conflict between the drive to fight—or at least, to engage in aggressive displays—and the drive to flee from the threatening rival. Tinbergen suggested that when a conflict like this became too powerful, the action-specific energy would build up too much, because it had no outlet; and so it would overflow into another instinctive system, producing these random actions.

Criticisms of the hydraulic model

Although on the surface, the hydraulic model formulated by Lorenz and Tinbergen appeared to explain what was going on quite adequately, a number of weaknesses in it quickly became apparent:

Using up action-specific energy.   One of the problems in the model was the way that it suggested that action-specific energy would be used up by the animal performing whichever consummatory behaviour was the appropriate one for that energy. Prechtl (1953) found that what actually happened was more like habituation: although the behaviour would die out in response to exactly the same stimulus, changing the stimulus would result in the re-emergence of the fixed action pattern. Young chaffinches gape their beaks widely when they hear the sound of an adult chaffinch. But they also gape if their nest vibrates, and Prechtl found that they were just as ready to do this even after their gaping response to sounds had died out through repeated stimulation. To do this, they must still have had action-specific energy available.

The alternative also seemed to happen: that the action-specific energy reservoir didn't seem to refill itself as it should. Hinde (1954), exposed chaffinches to continuous or repeated exposure to predators, and showed that their alarm calls declined. But this decline continued for a very long time—much longer than would have been needed for new levels of action-specific energy to build up. Again, what was really happening seemed to be much more similar to a learning process, of *habituation* to a single stimulus, than to the mechanical release of action-specific energy in response to a pre-programmed stimulus.

The role of displacement.   There were questions raised, too, about the role of displacement. In Lorenz and Tinbergen's model, displacement was essentially a random process—the excessive energy simply "overflowed" into other fixed action patterns. But other researchers suggested that displacement wasn't random at all. Räber (1948) showed that the immediate environment exerted an influence on displacement: if a turkey was engaged in an aggressive interaction with another, its displacement activities would concern drinking if there was water nearby, or eating if there was food instead.

Andrew (1956) proposed the *disinhibition hypothesis*, suggesting that what is happening in displacement is that when the two conflicting demands (to fight or to flee) become strong enough, they inhibit one another. But the animal must do something, so what it actually does is a brief resumption of the behaviour that it would have been showing anyway, if the aggressive episode hadn't been going on. The animal's normal routine has been inhibited by the aggressive encounter, but for a moment that inhibition lifts, and the animal goes back to ordinary activity. The fact that displacement activities generally tend to be very routine ones (preening, eating, drinking, etc.) lends some support to this idea.

Consummatory act or consummatory stimulation?   Another issue which became less clear as researchers looked more deeply into the hydraulic model was the distinction between appetitive and consummatory behaviour. Lorenz and Tinbergen had argued that action-specific energies were released when the animal actually performed the fixed action pattern: they saw the fixed action pattern as the *consummatory act*. One of the examples of fixed action patterns which they used was that of egg-rolling behaviour in the greylag goose. The sign stimulus was that the egg was missing from the nest, and the fixed action pattern was the way that the goose stretched out its neck and rolled the egg backwards until it was safely back in the nest. This action, they showed, was performed in exactly the same way each time.

However, Beer (1962) pointed out that the bird would only stop its egg-rolling behaviour when the egg was safely back. In other words, it wasn't the act itself that mattered, but the end result of the action. Beer proposed that fixed action patterns should be regarded as another kind of appetitive behaviour, making consummation more likely. Bastock, Morris, and Moynihan (1953) suggested that it is more appropriate to think of the end result (the egg back in the nest) as a *consummatory stimulus*, rather than to think of the fixed action pattern itself as a consummatory act. It isn't the action itself which satisfies the drive, it's the outcome of the action.

These challenges to the hydraulic model had one higher-order issue in common. Where Lorenz and Tinbergen were suggesting that these behaviours were entirely genetic in origin, researchers were discovering an interaction between the behaviour and the animal's environment.

Learning an instinct

Evidence for such an interaction was strengthened as researchers began to explore how genetic influences and environmental learning could act together. In a *Scientific American* paper entitled "How an instinct is learned", Hailman (1969) showed that even apparently entirely genetic behaviours improved with practice. The investigation focused on a particular behavioural interaction which Tinbergen had studied in 1959, Tinbergen had shown how adult and chick laughing gulls interact in a sequence of sign stimuli and fixed action patterns which results in the adult regurgitating food for the chick. When the adult returns to the nest, it swings its beak from side to side. This exposes a red spot, on the side of the beak. The chicks then peck at the red spot, and the pecking stimulates the adult to regurgitate food. By using models, Tinbergen showed that the positioning of the red spot was essential in eliciting the pecking behaviour from the chicks: if the red spot was anywhere else, for instance on the forehead, the chicks would not peck.

The laughing gull chick's pecking is a classic example of a fixed action pattern, in Lorenz's terms. But Hailman showed that even this was susceptible to environmental influences. As the young gulls aimed at the red spot, their pecking would become increasingly accurate with practice. Through further investigation with models it emerged that the sideways movement as the adult gull swung its beak was also a part of the sign stimulus, and it was very clear that the young gulls got better at hitting the moving target as they had more experience. On the first few occasions, they would miss the target entirely from time to time, but gradually they homed in on the spot, until eventually they would hit it each time. So even an instinctive response was one that had to be learned, to some extent.

As we saw earlier, Marler and Tamura (1964) showed that young American white-crowned sparrows would produce a regional "dialect" in their song only if they had heard it when they were less than four months old. Although the song itself was inherited, there was an environmental influence in the production of the finished article, as sung by birds in their natural environment.

What has become increasingly apparent, then, is that "purely" inherited behaviour as such is a bit of a fiction. Instead, behaviours that are instinctive in the sense of being shaped and/or produced by genetic influences are also influenced by an interaction with their environment. In many ways, this mirrors the distinction between genotype and phenotype which we examined at the beginning of this chapter: although the genetic blueprint of the genotype does exist in an idealised form, it doesn't actually manifest itself in reality, because everything develops within an environment, and interacts with it.

This interaction between genetic and environmental influences in the development of behaviour represents an important theme in modern comparative psychology. Hinde (1970) argued that to try to represent innate and environmental factors as "either–or" questions is impractical, because it is the interaction between the two that matters. Accordingly, we will now go on to look at some of the ways that environmental influences can shape behaviour, and in the other chapters we will be seeing how the two work together in producing specific kinds of behaviour.

Animal learning

While the European ethologists were exploring the characteristics of inherited behaviour patterns, American comparative psychologists were exploring the characteristics of the basic forms of animal learning which we have come to know as conditioning.

Classical conditioning

In 1903, the American behaviourist J.B. Watson showed that an animal would learn to perform an action if a connection between that action and an environmental stimulus was repeated often enough. He described this as the Law of Exercise—learning happens, he said, because the association between the stimulus and the response is exercised through repetition. Together with the work of Ivan Pavlov on conditioned reflexes, this produced the foundation of awareness of the kind of learning that became known as *classical conditioning*. Classical conditioning represents in many ways the most "primitive" kind of learning of all. A stimulus becomes able to produce a response simply because it has been associated with another stimulus which already has that effect.

Pavlov, in his book *Conditioned reflexes* (Pavlov, 1927) showed how autonomic responses, previously thought to be entirely inherited, could be conditioned to occur in response to a new stimulus. Working with the salivary reflex in dogs, he showed that dogs could be trained to salivate in response to just the sound of a bell, if for some time previously they had heard the bell at the same time as being presented with their food. The principle was of associating two stimuli by presenting them at the same time. One stimulus would already produce an autonomic response, and the other one was neutral. By being associated, the neutral stimulus would come to elicit the response (see diagram below).

Classical conditioning

Pavlov also found that this new learning would become generalised to other, similar stimuli: the closer the stimulus was to the original, the

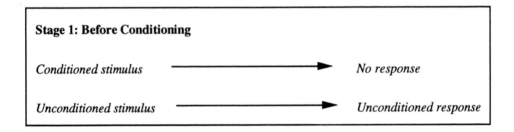

Stage 1: Before Conditioning

Conditioned stimulus ⟶ *No response*

Unconditioned stimulus ⟶ *Unconditioned response*

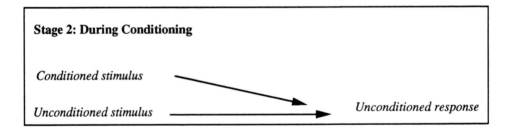

Stage 2: During Conditioning

Conditioned stimulus

Unconditioned stimulus ⟶ *Unconditioned response*

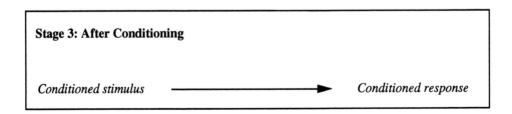

Stage 3: After Conditioning

Conditioned stimulus ⟶ *Conditioned response*

stronger the response. So, for example, a dog that had learned to salivate in response to the sound of one particular bell would also salivate when it heard the sound of a different bell. If the bell sounded very similar, the salivation response would be strong; if it was somewhat different in tone from the original bell, then the response would be weaker, as shown below. This process of generalisation seemed to be pretty well universal: any learned response was liable to be generalised to similar stimuli.

However, generalisation didn't just mean that the animal produced the response more and more often, because it would also learn to discriminate between different stimuli. Discrimination is based on the principle of *extinction*. In order for this type of learning to remain strong, the association between the conditioned stimulus and the unconditioned one has to be repeated from time to time. If it isn't, then the learning will die out—the learned association between stimulus and response will become extinguished. So when a response generalises to other stimuli, as a rule it

Stimulus generalisation

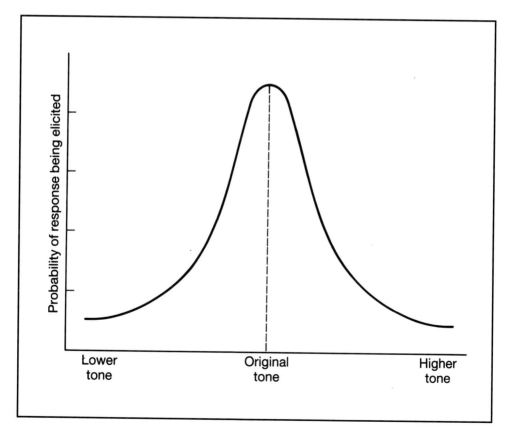

eventually dies out because it is not reinforced (strengthened), whereas the original learned response will be reinforced from time to time. This is the process of discrimination: as a result of selective reinforcement, the response is eventually produced in response to one stimulus, but not in response to a similar one.

Extinction doesn't always happen if a stimulus-response link isn't reinforced, though. There's a form of classical conditioning that is particularly powerful, and in which only one association of stimulus and response seems to be enough to create a very strong kind of learning indeed. This is known as *one-trial learning*. You may have had some experience of it yourself, if you have ever had the experience of eating a particular food and then being sick. After that, even the sight of that particular food can make you feel ill again. The association between the food and sickness is a strong form of learning, which doesn't extinguish easily at all—in fact, it can remain just as strong for years. We will be discussing the reason why this type of learning is so strong later in this chapter.

One of the most important characteristics of all forms of classical conditioning is the idea, at least in the orthodox, original version, that classical conditioning has nothing to do with cognition. In the case of one-trial learning, it doesn't matter at all if you know that the food is safe to eat this time—you still won't want to eat it. And more conventional classical conditioning for the most part tends to be concerned with autonomic responses, like fear, arousal, or salivation—responses and reflexes that are not generally under conscious control.

More recent work in this area has suggested that there might, in fact, be a cognitive influence in classical conditioning, at least in the sense that expectation and prediction seem to be important. Rescorla (1968) performed a series of studies which showed how it was important that a conditioned stimulus should predict an unconditioned one. In one study, groups of rats were placed in a situation in which they heard a tone from time to time, and there was then a 40% probability that they would receive an electric shock. The rats whose shock was always preceded by the tone quickly learned to associate the two; but those who only heard the tone at random intervals did not learn to respond to the tone at all. Rescorla (1972) argued that the important feature of the conditioning process was that it allowed the animal to predict what was likely to happen. Without prediction and expectation, Rescorla argued, even classical conditioning wouldn't happen.

Other work also supported the idea that prediction was important. Kamin (1969) showed that having a conditioned stimulus that can predict an unconditioned one seems to be quite enough in itself for learning to take place. If an animal learns that one conditioned stimulus is always followed by an unconditioned one—in other words, if it learns that the stimulus is a reliable predictor—then it doesn't condition to other stimuli that are available in the environment. For example, Kamin showed that if a rat has learned that a light reliably predicts an electric shock, then it will ignore other stimuli, like a tone. Having learned one reliable predictor, it doesn't seem to need any others, and so it blocks out new associations.

Seligman (1971) suggested that the conditioned stimulus forms a "warning" signal to the animal, indicating what an appropriate response will be. In a series of studies, Seligman showed that rats which have no reliable predictor that a shock is coming become continuously fearful, and may even develop ulcers from the stress. The value of the predictor, in Seligman's argument, is that it reduces uncertainty. By indicating to the animal when it is safe to relax and when it is appropriate to be alert and fearful, it allows the animal to perform more effectively in its day-to-day life.

Operant conditioning

Thorndike (1911) reported a series of investigations of trial-and-error learning, in which hungry cats were enclosed in a "puzzle box", and food was placed outside. The cat could release itself from the box by pulling at a piece of string which dangled down. Thorndike timed how long it would take the cat to escape from the box, and found that the time that each cat needed became shorter and shorter with the number of occasions on which it was shut in. This produced a classic learning curve when it was plotted on a graph, reproduced overleaf.

Thorndike argued that the reason why the cats were learning to perform the behaviour of pulling the string was because doing so had a positive effect: it allowed the cat to escape from the box, and to reach the food. This, Thorndike argued, was an illustration of a fundamental principle of learning: the *Law of Effect*. This principle states that if an action has pleasant consequences for the organism which performs it, then it will be more likely to be repeated.

Research into the Law of Effect was taken up by the behaviourist B.F. Skinner. In 1938, Skinner reported on a set of investigations designed to disentangle different aspects of this type of learning. For example, Skinner distinguished between two different kinds of positive effects: those which allowed the animal to avoid or escape from unpleasant stimuli—like escaping from a small box—and those which allowed the animal to reach desirable stimuli—like eating food. Both of these effects, Skinner argued, reinforced (strengthened) the learned behaviour; but they did so in different ways, and had different effects. Skinner referred to the positive

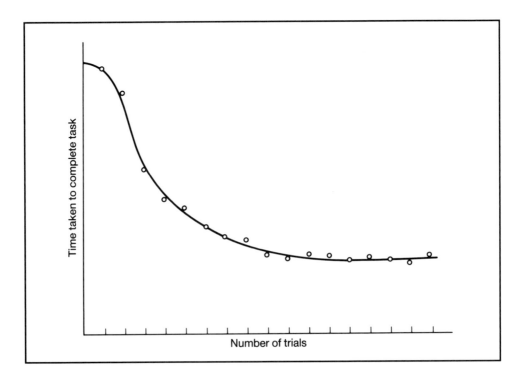

A learning curve

outcome of escape or avoidance as *negative reinforcement* (not the same as punishment, as we shall see later in this chapter), and the positive effect of receiving rewards as *positive reinforcement*.

One of the different effects of positive and negative reinforcement was in how resistant the learning was to extinction. If an animal has learned to avoid an unpleasant stimulus by performing some action—like, say, pressing a lever to stave off an electric shock—then it is likely to perform this action each time the situation seems to demand it. The learned response is particularly resistant to extinction, because the animal never actually gives itself an opportunity to learn that the unpleasant consequence is no longer likely to happen. But if an animal has learned an action to receive a reward—say, if it has learned to press a lever to receive a food pellet—then the response will begin to extinguish once the animal is no longer receiving the reward.

In later work, Skinner (1969) found that it was also possible to alter the resistance to extinction of behaviour learned through positive reinforcement. By manipulating the reinforcement contingencies—in other words, by adjusting what the animal had to do in order to gain a reward—he found that this type of behaviour could actually become quite resistant to

Schedule	Outcome
Continuous	Moderate rate of response; low resistance to extinction
Fixed interval (FI)	Slow rate of response; low resistance to extinction
Variable interval (VI)	Steady rate of response; high resistance to extinction
Fixed ratio (FR)	Very high rate of response; low resistance to extinction
Variable ratio (VR)	High rate of response; high resistance to extinction

extinction if trained in the appropriate way. The main ways that reinforcement contingencies are manipulated—known as *schedules of reinforcement*—are listed in the panel above.

The basic principle of this type of conditioning, according to Skinner (1938) is that an animal, naturally, is active. Just as part of being alive, it will perform different types of behaviour, which Skinner referred to as *operants*. If one of those operants produces a positive effect, then the animal will show an increased likelihood of performing again. Moreover, this conditioned behaviour will also be slightly variable in nature, so if only one variant of it is rewarded the animal will show that variant increasingly often, and so on. In this way, it is possible for quite complex forms of behaviour to be built up gradually, one step at a time. This process is known as *behaviour shaping*.

The process of behaviour shaping is important for two reasons: first, because it suggests a learning mechanism by which entirely novel forms of behaviour can be built up (classical conditioning can only deal with responses that the animal already has). Second, behaviour shaping deals with the training of voluntary behaviour, and not simply automatic reflexes (classical conditioning is mostly concerned just with autonomic functions). Skinner argued that behaviour shaping is the process by which both human beings and animals learn complex kinds of behaviour. Even human language, Skinner argued, develops as a result of parents and others reinforcing the child's operant behaviour of babbling, such that it becomes shaped to include an increasing number of word-like sounds, until eventually the child is able to produce whole words, and then sentences (Skinner, 1957).

Naturally enough, this claim produced a powerful reaction from linguists and many psychologists, spearheaded by the linguist Noam

Chomsky (Chomsky, 1959). It's not really appropriate to go into this debate here, but Skinner's claim was part of his extreme *behaviourist* outlook, in which he saw all human behaviour as explicable purely in terms of conditioning processes. The idea that all human—and animal—behaviour can be reduced to just a couple of simple processes is, in its own way, just as reductionist as Lorenz's view that human and animal behaviour could be reduced to the action of genetic mechanisms. Nowadays, few comparative psychologists would hold to either of these extreme views, for reasons which we will be looking at later on in this book.

Another aspect of operant conditioning that Skinner identified, and which formed a significant basis for his argument that all human behaviour could be understood through conditioning, was the phenomenon known as *secondary reinforcement*. Skinner observed that, if an additional stimulus was associated with a reinforcement (for instance, if a click sounded each time an animal received a food reward), then it seemed to acquire reinforcing properties of its own. After a while, in this example, an animal would press a lever simply to hear the sound of the click—the food reward wouldn't be necessary. One of the obvious parallels here is the way that money can act as a reward for human beings: at first, money is associated with rewarding things, like sweets or toys during childhood; but gradually it acquires reinforcing properties in its own right, so people will do things just to earn money.

Negative reinforcement. One of the important principles of Skinner's approach was the idea that it is better to reinforce desired behaviour than to punish inappropriate action, because punishing inappropriate behaviour doesn't provide any guidance as to what the human or animal ought to be doing instead. It might suppress the immediate behaviour, but they can just as well go and do something else equally inappropriate. Skinner (1972) argued that if this principle could be applied throughout society, so that people were systematically trained to act in socially desirable ways, a better society would result.

There are, of course, enormous ethical issues involved in that argument—such as whether we really want a society in which people are systematically manipulated to conform. Skinner argued that ideas about human dignity and freedom were myths anyway, as people were already being manipulated by their reinforcement contingencies. Other psychologists, however, took the view that human beings are not entirely driven by behavioural contingencies, as Skinner claimed. Instead, they argued that personal choice and social cognition are also significant factors in determining how people act, so there is far more opportunity for independence and autonomy in human action than Skinner allowed.

Although, on the surface, it may appear that punishment and negative reinforcement are quite similar, the important thing to remember is that operant conditioning works through the Law of Effect. Negative reinforcement strengthens learning because it has a positive outcome—allowing the organism to escape from, or to avoid, unpleasant effects. So the behaviour that the animal performs is actually encouraged, whereas in the case of behaviour that is punished, it is suppressed.

Rescorla and Solomon (1967) argued that avoidance learning through negative reinforcement actually represents a two-stage conditioning process. The first stage is where the animal or human learns to identify that the aversive stimulus is likely to happen. This stage, they said, is classically conditioned, arising from the link between the warning and the fear produced by the unpleasant event. The second stage is where the organism learns to reduce its fear by taking action of some kind, and this occurs through operant conditioning: the behaviour that the organism undertakes is rewarded by the fact that the fear goes and it is more able to relax.

For example: if an experimental rat learns to jump into a shuttle box in order to avoid receiving an electric shock, there are two stages of learning. In the first stage, the rat learns to associate the warning (such as a light), with its response to the electric shock. So it becomes fearful (its response to the shock) when it sees the light. This happens by classical conditioning. Then it learns that by jumping into the box, the fear is reduced, because the shock doesn't happen. In other words, jumping into the box has a pleasant effect: the rat learns this behaviour by operant conditioning.

This explanation provides an interesting example of what can happen to explanations if one aims to stick strictly within one level of analysis. In order to explain negative reinforcement purely in stimulus-response terms, it becomes necessary to evoke two different stages and two different kinds of learning to make sense of what is going on. So the explanation has become quite complicated. But if one is prepared to accept a higher-order level of analysis, involving the cognitive process of expectation, then explaining negative reinforcement becomes much less convoluted. A behaviourist would not accept saying that the signal allows the animal to anticipate the response as a valid explanation, because that would imply that the animal was somehow doing some mental processing of the information. But most modern comparative psychologists accept that animals do have some capacity for cognition, and that using a slightly higher-order level of explanation can often help us to understand what is happening much better.

Superstitious learning.   Another phenomenon of operant conditioning which illustrates the conflict between purely behaviourist and cognitive explanations is that of *superstitious learning*. Skinner had observed that experimental animals sometimes picked up odd habits: a pigeon might preen its wing briefly before pecking at a target, or a rat might turn to the left before pressing a lever. These habits seemed to have been acquired because they were associated with successful action—i.e. actions that had actually been rewarded. The pigeon, Skinner explained, had happened to preen its wing before pecking at the lever and being rewarded, and so continued to do so. This seems to be a kind of one-trial learning, based on a single performance of a successful action.

Skinner explained this phenomenon simply in terms of classical-style association, with the action producing the reward. But other researchers argued that this showed that there was some kind of expectation on the part of the animal. Rather than a mechanical link between stimulus and response, there were cognitive factors involved. Brown and Jenkins (1968) showed that pigeons will learn to peck at a light which signals that food is coming, even if their action makes no difference to whether food actually comes or not. And Schwartz and Gamzu (1977) showed that in this type of situation, the pigeons act as if they are expecting the food: those who learned this behaviour associated with food rewards would peck with beaks that were open in a feeding position, whereas those who had learned it in association with water would peck with their beaks open in a drinking position. So the implication was that the animal was in some way anticipating the reward: that there are cognitive factors involved in conditioning, even in pigeons.

Learned helplessness. Maier and Seligman (1976) found that, under certain circumstances, passive responses to stimulation appeared to generalise, so that an animal would remain passive even when taking action would have helped it considerably. In one study, dogs were linked in pairs, and given a series of electric shocks. One dog in each pair could push a panel to turn off the shock, but the other received the same shocks and was unable to do anything about them. Later, the two dogs were placed in a different situation, where they also received shocks. This time, however, a light shone before the shock came, and they could avoid the shock by jumping across a barrier into the next area. The dog that had previously been able to turn off its shocks learned to escape in the new situation very quickly; but those who had been the passive victims in the previous condition didn't learn the avoidance response at all. Instead, they just remained where they were, passively, even though it was clear that they found the shocks very unpleasant.

From this study and others, Seligman argued that learning and control were closely linked: an animal or human would only learn if it were possible to exert some control over a situation (Seligman, 1975). If no control was possible, then the animal would remain passive. As operant conditioning depends on the animal emitting operant behaviour, it can't begin to take place if the animal doesn't do anything! Seligman compared this with the apathy and inertia that is a characteristic of depression, and argued that it might be useful to think of some kinds of depression as similar to the animal phenomenon of *learned helplessness*. His argument was that depressed people become depressed because they have experienced so many disheartening situations which they were powerless to influence. This means that they cease to perceive themselves as being able to control events, and so become passive and apathetic.

The concept of *control* is another one that is difficult to interpret in a purely behaviourist framework, and yet is very useful for making sense out of what seems to be going on when we investigate these types of learning more deeply. Like the constructs of expectation and anticipation, control requires an acceptance of some kind of cognitive activity; and it adds weight to the idea that strictly behaviourist explanations for what is going on in animal learning are not really adequate.

Insight learning and learning sets

Even higher-order levels of animal learning were described by Köhler, in 1925. Köhler, a Gestalt psychologist, was interested in those holistic forms of learning in which people perceive the complete solution, all at once. He was particularly interested in *insight learning*—in which the individual gains a sudden insight into the nature of the problem, which means that from then on the solution is easy, and just fits into place. When Köhler was given the opportunity to study learning in a group of adult chimpanzees, he was concerned to find out whether this kind of learning would be possible for them.

Köhler set up a series of problems that could not be solved gradually through trial and error learning. In these problems, a goal—usually a piece of fruit—was placed out of reach of the animal, either by suspending it from the ceiling, or by placing it outside the bars of the cage. Materials with which the animal could reach the fruit were provided: boxes scattered around the cage in the case of the fruit which was hanging up, or sticks that could be poked through the bars.

In each case, Köhler found, the animal would make some unsuccessful effort to reach the fruit, and then would seem to give up. Then, quite suddenly, it would get up and begin to take the necessary actions to solve the problem. Sometimes, these solutions were quite complicated. For example, in one trial, the animal had to reach a piece of fruit outside the bars, but was only provided with a short stick—too short to reach the fruit.

However, it could be used to reach a longer stick, which was also outside the bars, and which could then be used to reach the fruit. In each case, however, the chimpanzee would manage to solve the puzzle—generally quite suddenly. Köhler argued that what was happening here was a purely *mental* kind of learning: that the animal had an insight into the nature of the problem, and was applying its understanding to it.

Perhaps naturally enough, this argument produced a strong reaction from the behaviourists. They argued that there were other possible explanations—for example, Köhler's chimpanzees had been caught from the wild, and could have learned similar solutions (reaching fruit that was too high up on a branch) by trial and error. They would be generalising this learning to the new situation, but it would still have been acquired through conditioning.

Harlow (1949) investigated the mechanisms by which trial and error learning could generalise into something that looked very like insight learning. In one of these studies, Harlow gave monkeys a series of odd-one-out puzzles, in which the animal was rewarded with a raisin or a peanut if it chose the object that was different from the other two. Very quickly, the monkey learned to solve these problems, even though the actual stimulus that formed the correct solution would be different each time. Harlow argued that what had happened was that the monkey had developed a *learning set*—a state of readiness to solve this particular type of problem. Harlow went on to show that the problems could become even more complex, but monkeys who had had prior experience in this type of learning would still be able to solve them very quickly—in most cases, after the first trial.

In some cases, an animal would learn to solve a problem that involved taking into account several additional factors. For example, it might be provided with a set of three objects such as a red square, a blue square, and a red circle. If the puzzle was presented on a tray with an orange background, then the monkey would be expected to pick out the odd colour, whereas if the tray had a green background it would be expected to pick out the odd shape. With enough experience, Harlow found that monkeys could develop a learning set that would enable them to solve puzzles like this correctly after just one attempt.

The point that Harlow was making was that it was possible to develop what appeared to be insight learning through trial-and-error learning based on operant conditioning: it wasn't necessary to invoke cognitive explanations. But that still begs the question of how a learning set is represented in the brain, or mind. As with latent learning, it doesn't show up in the animal's behaviour until it is appropriate, and that assumes that it is stored somewhere. Effectively, what Harlow's work seems to be implying is that the monkeys had learned the *concept* of odd-one-out, rather than just developing stimulus-response associations

Pearce (1987) suggested that it might be the case that insight learning involves putting together familiar components into new combinations. If this is the case, it might be that most kinds of animal would be able to perform something that resembled insight learning. Epstein et al. (1984) taught pigeons two different skills (through operant conditioning), and then put them in a situation where they would need to combine those skills. One of the skills was to push a small box towards a spot on the wall; the other was to peck at a suspended banana while standing on a box. Then the birds were given a problem in which there was a banana hanging down, and a box, but the box was some way from the banana. Although at first, the birds seemed to be "confused" by the problem, according to the experimenters, after a minute or so they would begin to push the box towards the banana so that they could peck at it. By combining the two things they had learned into a new synthesis, they had demonstrated something that looked very similar to insight learning.

Research with "higher" mammals does seem to show that a level of insight into the nature of a problem often occurs. Pryor (1981) reported on the behaviour of a killer whale in an oceanarium, which was being trained to jump over a hurdle at exactly the same time as another whale, but travelling in the opposite direction. The whale was being trained using conventional reinforcement, but it had taken to jumping late. Pryor reported that, when the trainers attempted to correct this through selective reinforcement, the whale instantly conducted a precise set of hypothesis-testing jumps, to establish the situation.

First, the whale made a perfect jump and was reinforced; second, it made a late jump and was not reinforced; third, it made a perfectly timed jump but from the wrong side of the hurdle (something it had never done before and had not been trained to do); fourth, it made a correct jump that was just a little bit late and received a very small reward; and fifth it made a correct jump that was perfectly timed, and received a large reward of fish. From that point on, it performed the action perfectly. In just five jumps, the whale had established the criteria on which it was being reinforced. This ability to check out the nature of the problem clearly showed an insight into the nature of the problem, according to Pryor (1986).

Whether or not insight learning involves abstract understanding, or whether it is simply the association of different sets of prior learning, it still seems clear that some kind of cognitive level of explanation is needed to understand what is going on—even if it is only how the animal goes about mentally representing actions.

Recent research in both classical and operant conditioning, then, tells us that animal learning is much more cognitively complex than was envisaged by Watson and Skinner. Simply seeing it as mechanistic associations between stimuli and responses is not enough to explain the evidence. In both cases, cognitive factors have been shown to be involved in this type of learning. In Chapter 6, we will be taking up the question of animal cognition, and looking at some other kinds of animal learning which suggest that animals may be more cognitively sophisticated than was previously thought.

Learning by instinct

The more we look at inherited behaviour, the more it seems that there is no such thing as behaviour that is "purely" inherited, and has no learned or environmental component at all. As we have seen, even the egg-rolling behaviour of the greylag goose, discussed by Lorenz in 1958 as a classic example of a fixed action pattern, shows some responsiveness to environmental stimuli, because the bird will also make sideways movements of its beak if the egg seems to be slipping out of line. And Hailman's work on young gulls' pecking for food showed how practice refines the instinctive behaviour, even though the fundamental response is itself innate.

But what about learning? Is there such a thing as "purely" learned behaviour, which shows no influence of genetic factors at all? The behaviourists viewed the animal, and the human being, as a *tabula rasa*—a blank slate, on which experience could write its message. Any behaviour could be trained, they believed, given the right environmental contingencies. Other researchers, however, find this view more questionable. Gould and Marler (1987) proposed that learning is constrained by instinctive predispositions: some things are learned very much more readily than others, because the animal is biologically prepared to undertake certain forms of learning.

One-trial learning

We have already encountered one form of prepared learning, when we looked at one-trial learning, and how resistant it is to extinction. Seligman (1971), investigating this phenomenon, interpreted it as a basic survival mechanism. If you are sick after having eaten something, the odds are there was a reason for it, in that it is likely that the food was bad, or poisonous. Therefore, in evolutionary terms, it increases your chances of survival if you learn never to eat that sort of food again. Similarly, if a stimulus is accompanied by a particularly traumatic or extremely painful event, the chances are it was very dangerous for you, so the more you avoid it the greater your chances of survival. And in both these cases, the faster you learn, the more your chances of survival are increased.

The implication of this phenomenon is that animals (and humans) may be genetically prepared to undertake certain kinds of learning, because it helps them to survive. Gould and Marler (1987) argued that animals are innately programmed to attend to specific cues in specific behavioural contexts. This means that they will be far more ready to link certain kinds of stimuli with certain kinds of responses.

Garcia and Koelling (1966) showed that rats would refuse to drink salty water again, if the first time they drank it, they had previously been injected with a substance which made them sick. But rats that had experienced the same conditions except for receiving an electric shock instead of an injection were not put off the salty water at all. They did, however, link the electric shock with different stimuli: the animals had first been given the salty water in the presence of a light and a clicking sound. Later, when they were given ordinary water to drink, the rats that had been made ill would drink it regardless of the situation, but those which had been given an electric shock would not drink it if the light or the click were present.

In other words, the rats had been selective as to which cues they would link with which stimuli. They were fully prepared to link the taste of salty water with being sick, and would learn from this not to touch the salt water again. They were also prepared to link an electric shock with the presence of a light or a sound; but not with a taste. The animals were more ready to link certain cues with certain other cues.

This challenges the behaviourist idea of the *tabula rasa*—the blank slate, ready to be inscribed by learned associations. The behaviourist model assumes *equipotentiality* between stimuli—it assumes that any stimulus will have equal value to any other stimulus, in terms of whether it will form an associative link or not. But Garcia and Koelling's study—and the many other studies showing similar outcomes—showed that this was not the case. Some stimuli are simply more effective than others for certain forms of learning. Seligman (1970) linked this observation firmly with evolutionary survival mechanisms: as we have seen, those stimuli and responses that are most easily connected are those that are most likely to help the animal to survive.

There have been several other studies, both ethological and laboratory-based, which have supported this idea. Von Frisch (1950) showed how bees will learn to recognise particular smells: if a bee has been fed with, say, lavender-scented food, it will then seek out lavender-scented sources in preference to other types of food. Menzel and Erber (1978) showed that the tendency for this learning seems to be particularly powerful: even after just one exposure, a bee will learn to choose a familiar scent 90% of the time—at least, if it is a flower scent. They take longer to learn non-floral scents.

If the scents are the same, bees also learn to identify food sources by their colour. They don't learn this quite as quickly as they learn about scent, but it still seems to be reasonably fast: Menzel and Erber showed that bees needed roughly three training visits to flowers of a particular colour before they would choose that colour 90% of the time. Bees will also learn to identify the shape of a flower, but they needed five or six learning trials to achieve 90% accuracy.

There are some stimuli, however, that bees will not learn at all. Although they can detect polarised light, and use it in navigation to and from the hive, bees will not learn polarisation patterns of flowers. They are very sensitive to direction in terms of which way the hive is facing, and will become very confused if it is turned round; but they are not able to learn about the direction that a flower faces.

So we can see that bee learning is not random: bees learn in response to certain kinds of cues, and these are arranged hierarchically: they are most ready to learn to forage for food in response to scent, then to colour, and then to shape; but they are not at all responsive to other kinds of stimuli. We can see how these findings make sense in terms of evolutionary processes: although the bee learns from its experience, the learning that takes place is genetically constrained so as to maximise the bee's chances of survival.

Critical and sensitive periods

Genetic factors are able to constrain learning in other ways, too. Perhaps the clearest example of this comes in the idea of the sensitive learning period: a time in the animal's development when it is particularly sensitive to certain environmental stimuli, and when the learning that results from exposure to them is rapid and (under normal circumstances) lasting. We will be looking at research into critical and sensitive periods in early infancy in the next chapter, but to illustrate the idea, we will take a well-established study of how young birds learn to sing.

Marler and Tamura (1964) reared white-crowned sparrows in isolation. They found that, when the young male birds reached a certain stage of maturity, they would begin to sing, as others of their species did. But the song that they sang was noticeably different from the songs of wild birds of that species. It was more basic, containing the fundamental features of the song but only in general outline. Moreover, adult wild birds have distinctive regional variations in their songs: the basic pattern of the song is similar, but there are embellishments, such as trills or extra notes, which are sung by all sparrows in that area, but not by sparrows from a different region.

By experimenting with exposure to the songs of wild birds at different times of life, Marler and Tamura demonstrated that there is a period when the birds are between 30 and 100 days old, during which time they are particularly sensitive to the song of the adult birds. If they hear a normal white-crowned sparrow's song during that time, then when they eventually begin to sing themselves they will show the regional dialect. If they do not, then as adults they will only produce the basic song.

This time period, therefore, is one in which the animal is very ready to learn that particular ability, and as long as it experiences the appropriate stimulation at that time, it will do so. In the wild, young white-crowned sparrows will hear their father and neighbours singing for their first 100 days or so. The birds stop singing for the summer and autumn, and begin again in late winter. So the period of sensitivity of the young bird is matched to the period when it is most likely to experience the appropriate stimulus.

A sensitive period, then, is one when the animal is in a strong state of readiness to learn something, if it experiences the right kind of stimulation. A critical period operates on the same principle, but also includes the idea that this is the only possible time for the animal to learn. In the case of the white-crowned sparrow, there seems to have been a critical period for song learning, but in many other instances it is still possible for the learning to take place outside that period, though usually only in relatively artificial situations. The important thing, however, is that both of these periods are genetically determined. The animal is learning from its environment, but how it learns and when it learns are constrained by genetic factors. In a sense, we can interpret the critical period as nature's insurance: the animal needs to be sensitive to environmental stimulation, but through the critical period the risk of this important aspect of learning going wrong somehow is minimised.

We can see, then, that just as Lorenz's model of instinctive behaviour proved to be too mechanistic, ignoring the interaction between the individual and the environment, so also did the behaviourist *tabula rasa* approach to learning, ignoring both the cognitive abilities of the animal and the influence of genetic factors in what is learned and how. In both cases, though, the extreme positions provided a starting point for subsequent investigation of animal behaviour, and became modified in the light of further research. Throughout comparative psychology, we see how innate factors, experience, and environment operate together to produce the behaviour that a given animal is showing at a given time.

In the next three chapters, we will look at some of the specific aspects of animal behaviour that have been studied in detail by comparative psychologists. We will return to the question of animal cognition in Chapter 6, where we will also examine the implications of some of these findings, to see if it is possible to identify unifying themes underlying different aspects of research in comparative psychology.

Summary: The basis of behaviour

- Individual characteristics are passed from one generation to the next by genetic transmission. This may occur through mitosis, in which case the new animal is genetically identical to one parent; or meiosis, in which case the individual inherits characteristics from two parents.
- Genes are units of heredity that take the form of sequences of DNA. They initiate protein synthesis, for growth and other functions. Genes are not considered to change much through life, but their physical expression is a result of a constant interaction with the environment, and so may vary considerably.
- There are a number of indicators of genetically determined behaviour, such as that it is fixed in form, does not vary, and will not need to be practised. It often takes the form of fixed action patterns which are triggered off by distinctive sign stimuli.
- Lorenz's hydraulic model envisaged innate behaviour as resulting from a constant flow of action-specific energy which would need to be released from time to time. There are a number of weaknesses to this argument.
- Classical conditioning is a form of animal learning which is based on the idea that a stimulus can trigger off a response as a result of association. Such learning also generalises to similar stimuli.
- Operant conditioning is a form of learning based on the idea that an action that has a positive effect for the organism—either through allowing escape or avoidance of unpleasant stimuli—is more likely to be repeated.
- Other forms of animal learning include insight learning, learning sets, and latent learning. Studies of one-trial learning and of critical and sensitive periods suggest that animals are genetically prepared for some types of learning, and so will learn them more readily.

Courtship, mating, and reproduction 3

The fundamental imperative of species survival is that the species should be continuous: that members of the species should be able to reproduce themselves. Individuals must produce young, and enough of those young must survive to ensure that an adequate number will be able to produce the generation after that. Without this process, a species will inevitably die out.

There are other criteria, too—perhaps less fundamental, but still advantageous to a species in the long term. In the last chapter, we saw how genes become mixed up into different combinations through sexual reproduction: the larger the gene pool, the more likely it is that "aberrant" genes, which carry physical disorders, will be paired with "healthy" ones. In such cases, it is the "healthy" genes that are expressed in the phenotype, and the disorder doesn't develop. But if the species has only a limited range available in the gene pool, then the chances of two aberrant genes pairing together are much higher, so that, over generations, the individuals of the species are likely to become much less healthy as these disorders accumulate. This makes it important that, whatever reproductive strategy the species uses, it is open to genetic contributions from individuals who are not part of the immediate family group.

These two principles—that enough of the new generation must survive to reproduce in their turn, and that the gene pool should be as wide as possible—have produced a huge diversity in reproductive strategies. In this chapter, we will be looking at some of the different aspects of reproductive behaviour that have been studied by comparative psychologists; but we have to remember that we are only touching on the very tip of the iceberg—that there are far more reproductive strategies taking place in the animal world than early comparative psychologists ever suspected.

Courtship and mating

Animal species take a number of different approaches to the question of mating. In some species, two animals will pair together for life—a process known as *pair-bonding*. They will spend their time together, share in the raising of the young, and refuse to mate with others if their own partner dies. In other species, two animals will pair together for just one year: they will pick out their mates at the beginning of the season, and stay together until the young have been raised and are independent. At that point, they will separate, and will select new mates the following year. In some species, mating only occurs in the season, then either the female or the male brings up the young while the other leaves to resume its single life. Yet other species engage in versions of polyandry (one female with several males) or polygyny (one male with several females). And in some species, like ants, mole-rats, or mongooses, only one or two individuals in a colony mate, and the others combine their efforts to help to raise the young.

One of the problems of trying to make sense out of this diversity of behaviours is the fact that we are not actually very well informed about how common the different practices are, and so we tend to fill in the gaps by using our own imaginations. As this often involves drawing parallels with human society, the picture that results can easily become very distorted. For example, Dawkins (1976) argued that adult animals will not raise offspring that are not related to them, because they will only protect those that share some proportion of their genes. This argument rested on two cases: first, that male mice have been known to secrete a pheromone which causes females to abort if they are pregnant with offspring not related to that male; and second, that male lions joining a pride will sometimes kill the young cubs.

However, there are numerous cases in the animal world in which non-related adults do raise individuals that are not related to them. Three of the most well-known ones are baboons, in which non-related "aunts" will often care for infants or youngsters; mongooses, which live in colonies where the young are cared for by special "aunts" who are often not related to them at all; and ostriches, which care for their young in large crèches, containing anything up to 200 young birds from many different pairs. In developing his argument, Dawkins simply ignores these examples—if it doesn't fit the explanation, it doesn't count. And this, regrettably, seems to be a major tendency when people are trying to develop theories to "explain" animal behaviour: they make sweeping generalisations which end up ignoring the enormous diversity that exists in nature.

In part, this occurs because we have not, traditionally, been very well informed about the diversity of practices: we hear a great deal about some versions of animal behaviour, and almost nothing about others. There seem to be quite a large number of species, for instance, in which the father looks after the young, and yet we hear relatively little about these—so much so, that it is not uncommon to hear the argument that mothers are biologically compelled to look after children because "that's what animals do, after all".

There are two reasons for our relative lack of knowledge about the diversity of animal behaviour. One of these concerns *anthropomorphism*. As I suggested earlier, human beings have a powerful tendency to impose their own value systems and ideas on their observations of animals. It is only very recently that researchers have been more systematic in identifying their own unconscious biases and assumptions, and some of these are still apparent even in current research (Rose et al., 1984). So the bedrock of established knowledge on which modern theory is built is often a little questionable. We will be looking at this more closely in the next chapter, when we consider theories of animal social organisation.

The other reason is related, though not the same. It is that observers of animal behaviour have tended to be attracted to studying those forms of behaviour that seem to have some human parallels. This is partly because they provide us with some useful metaphors for understanding what is going on: it would be hard to make sense out of practices that were so totally alien that they didn't connect with any aspect of our experience. And it is partly also because researchers have tended to look to studies of animal behaviour to help us to explain our own. So behaviour that has little connection with human behaviour does not attract as much attention, except from among those dedicated biologists or ethologists who have an interest in that type of species for its own sake. An example of this can be seen in studies of how animals actually mate. There are innumerable ways of combining eggs and sperm, some of which don't even require the two donors to be together in the same place at the same time. But it has been the study of *courtship*, in which two animals come together and follow some kind of ritual, which has been the focus of attention in comparative psychology.

Courtship rituals

It was animal courtship that first attracted the attention of many of the early naturalists, and later the first ethologists. In many species, the process of finding a mate and attracting it is an elaborate one, and the displays and rituals involved in courtship behaviour in different species are fascinating. One of the first formal ethological studies was Huxley's observation of the courtship behaviour of the great crested grebe, with its elaborate rituals and exchanges between the two animals. Huxley (1914) provided a detailed scientific description of this process, timing the sequences of behaviour and showing how each action acted as the signal for the next one.

Huxley's work was particularly meticulous in terms of the quality of the observation; but it also fell within a long-established European tradition of observing nature. As one of the readily available intellectual hobbies of the middle and upper classes in the 18th and 19th centuries, a considerable amount of knowledge had built up about the range of animal habits and curiosities to be found in the natural world. This well-established tradition, of course, was the basis on which both Lamarck and Darwin founded their theories of evolution, as well as being the milieu of the enormously influential Victorian naturalists like Hooker and Henslow.

With such an interest in nature in general, it was to be expected that courtship would attract special attention; and with the general acceptance of evolutionary theory, with its implication that one of the most important tasks for an animal is to reproduce itself, this interest grew. In 1951, Tinbergen reported the outcome of a series of detailed investigations of the courtship behaviour of three-spined sticklebacks. Beginning with observations of the stickleback's behaviour in its natural environment, Tinbergen had then gone on to re-create similar environments in tanks, and to perform experiments to see which factors would influence the fish's behaviour.

In the wild, at the beginning of the season the male stickleback chooses a suitable territory, and builds a tunnel-shaped nest in the centre of it. From then on, he patrols the outer limits of his territory. If a female stickleback approaches, he swims towards her in a zig-zag fashion. If she is receptive to his advances—other words, if she has eggs—she responds by lifting her head and tail, and swimming with her swollen belly protruding. The male then leads her to the nest, and nudges her when she lies in the tunnel which seems to stimulate her to deposit her eggs. Then she swims out of the nest, and the male enters the nest and releases his sperm, to fertilise the eggs (as illustrated opposite). Once this has been done, he chases the female away and resumes his patrolling, on the look-out for another female.

If a male stickleback approaches—distinctive because all males develop a bright red belly in the courtship season—the stickleback responds quite differently. He immediately begins an aggressive display, attacking the intruder to drive it away. As we saw in the last chapter, Tinbergen showed that the red belly of the male acted as the sign stimulus to the stickleback, indicating that it should act aggressively. Tinbergen also believed that the swollen belly of the female acted as a sign stimulus for the courtship ritual, and that this was why her first response to the male's approach was to raise her head and tail, making it plain that she was swollen with eggs.

In fact, Tinbergen argued, the whole sequence consisted of a chain of innate behaviour patterns, with each action forming the sign stimulus to release the next one. The male's zig-zag dance acts as a sign signal for the female to show her abdomen; this acts as a sign signal for him to lead her to the nest, which in turn acts as a sign signal for her to enter the nest; her being in the nest acts as a sign signal for him to nudge her, which acts as the signal for her to release the eggs.

Co-operation and courtship

Courtship is often thought of as an entirely individual affair: a question of one female animal and one male animal coming together to mate. If any others are involved, it is generally assumed that they are competitors, and that the purpose of the display or ritual is to exclude them from the possibilities of mating. But the long-tailed manakin has a display in which two male birds co-operate to produce an impressive auditory and visual display designed to attract a female (Foster, 1977). The display begins with a triple-syllable call, which sounds as if it were just made by one bird, but is really produced by the two individuals singing in perfect synchrony. In this way, the pair can produce as many as 300 calls an hour. If a female is attracted to the area by the call, the birds then begin an elaborate display in which the two males cartwheel around one another: one leaps into the air to come down on the other side, while the other simultaneously slides along the branch that they are on, to make room for it to land. They repeat these manoeuvres several times, then the two males, in sequence, will jump over the head of the female (who is perched on the same branch) to repeat the manoeuvres on her other side (see below).

There are variations to the display, too. At some points, the males will fly up from the perch and produce a showy, fluttering flight, holding their wings above their heads while almost hovering in one place. Then they both dart backwards and forwards, at top speed, over the female's head. The total display can last for 10 minutes or so. If, towards the end of this, the female signals that she is ready to mate by jumping about on the perch, one of the partners leaves, while the other produces a brief flight display before mating. Foster (1977) showed that this was almost always the same male: the helper rarely gained a chance to mate.

On the surface, then, there is little evolutionary benefit to the second male in helping the first in its courtship display. But one possibility is that in this way the helping bird gains a claim to the territory. There is considerable competition between manakin birds for display purposes, and other males frequently come to the area and will display in co-operation with either bird. But only the resident pair get to display regularly. It is thought that by maintaining its status as the regular "helper", the second bird maximises its chances of inheriting the site, so eventually becoming the senior bird of a new partnership, and achieving reproductive success.

Courtship of the long-tailed manakin

At present, though, this explanation is only speculation: whether it is true or not can only be discovered with further long-term research.

Courtship as ensuring appropriate mating

There have been a number of different theories put forward to explain why animals develop elaborate rituals of this kind. Tinbergen (1951) believed that one of the advantages of a complex chain of behaviour and responses of this kind was that it manages to ensure that mating occurs only with members of the right species. As the behaviour pattern seems to be innate, an animal that doesn't carry the appropriate genes would not make the appropriate responses, and even if it did so once, it would not be able to carry the whole sequence through.

If there are other similar species also resident in the area, having distinctive rituals of this kind can be a distinct advantage. For example, as Tinbergen observed, the courtship display of the ten-spined stickleback contains a number of elements which are quite similar to those of the three-spined stickleback. But there are also some crucial differences in the sign stimuli the animals present to one another. One of these differences is contained in the colouring: male ten-spined sticklebacks are completely black during the courtship season, whereas three-spined males, as we have seen, have a red belly. Because the red belly as well as the zig-zag dance acts as a sign stimulus for the female, mating with the wrong species is unlikely to take place.

Courtship as enhancing survival of the participants

Another explanation for courtship rituals which has been suggested is the idea that the content of the ritual will allow each individual to protect itself from the other partner. In the case of the sticklebacks, it has been argued that the curious posture of the female as she swims with head and tail upwards is a defence against the male's attack: by appearing obviously egg-heavy and vulnerable, she wards off the male's natural response, which is to attack any intruder. Similarly, the male's zig-zag dance has been described as the result of a conflict between the natural tendency to rush at the intruder to attack, and the tendency to lead the female to the nest in the centre of the territory. The ritualisation of these actions protects the female from attack by the male, and allows the two normally solitary animals to share the same space for long enough to fertilise the eggs.

In spiders, it is the female who represents the danger to the male: it isn't uncommon in many species of spider for the male to be eaten after mating—and sometimes even while mating is still taking place! So several species of spider have developed elaborate courtship rituals, in which the male approaches the female very cautiously indeed, in such a way as to maximise its chances of survival. The male ground-nesting spider *Pisaura mirabilis*, for example, begins the courtship by catching a fly and wrapping it up in silk. Then he presents this to the female, and quickly copulates with her while she is eating it. As soon as he has finished, he escapes—thus surviving for another time. In another species, the male spider approaches carefully in an elaborate weaving dance and gradually wraps the female herself up in silk, so that he can mate with her safely and escape before she frees herself and catches him. The survival value of this type of courtship is very clear; although, of course, it only applies to certain species.

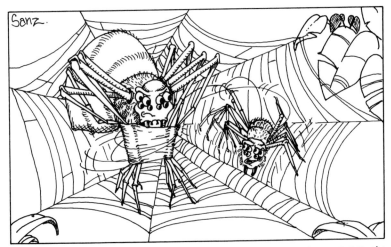

"FORGIVE ME, VERA...BUT I ALWAYS PRACTICE 'SAFE SEX'..."

Courtship as improving the species

Several studies of animal courtship have shown how courtship rituals may be a way of improving the breed. Lewin (1978) reported a study of the ritual roaring contests of male red deer, which occur at the time of the rut. Roaring forms a precursor to actual fighting: a male will approach a group of hinds and challenge the male who is with them by roaring. The incumbent male roars back, and the newcomer will then either move away, or go on to approach the male. If that happens, they will walk together, shoulder to shoulder, separated by a distance that can range from three to fifteen yards. At this point, the newcomer also sometimes withdraws, although Lewin did not see any of the incumbent males doing so. After they have walked for some distance, to a clear area, the newcomer lowers his head, and the two fight by running at one another and wrestling with their antlers.

The actual fight can be very dangerous, and animals are often severely injured. But the displays of strength beforehand mean that often things don't actually come to a fight. By measuring the roaring behaviour, for instance, Lewin and colleagues found that the rate and volume of roaring correlates very closely with how strong the animal is; and so the two are able to gauge from the roaring contest whether they are unequally matched. If the newcomer is weaker, it will withdraw from the contest: Lewin found that it is only if they are reasonably equally matched that they go on to the other stages.

The argument is that these contests of strength mean that only the strongest animals get to reproduce, which means that the species as a whole benefits. In the case of deer, which used to have natural predators like wolves as well as human beings, breeding for size and strength would have been an evolutionary advantage, because a strong animal was more likely to escape from predators. But, although this sounds reasonable in theory, it isn't nearly as clear in practice. For example, Lewin showed that it wasn't at all unknown for younger males to seize the opportunity to mate with one of the hinds while the incumbent male was off fighting with a competitor. In such cases, it clearly isn't the strongest animal that gets to breed.

Courtship as a fitness display

A related explanation for why animals engage in courtship rituals is the idea that they do so because in that way they can show their prospective partner how strong and well-adapted they are. Darwin suggested that female sexual preferences might have produced exaggerated characteristics through the evolutionary pressure of increasing the possessor's likelihood to mate. However, Hamilton and Zuk (1984) proposed that a more likely evolutionary mechanism was that such signals allowed the animal to advertise the fact that it was strong, fit, and healthy. Effectively, the animal is saying "I would make a good parent for your offspring, because I am fit and strong, and would therefore produce fit and strong young".

Courtship displays of this kind show off the animal's physical characteristics to the best advantage on the principle that a prospective mate will choose the partner who has the best display. Durrell (1966) described the courtship display of the Australian lyrebird. In this species, the bird first clears an area of ground in the forest where it lives, so there is bare earth without vegetation. Its display includes a loud, elaborate song, which is likely to attract the attention of any female lyrebirds in the vicinity, accompanied by a complex "dance", in which the bird stamps on the ground, waves its tail feathers, and even jumps onto branches and swings upside down from them. By the end of the display, any watching female would have gained a good picture of the male lyrebird's physical capability.

In general, courtship displays of this kind seem to involve males demonstrating to females, rather than the other way round. It has been argued that, in species where the female rears the young and the male doesn't, an impressive physical display indicates genetic fitness, which is what the female actually requires of the father. But a great deal more research is needed to see if this type of courtship display does actually correlate with that type of infant-rearing practice. There is so much variability in the ways that animals look after their young—in some species it is the father who cares for them, not the mother, for example— that it is too easy to jump to conclusions just because something sounds plausible, without looking carefully at whether there is actually evidence for it.

Courtship as reinforcing pair-bonding

A further explanation for courtship which has been put forward is that it strengthens the pair-bond between two mated animals. Some species mate for life, and some others remain with the same partner throughout the season. It may be that the mutual courtship rituals, which involve interaction and turn-taking between the two animals, strengthen their attachment. In Huxley's observations of the great crested grebe (Huxley, 1914), he noted that the birds would begin their courtship displays in January, and continue throughout the next six months. If they had been separated for any time, they would perform the ritual particularly intensely, which gave Huxley the idea that performing the ritual acted as a reaffirmation and strengthening of the relationship between them.

Mutual courtship rituals often involve a variety of actions, performed either in sequence or simultaneously. For example, one of the elements in the great crested grebe's courtship display was what Huxley called the "penguin dance". The birds would submerge in the water, and then they would reappear very close together, breast to breast. Each bird would have water-weed in its bill, which they would present to one another. Another part of the ritual which Huxley observed was what he described as the "head-shaking ceremony". The two birds would face each other in the water, remaining still with their crests and neck frills raised. Then they would suddenly lower their beaks, and shake their heads from side to side. A third element in the ritual was the "cat position", in which each bird would crouch low in the water, wings spread out to the side; and a fourth was what Huxley referred to as the "ghost position", in which both birds would rise up out of the water almost vertically, becoming as tall and thin as possible. The ritual consisted of a stately "dance" involving different combinations of these actions, sometimes repeated several times (see below).

As we saw in Chapter 1, these actions often resemble the actions of everyday life. For example the "penguin dance" part of the display seems to be a form of ritual feeding. But the ethologists were more interested in those parts of the ritual that seemed to resemble aggressive behaviour. Huxley suggested that the "head-shaking" part of the display was actually an example of ritualised aggressive and appeasement gestures, on the part of the two birds, and that the arousal of aggressive and appeasement mechanisms might be an important part of how the attachment was strengthened by the ritual.

Again, it isn't really possible to evaluate this explanation of courtship until we know a great deal more about the parenting and social habits of species which have elaborate mutual rituals, as opposed to those where the males compete or those where the male displays. It may well be that strengthening the pair-bonding would be important, particularly for spe-

Courtship of the great crested grebe

cies where both members of the pair devote considerable time to looking after their young; but first we need to know whether it is actually in those species that this type of ritual happens.

As you can see, these different explanations of courtship aren't mutually exclusive. There is so much diversity in the animal world, that there is room for a number of different evolutionary mechanisms and evolutionary explanations. It seems likely that, in any species with elaborate courtship rituals, the rituals will serve some kind of function for the animals concerned. However, precisely what that function is will depend very much on what members of that species need in order to maximise evolutionary survival—and that varies so much from one species to another that to look for just one single explanation for the existence of courtship rituals would be simply unreasonable.

Reproductive behaviour

Any species needs to produce enough young to ensure that some survive to produce a further generation. But there are a number of different ways of going about this. At one extreme, an option is to produce just one infant at a time, but then to invest a great deal of effort in looking after it, to maximise its changes of survival. At the other extreme, an option is to produce young in vast numbers and leave them to fend for themselves, so that even if they are preyed on in quantity, a few will survive to adulthood. And, of course, there are all sorts of variations in between. The reproductive strategy that a species adopts will depend on numerous variables, including immediate environmental demands and the animal's place in the food chain (Colinvaux, 1980).

We can find examples of almost every type of reproductive strategy in the animal world. As with the study of courtship, however, most research in comparative psychology has tended to focus on the type of reproductive strategy that shows the closest parallel with human beings.

Parenting

Although most comparative research into parenting has looked at maternal behaviour, it is important to remember that there are many species in which the males take as much share as the females in raising the young; and that in some species, like crocodiles and seahorses, it is the male who takes entire responsibility for the young—the female's task is over once she has produced the eggs and they have been fertilised.

Of course, it seems likely that there will be more species in which the mother takes prime responsibility for the rearing of the young than there are species where it is the father who is responsible. However, it is important to recognise that this is exactly one of those cases where our lack of knowledge means that we fall back on what seems reasonable to us. And as I mentioned at the beginning of this chapter, that is based as much on our own social experience as on the evidence that we have available. Without far more systematic evidence than we have at present, we cannot take this idea as axiomatic, no matter how plausible it may be as a theory. We can, though, use it as a hypothesis, as long as we bear in mind that it is just that, and not an absolute truth.

Falling back on what seems reasonable has also produced another problem. Even for species that have been studied, we know relatively little about paternal behaviour, or the behaviour of unrelated males. Because social assumptions for the first half of the 20th century (at least) were that it was really only mothers who did the child-rearing, researchers tended to focus on maternal behaviour when studying animals, and didn't really collect systematic data on the involvement of other individuals. Although there are examples in the literature of both male and female chimpanzees in a colony playing with youngsters, and the same observations have been made with some baboon troops, these have been informal observations, and haven't been the subject of study in their own right. In laboratory studies of maternal behaviour, too, animals were often kept in such a way as to restrict the opportunities for the involvement of others in infant care, so we really know very little about these broader relationships.

That doesn't mean that we are unable to learn from conventional studies of maternal behaviour. By comparing research into different mammalian species, we may find that there are regularities or general principles emerging. As with courtship, though, we need to bear in mind that any general principles that might emerge are far from reflecting the whole range of possibilities in the animal world.

Parenting in rodents

Perhaps the two most extensively researched animals in the whole world are the fruit fly and the albino rat. The fruit fly has particularly large chromosomes, and so has been extensively studied by genetic researchers; the reasons for the choice of the albino rat on the part of behavioural researchers are more obscure. Be that as it may, almost every facet of its behaviour, including its maternal behaviour, has been the subject of research.

Rosenblatt and Lehrmann (1963) described the apparently innate nest-building behaviour of the female rat. Shortly before birth, the female rat gathers nesting material into a secluded spot. She begins to lick herself repeatedly just before the birth, and continues to lick the young as they are born. Noirot (1972) proposed that this licking serves as a sign stimulus, to "prime" the onset of maternal behaviour, through exposure to the scent of the pup.

In a study designed to investigate this idea, Noirot enclosed a pup in a perforated metal box, and put it in with an adult female for a short period, so that the female could become accustomed to the pup's smell. Then the pup was removed, and a little later the female was presented with a different pup. The females immediately carried out maternal behaviour, unlike the control females, who had not had previous exposure of any kind to a pup.

The maternal behaviour of the rat in the first week or so after the pups are born consists mostly of nest-building, licking and suckling the young, and retrieving them if they stray from the nest. There appears to be a strong genetic component in this, in that this behaviour is even shown by rats that have been brought up in isolation from birth; although not if they had been prevented from ever being able to hold or manipulate objects. As usual, however, the behaviour is not purely mechanical: Kinder (1927) showed that there was some environmental interaction, in that rats would build thicker nests if the temperature was cold than they would if it was warm.

In the second week, according to Rosenblatt and Lehrman (1963), the female rat adds more material to the nest, extending it sideways. As the pups begin to crawl around more, the mother is called on to produce more complex behaviour, in retrieving sometimes unwilling pups and dealing with their attempts to suckle while out of the nest. By the third week, as the pups are beginning to eat other kinds of food, the mother becomes less tolerant as they suckle, rarely lying down for them and often moving away. She also ceases to bring the pups back to the nest, or to repair it—effectively encouraging the pups in their growing independence.

Other species of rodents show maternal behaviour adapted to their environmental situations. Young rabbits are born in a burrow, in a nest which their mother builds from her own loose fur. Unlike rats, female rabbits do not retrieve their young if they stray from the nest, although in many other respects their maternal behaviour is quite similar. Ross et al. (1963) performed a study in which infant rabbits were removed from the nest box, and placed just outside it. The mother rabbits showed a variety of reactions: sniffing, licking, and even trying to suckle the young ones, but none of them tried to retrieve them. Because, in the wild, young rabbits are reared in an enclosed space which they can't really stray from, retrieval of young who have strayed doesn't form part of the rabbit mother's behavioural repertoire.

Parenting in cats

Moving higher up the phylogenetic scale—or perhaps it would be more accurate to say moving from looking at foragers and herbivores to carnivores—the maternal behaviour of the cat seems to be more complex. After the first day, the mother cat will leave her kittens for anything up to two hours at a time, and when she returns, she licks them vigorously, which arouses them. Then she lies down, encircling them, and suckles them. Schneirla, Rosenblatt, and Tobach (1963) argued that this behaviour provides the basis for later more complex interactions. They found that the feel of the mother cat, and her smell, had a definite quietening effect on the kittens.

Mother cats do retrieve their young to the nest, at least for the first couple of weeks or so. From a series of experimental investigations, Leyhausen (1956) found that the salient cue for this is the sound of the kitten's mews: mother cats would ignore their young if they could see them but not hear them. The functional explanation for this sign stimulus links with the idea that the mewing of the kittens indicates that they are in distress and require aid from their mother. If the kittens make no noise, they are unlikely to be in distress, and therefore retrieval would be inappropriate.

As the kittens grow, and become more active, the mother spends increasing amounts of time away from the nest, and becomes less responsive to their approaches. By the end of the fourth week, she will often actively evade the kittens, deliberately remaining out of reach. This behaviour increases over the next couple of weeks, and also correlates with weaning: the young kittens are beginning to take an interest in other forms of food by the time they are four weeks old, and they become fully weaned by about six weeks of age.

By the time the kittens are independent, they accompany their mother more often. Kuo (1938) suggested that this behaviour marks the beginning of an extended learning period, in which the kittens learn from their mother the skills that they will need as adults. Kuo observed that young kittens who had watched their mother hunting mice were far more likely to hunt mice themselves as adults than those who had not; and would begin signalling interest in this type of behaviour earlier.

The mechanism by which this learning-through-observation happens has also been the subject of investigation. Kuo supposed that the mother "taught" the kittens to hunt, and that they learned through imitation; but Wilson and Weston (1947) argued that the kittens acquire the behaviour because they become aroused and excited when their mother makes the kill, and so they learn to hunt in later life as a sensation-seeking behaviour.

Parenting in sheep

The maternal behaviour of herd animals must respond to different types of environmental demands. Where young rodents and cats are effectively passive and helpless at first, many herd animals are able to move around shortly after birth—a survival mechanism that is necessary if they are to follow their herd as it moves around. In addition, whereas rodents and cats tend to care for their offpring in relatively solitary conditions, in a herd, many other animals will be present.

One of the questions, then, which needs to be answered for herd animals is: how do the individual parent and infant come to recognise each other? On the part of the young animal, this generally involves the mechanism of *imprinting*, which we will be looking at later in this chapter. But there is also the question of how the mother comes to recognise her own offspring. Hersher, Richmond, and Moore (1963) suggested that there is a sensitive period for recognition of young in sheep. Immediately after she has given birth, a mother will accept any newborn lamb, but within a few hours her maternal behaviour has become restricted to just her own lamb and no others. Although this can be forced—for example, if the mother and the strange lamb are kept very close together and the mother prevented from butting the lamb away—the dominant tendency is to reject any other individual. And, of course, in the wild state such restrictive conditions would be extremely unlikely to occur.

Lamond (1949) found that the sense of smell was very important in this process. Mother sheep could be persuaded to accept a strange lamb the day after they gave birth, if that lamb had been sprayed with their own milk. However, after a full day had passed, this technique was less successful. Other researchers found that other sensory modes were involved too: Hersher et al. (1963) found that the appearance of the lamb seemed important: mothers would spend far more time sniffing at a strange lamb that resembled their own than they would a lamb that looked different; and they were also more likely to accept a visually similar lamb for adoption.

As the lambs mature, and begin to mingle more with the flock, the auditory stimulus becomes significant. When the mother notices that her lamb is not present, she begins to call loudly, which acts as the signal to the lamb, who in turn responds by running to the mother. Murie (1944) observed that lambs would always respond to the calls of their mothers, although mothers would sometimes respond to calls from lambs that were not their own.

When the young lambs are between three and six months of age, the mother appears to lose interest in them. She ceases to call them when they are missing, and will not always allow them to suckle. At this time the young lambs begin to spend increasing amounts of time in "schools"— groups of youngsters of the same age—and the amount of time that they spend with their mother becomes less and less, until by eight months or so, they are fully independent.

Parenting in rhesus monkeys

Moving even further up the phylogenetic scale, as it were, we find even more complexity in the maternal behaviour of the rhesus monkey. Harlow, Harlow, and Hansen (1963) performed a number of studies of maternal behaviour in rhesus monkeys which were kept in various combinations in the primate laboratories at Wisconsin. The assumption underpinning the research programme was, at least initially, that the maternal behaviour of these animals would be likely to be largely genetically determined, in that it would be expected to remain reasonably consistent even in an artificial environment.

Harlow et al. identified three distinct phases in rhesus monkey maternal behaviour, which they described as projection, ambivalence, and rejection. In the projection phase, which lasted until the infant was about two months old, as a general rule, the mother would keep in close physical contact with the infant, cradling and grooming it frequently. In the ambivalent phase, from about two to about fifteen months, she would sometimes show affectionate, projection-type behaviour, but at other times would push the infant away or act punitively towards it. The amount of rejection would increase steadily through this phase, until from about fifteen months onwards the mother would actively reject the infant most of the time.

Although they did identify these general trends in monkey maternal behaviour, Harlow et al. also found that there was a considerable amount of individual variation in the different ways that mothers interacted with their infants. Not every mother went through the phases at the same times, and they varied considerably in how much they rejected the infant in the second and third phases.

This led on to investigations as to the source of these variations. Ruppenthal et al. (1976) proposed that they might be something to do with a lack of attachments in early infancy: perhaps the mothers had not learned how to act maternally from their own mothers. As a result of studies into the nature of attachment, which we will be looking at later in this chapter, there were some 50 young monkeys in their laboratories which had been reared without contact with their mothers. Instead, 25 of them had been reared with only wire mesh models to act as "surrogate mothers" in their cages, 17 had been reared with towelling-covered models, and 8 had been reared with others of the same age, in two groups of four. These young monkeys had been isolated from any actual contact with other monkeys as they grew up, but they had been able to see and hear other monkeys in the laboratory, through the mesh of their cages.

When they became sexually mature, each of these monkeys was impregnated—the more disturbed ones by artificial insemination—and their behaviour with their infants was closely observed. This was coded into three categories: adequate, in which the young infant was fully cared for by the mother; indifferent, in which the mother showed little interest in the infant and it had to be fed by laboratory staff (although many of these mothers did seem to develop an attachment to their infants after a few days); and abusive, in which the mothers showed a violent rejection of the infant, requiring the intervention of laboratory staff to protect it.

Perhaps not surprisingly, Ruppenthal et al. found a close correlation between the monkeys' upbringing and their treatment of their infants. Monkeys reared with the surrogates tended to be either indifferent or abusive as parents; and those reared with wire models were more abusive than those reared with the cloth ones. Monkeys that had been reared with others of their own age generally managed adequate care of their infants, and the earlier they had been put with the others, the better they would manage.

However, there was also some evidence that later experience could manage to undo some of the damage caused by the early upbringing. Some of the group had spent a period of time on a "monkey island" in a zoo with a normal adult male monkey, in an attempt to investigate whether their disturbance was irreversible. These monkeys showed better mothering than the others of their groups. Interestingly also, when they were impregnated for a second time, most of the monkeys managed to care for their infants adequately—it was only those who had been so severely abusive that they had lost their infants within 48 hours of birth (because they had killed them, or because they had been in so much danger that they had to be taken away) who were still inadequate as mothers.

The implication, then, is that in primate maternal behaviour, adequate mothering is extremely dependent on social contact and learning: a situation that contrasts sharply with what appears to be the highly instinctive maternal behaviour of rodents. Savage-Rumbaugh and Hopkins (1986) emphasised that there is little point in thinking in terms of fixed behavioural patterns of maternal care when dealing with monkey behaviour, because what they do is so readily adjusted to the demands of the situation.

For example, a study by Rumbaugh (1965) of maternal behaviour in the squirrel monkey showed that, for the most part, it is the infant that is responsible for maintaining contact with the mother, which it does by clinging tightly to the mother's fur. The mother leaps rapidly around, and shows no apparent concern for whether the infant is hanging on successfully or not. However, if the infant's arms are bound, so that it is unable to cling, the mother will pick the infant up and carry it—even though this impedes her ability to move around, and means that she has to walk bipedally. So in this case, maternal behaviour is clearly not just a matter of inherited fixed action patterns, but of a more general concept; of keeping the baby in contact. The monkey's behaviour is adapted in order to fit the concept.

Another facet of maternal behaviour in primates, and perhaps some other mammals too, seems to be the growing ambivalence of the mother towards the youngsters as they grow older. Bowlby (1969) argued that it was an evolutionary advantage for mothers to promote dependency in their infants, so that they would stay protected for longer. But Hinde (1983) suggested that, in some species at least, there is an evolutionary advantage if mothers actively promote independence on the part of their infants—sometimes even before the infants themselves feel ready for it. Hinde suggests that early independence may maximise both the mother's and the youngster's chances of escaping predators and of finding good food supplies.

Altmann (1980), in a study of baboons, showed that mothers who were more protective of their infants and restricted their actions more had infants who survived better in early life than others, but were less likely to survive if they were orphaned. Mothers who were less protective had youngsters who were better able to survive on their own from quite an early age.

We can see, then, not only that there are marked individual variations within one species (the different mothering styles Altmann observed were within the same baboon troop) but also that both strategies have some advantage. Hinde emphasised that no one ideal mothering style is likely to emerge from the pressures of natural selection, because there are so many other variables which will affect the optimal strategies. Factors like the infant's position in the family, the food supply and whether there is competition for it, the infant's gender, and the social structure of the troop are all likely to contribute to the infant's chances of survival, and to affect optimal mothering strategies.

Altricial and precocial mammals

One major distinction made by ethologists in terms of patterns of caring for the young was made by Portmann (1945), and concerns a distinction between *altricial* and *precocial* mammals. Altricial mammals have evolved a reproductive strategy which involves a relatively short gestatory period, large litters of poorly developed young, short lifespans, and small brains. A classic example here might be rats or rabbits, with their large litters of blind, hairless, and helpless young. Precocial mammals, on the other hand, are born in a state that fits them better to survive. Typically, precocial mammals have long gestations and lifespans, bigger brains, and more complex social behaviour. The classic example of this type of strategy is in primates, and particularly monkeys and apes. Portmann thought of them as more "advanced" evolutionarily, but nowadays we would simply consider them to be adapted for a different type of interaction with their environment.

The exception to this, though, is the human infant, which seems to combine characteristics of both altricial and precocial mammals. Human infants are extremely helpless at birth, like altricial animals; but they are also large-brained and develop complex social behaviour, like precocial animals. One of the most striking characteristics of human infants is their very extended period of dependency—unlike other primates, human infants need to be physically cared for a very long period of time. Gould (1978) argued that this is because of *neoteny*—because human infants are born prematurely, with respect to their developmental stage. There are all sorts of characteristics of human infants which are only half developed at birth, such as the ossification (hardening) of the bones in the fingers and toes, or the closing of the skull plates. In other primates, birth takes place at a particular stage when the young animal is fully formed in some crucial respects. For example, unlike a human infant, a young monkey is able to cling independently to its mother, and to move around her body to find the breast, from almost as soon as it is born. A human infant, on the other hand, needs to be supported for months, and doesn't become capable of independent locomotion for a year or more.

The reason for this, Gould argues, is in the development of the large human brain. If we were to be born at the same time as other primates, relative to the lifespan and stage of development, human beings would have a gestation period of something over eighteen months. But as it is, the infant's head is as large as possible for birth: if it was any larger, giving birth would become impossible. Accordingly, the period of gestation has become relatively shorter in human beings than it is in other animals (by comparison with their lifespans), and the human infant does much of its further development while being cared for outside the womb.

This extended period of dependency also allows for much greater plasticity in acquiring knowledge. The human brain continues to grow at an extremely rapid rate after birth, but the infant is also very receptive to environmental contingencies and transactions (Stratton, 1983). The potential for learning that this implies is considerable, and likely to be quite different from that of other primates—a point that is worth bearing in mind when we are thinking about generalising from animal parental or infant behaviour to that of humans.

Attachment

It is difficult, in many cases, to make a sharp distinction between the mother's behaviour and that of the infant, because the two interact together so closely. Looking at how mothers act almost inevitably means looking at how infants act as well. So, for instance, Harlow et al. (1963), looking at maternal behaviour shown by monkeys, found that although a young kitten would elicit maternal responses for a short time—in other words, a young female monkey would cuddle a kitten—this wouldn't last very long, because the kitten didn't act in the same way that a young monkey would. In particularly, it didn't cling to the monkey's fur, and so every time she released her grip it would fall. After a few days, the monkey would abandon her nursing of the kitten: unless the young one was giving the correct responses the behaviour couldn't be maintained. Mother and infant act as a *system*—each shows behaviour that links with and stimulates the other.

Imprinting

There have been several theories put forward about how attachments develop between the young animal and its parent. One of the first of these was the concept of *imprinting*. The idea that staying close to the mother can be an evolutionary advantage became particularly apparent with investigations of a different form of attachment, in young ducks and geese. As a child growing up on a farm, Konrad Lorenz had observed how young ducks and geese follow their mother around, and also how a female bird from another species, like a hen, could "adopt" a brood which were not her own, as long as she was there when they hatched, or soon afterwards. As an adult biologist, Lorenz conducted a number of investigations into this phenomenon.

He began by becoming a surrogate "parent" to a set of young geese, and observing their behaviour as they followed him around. One thing that was immediately apparent was that they were determined to keep him in view, and would follow him wherever he went, becoming distressed if they lost sight of him. Their behaviour indicated that they had formed an attachment, and one that obviously couldn't simply have been inherited. Instead, it was as if the new parent had made a deep impression on them, very rapidly after they had hatched. For this reason, Lorenz called this new form of attachment *imprinting*.

Researchers went on to investigate the different characteristics in imprinting, beginning with the information from Lorenz's studies. It was quickly found that a young chick, gosling, or duckling had a powerful inherited tendency to follow the first large, moving object that it saw. After it had followed that object for a continuous period of about 10 minutes, it would then develop an "attachment", avoiding other large moving objects and following only that one. Researchers showed that this didn't even need to be a live figure: ducklings would imprint on a large box that was dragged across the floor, and even—if they were kept in total isolation—on a stationary, brightly illuminated one. It seemed that the young bird was born "pre-programmed" to attach itself to some large object, and preferably one that moved.

Such an inherited mechanism might seem a little chancy—after all, what would happen if the mother were out of the nest when the young bird hatched? But Hess (1972) showed that there was an auditory component too. By secreting microphones in nest boxes, similiar to the picture below, Hess showed that, as the time of hatching draws close, mother ducks make a repeated "cluck" call to their eggs while they are incubating them. When the young hatch out, they imprint most readily on the large object making the familiar noise—in other words, on their mother. By sitting next to a clutch of eggs and calling "come, come" to them, Hess

Studying sounds during imprinting

showed that this auditory stimulation isn't totally pre-programmed—although the chicks are ready to respond to an auditory signal, which signal they respond to is a matter of experience. Hess's ducklings turned towards him as soon as they heard his voice, and were very ready to imprint on the stimulus that made the familiar sound.

What was happening as researchers investigated imprinting indepth was very exciting, in terms of our evolutionary understanding of animal behaviour. Imprinting appeared to be a special form of learning, but one with a very strong genetic component. In the ethological world of that time, where animal behaviour seemed to be strictly "either–or" (either learned or inherited) the discovery of a synthesis between the two, as represented by imprinting, was fascinating.

Lorenz, perhaps not surprisingly, argued that the genetic component was quite rigid. For example, Lorenz argued that there was a *critical period* for imprinting—in other words, if imprinting didn't happen during a certain time, then the genes would "switch off", and the learning would never happen. By keeping young birds without the opportunity to imprint on any large moving object, Lorenz showed that after about 25 hours, they would avoid all such objects, and so they wouldn't imprint. As research developed, however, it became apparent that there was more flexibility than this.

Lorenz, knowing that young birds imprinted optimally on large moving objects, had kept them away from contact with such things. However, the young birds in his investigation were kept together. Sluckin and Salzen (1961) kept young ducklings in isolation, and found that the period during which imprinting was possible could be significantly extended under those conditions. They suggested that the young birds of earlier experiments had imprinted on one another, which was why they avoided large moving objects after the "critical" period.

Other studies also showed that the period for imprinting could be lengthened. Although this period varies from one species to another, Ramsey and Hess (1954) had shown that in ducklings it is generally from about 5 to 25 hours after hatching, and is most likely when the chick is between 13 and 16 hours old. But Guiton (1959) showed that if the environment in which young birds were kept is extremely monotonous and unstimulating, the imprinting period can be extended to a few days; and Moltz (1960), investigating whether the visual experience was the crucial factor, found that fitting ducklings with translucent hoods could also extend the period for as much as four or five days.

The consensus, then, was that imprinting didn't take place during a critical period, rigidly and mechanically controlled by the genes; but during a *sensitive period*, in which the animal was optimally responsive to a specific kind of stimulation. This sensitive period is genetic in origin, but is modifiable by environmental circumstances, rather than being the mechanistic, automatic process initially envisaged by Lorenz. The genes establish a "state of readiness to learn" in the young animal; but it is the animal's own circumstances that determine how and when that learning occurs.

One reason why the concept of the critical period was initially a popular one was to do with the idea that such periods also determined adult behaviour. Lorenz proposed that the imprinted parent was the essential source of information for the young animal: by following its parent around, the young animal would learn all the appropriate behaviours for its species, which it would need in later life.

In the normal state of affairs, of course, this was not an important issue. But many of Lorenz's studies had been conducted with adoptive parents—as I mentioned before, he had become adopted parent to a group of young goslings, and had found as they were growing up that, in order to get them to show the appropriate behaviour, he often had to demonstrate it for them. For example, they wouldn't learn to swim until he went into the water with them. The prediction from Lorenz's idea of a critical period, then, with its emphasis on the importance of early learning, was that such animals would never learn to interact appropriately with members of their own species.

Desmond Morris (1967) took this notion of imprinting even further, and argued that this accounted for a number of instances of obscure sexual behaviour, including fetishism in human sexual behaviour, and even why the two giant pandas Chi-Chi and An-An had failed to mate—a major news event of the 1960s. (Morris argued that Chi-Chi had imprinted on her human keepers, and was therefore not interested in another panda as a potential mate.) This type of argument, despite receiving a great deal of popular attention, rested on some very questionable evidence; but provides a good example of how ideas in comparative psychology have often been misapplied in "popular" science to produce speculative and very deterministic explanations.

As with the idea of the critical period itself, serious research established that there was a great deal more flexibility in an animal's capacity to learn than had previously been thought. In one of these studies, Guiton (1966) showed that ducklings who had imprinted on the yellow rubber gloves worn by their keeper as they were fed had no problem adjusting to normal adult duck behaviour when they grew older. The important factor was that they should have the opportunity to learn through contact with members of their own species at some period in their lives—not that the imprinted learning determined everything from then on.

"WHAT'S THAT GUY GOT THAT I AINT GOT?..SKINNY LEGS? YOU LIKE SKINNY LEGS?... *I* GOT SKINNY LEGS!..SEE?..."

Another area of work concerned the physiological mechanisms by which imprinting happened. Lorenz had observed that the goslings would become distressed if he went out of their sight—implying that their visual image was important. A study by Bateson (1966), illustrated on the next page, showed that young birds tend to maintain a fixed distance between themselves and the mother figure, and that if their mother figure is larger than usual (for instance, by being a human being) then that fixed distance is also longer. Bateson showed that these distances always produced a retinal image of approximately the same size, and hypothesised that there is a link between the gosling's anxiety or distress mechanisms, and a "pre-programmed" size of retinal image. As long as the retinal image that the chick or gosling received is within the pre-programmed size limits, there will be no problem; but if it becomes smaller than that, then anxiety responses will be triggered off and the chick will hurry to get closer to its parent. As it does so, the retinal image will resume its former dimensions, and the young bird's anxiety will be reduced.

Behavioural investigations of the anxiety mechanisms showed that, if anything, arousing anxiety tends to strengthen the imprinted bond. Hess (1958) imprinted young ducklings on to a model "duck" which moved

around the inside of a large circular path. The ducklings had to run around
the path to follow the model. Hess placed a series of obstacles in their way,
which they would have to scramble over to keep following, and found
that these obstacles seemed to make the young chicks even more determined to follow the model. When these chicks were later tested for how
strong their attachment seemed to be (how long it would last before it
disappeared), Hess found that those which had had to put in more effort

had developed stronger attachments to the model duck than those which had simply followed it around unimpeded.

One possibility is that this is another manifestation of Bateson's findings: as the model receded from the chick, the retinal image became smaller and the chick became more anxious, and so struggled to overcome the obstacle and run to the mother figure. Some researchers suggested that this strengthened the attachment because the struggle to overcome the obstacle aroused the young chick physiologically, through its anxiety, and that it was this arousal that influenced the strength of the attachment directly. Hess described his finding as the Law of Effort—the more effort, the stronger the bond—and it is apparent how such a principle could be an evolutionary advantage. But identifying the precise mechanisms of its operation is not so easy.

There are obvious parallels that can be drawn with human infants. For example, Ainsworth, Blehar, Waters, and Wall (1978) showed how infants with insecure attachments tend to cling more to their mothers, whereas those with secure attachments explore more freely and wander further. For a tender young gosling or duckling, wandering freely would not be an evolutionary advantage—quite the reverse! It would make them very likely to be eaten by some predator. So having an "insecure" attachment based on anxiety about getting left behind might help the young animal to survive.

But we need to be very careful about drawing these simplistic parallels. Analogy is not homology—many of the different behaviours that animals and human beings show look similar, i.e. they are analogous to one another. But that doesn't mean that they are homologous—that they are genetically related because they have evolved from the same mechanism. Although in their popular writings, many biologists (particularly Lorenz, Morris, and Dawkins) have talked as if the two are the same thing, this is very misleading. It's not at all uncommon in nature for two species to show behaviour that looks similar on the surface but actually comes from totally different roots.

Neurological studies of imprinting

In behavioural terms, the process of imprinting in chicks can be summarised as follows: shortly after hatching, a young bird shows a tendency to approach almost any visually conspicuous object, especially if it is moving. If the object remains in the chick's vicinity for a period of time, the chick develops a social attachment to it. The attachment shows itself by the chick producing contentment calls and approach behaviour if the object is nearby, and following it if it moves away. It is also shown by the way that the chick now avoids other visually conspicuous objects.

Recognising individuals

Horn (1991) reported a series of studies which investigated the neurological basis of imprinting. As a result of these studies, two distinct physiological mechanisms had emerged. The first of these was to do with the way that a young bird learned to recognise a particular object. The basic procedures used in these studies were very similar: young chicks from the domestic fowl were hatched and reared in darkness in individual compartments in an incubator, until they were between 15 and 30 hours old. Then each was placed in a running wheel, and exposed to some kind of distinctive training object for a period of between one and four hours. The researchers tested whether the chick had imprinted on the object on a later occasion, by giving the chick a choice between approaching the familiar object or an unfamiliar one.

McCabe, Horn, and Bateson (1981) showed that there seemed to be a particular region of the chick's brain which was involved in the process of recognising the familiar object. This was the intermediate and medial part of the hyperstriatum ventrale, referred to as the IMHV for short. Birds' brains are quite different from those of mammals, in particular in the fact that they do not have cerebral hemispheres as mammals do; but the IMHV region is located in a part of the brain that may roughly be seen as a kind of evolutionary equivalent. McCabe et al. showed that chicks with the IMHV lesioned—i.e. destroyed—did not learn to recognise an object if they had not yet imprinted; and did not continue to recognise an object that they had previously imprinted on.

Following this discovery, researchers looked for specific changes in the structure of the IMHV which occurred as a result of the learning. Horn, Bradley, and McCabe (1985) found that imprinting seemed to produce changes at the synapses—the junctions between nerve cells—of neurones in the IMHV region. In particular, receptor sites on neurones in that area became thickened as a result of the learning. Receptor sites are located at the synapse and are where a chemical message from one neurone is received by the next one (see also *Principles of Biopsychology*, in this series). The thickening of these receptors appeared to result in an increased sensitivity to the neurotransmitter L-glutamate. L-glutamate is an excitatory chemical, which makes the neurone that receives it more likely to fire, so the implication of this finding is that as a result of the learning process, certain cells in the IMHV region of the chick's brain had become much more ready to respond to certain kinds of stimulus. The rapid individual-recognition aspect of imprinting, then, seems to have a distinct and identifiable physiological basis.

Predispositions towards conspecifics

The other physiological mechanism that gradually became apparent was a predisposition for a young animal to approach a member of its own species (known as a *conspecific*), in preference to approaching any other type of stimulus. Although, as Lorenz had shown, a chick could be induced to imprint on almost any moving or visually distinct stimulus, that didn't mean that all stimuli were equally effective. Some of the studies of IMHV lesions had used a stimulus of a brightly illuminated box for the first stimulus, but others had used a stuffed jungle fowl (the "wild" relative of the domestic chicken). This had not seemed to influence the outcome of the studies, as far as investigating the effects of IMHV lesions were concerned.

Part of these experiments, however, had involved the IMHV-lesioned chicks being given a preference test, which involved choosing between the box or the fowl. When Horn and McCabe (1984) re-analysed findings from these studies, they found that there was a difference between the box-trained chicks and the fowl-trained chicks. IMHV-lesioned chicks that had been trained on the box showed no preference—they were equally likely to approach either the box or the fowl. But those that had been trained on the fowl showed a clear preference for it: they largely ignored the box and would approach the fowl when given the opportunity. Although they didn't retain a specific memory for the object on which they had trained, they did seem to retain a preference. This implied that perhaps the early training had made some difference after all.

Johnson, Bolhuis, and Horn (1985) performed a set of studies in which chicks of domestic fowl were raised, entirely in darkness, in an incubator until they were about 24 hours old. Then, still in darkness, they were placed in a running wheel for two hours, before being returned to the incubator (earlier studies had shown that the exercise of running seemed to stimulate a readiness to imprint). Then, for the first time, the chicks were exposed to a visual stimulus, and given the choice of approaching the brightly illuminated box or the stuffed jungle fowl. Neither stimulus was moving, but both were very distinct, and their relative "attractiveness" had been carefully balanced during earlier studies conducted by Horn, McCabe, and Bateson (1979).

Half of the chicks in the study were exposed to the two stimuli just two hours after leaving the running wheel. These chicks performed at chance levels in the test—they were equally likely to choose the box or the fowl. Chicks that had no experience of the wheel beforehand were also likely to perform at chance. But those that were not tested until 24 hours after they had been removed from the wheel showed a very clear preference for the stuffed jungle fowl. As they had been kept in darkness all the time, this could not have been the outcome of prior visual learning. Nor did it appear instantaneously. Horn (1991) referred to it as an *emerging predisposition*: the chick was predisposed to approach a member of its own species, and this predisposition emerged gradually, with the chick's experience.

The process of learning to recognise a particular individual and the predisposition to approach a member of the same species seem to involve entirely separate physiological mechanisms. Johnson and Horn (1987) showed that chicks with lesions of the IMHV area of the brain were not able to learn to recognise specific individuals—an effect that persisted into adulthood—but still showed a tendency to approach members of their own species. In the natural state, of course, both of these mechanisms would be involved, and both would contribute to ensuring that the imprinting mechanism was operating appropriately.

Monotropy

When imprinting as a mechanism became known, it wasn't just the "pop biologists" who seized on the concept. Bowlby (1951) used this idea as the basis for a theory about attachment, in which he proposed that human infants, too, formed an imprinted bond with their mother, a process that he referred to as monotropy. This made the relationship between the mother and her infant qualitatively different from all other relationships, and could, Bowby said, result in psychological damage lasting into adult life if the bond was broken. By going on to relate juvenile delinquency to early maternal deprivation, at a time when the British Government was trying to close down the day-care nurseries of the war years and shift women back into the home, Bowlby's ideas quickly took the debate into the political arena.

Not surprisingly, this also stimulated a considerable amount of research into which species did form attachments through imprinting, and which didn't, and also into how other kinds of attachments developed. Research into parent-infant interaction in humans showed that the basis for infant attachments was established gradually, and could apply to more than one individual (e.g. Schaffer & Emerson, 1964), so imprinting seemed an inappropriate model for this type of process. But human beings are relatively helpless, physically if not psychologically, at birth. Those species that did imprint, it emerged, were those in which the young were able to move about soon after birth.

We have already seen the evolutionary advantage of a sudden attachment, based on locomotion, which appears almost as soon as the young animal becomes able to move about. Researchers found evidence for imprinting in herd animals like goats, deer, sheep, and horses, as well as in the precocial birds studied by the early researchers. But the evidence for imprinting in animals where the young are static or helpless for their first period of life was less apparent, and could only really be obtained by broadening the definition of imprinting to mean almost any kind of attachment at all. (This, of course, is the real argument against Morris's "pop" theory of imprinting—he was applying the concept to species that seem to use quite different mechanisms of attachment.)

To the comparative psychologist, however, imprinting is an exciting concept, mainly because of the way that it represents an intermediate situation in the control of behaviour. Imprinting is both genetic and environmental, and although that can really be said about all forms of learning (without genes to establish the potential to learn, how could we learn at all?) it is so in a very special sense. Genetic factors establish a state of readiness, environmental factors establish what should be learned, and to some extent when. So the learning isn't just a random process of trial and error inscribed on a blank slate: it's a tightly prescribed process, which results in the animal maximising its chances of survival. We will be coming back to this issue in Chapter 6.

Attachment in rhesus monkeys

Another important implication of research into imprinting was the way that it challenged the behaviourist model of attachment. Behaviourists had always argued that the attachment which develops between mother and infant was simply a learned association— generalisation from a classically conditioned response, which involved associating the mother with food and therefore with a feeling of satiation and comfort. This association led to a behavioural tendency in the young animal to approach the mother. According to the behaviourists, attachment could really be reduced simply to a tendency to approach.

Because this explanation fitted with Lloyd Morgan's canon (see Chapter 1), that explanations should always use the "lowest" form of mechanism on a scale of psychological complexity, it remained popular for a considerable period of time. But in 1959, Harlow reported a series of studies which were designed to investigate whether food alone was sufficient to produce attachments. In these studies, young monkeys were brought up in isolation. Although they could see and hear other monkeys in other cages in the laboratory, they did not have any physical contact with them, not even to the extent of having adjacent cages. Harlow provided food through a feeding bottle attached to a "model" in the cage, which was referred to as "surrogate mother".

There were two kinds of models, which are illustrated in the picture below. One kind was composed of bare wire mesh, with a rectangular "head". The other was composed of mesh covered in towelling, with a rounded "head" which had large eyes. Some of the monkeys had only the mesh figure, whereas others had both in their cages. All of them, however, were fed from the wire surrogate. If the behaviourists had been correct, and attachment was simply generalised classical conditioning to food provision, their attachment would have developed to the wire mother, as that was the source of food.

What Harlow found, though, was that the young monkeys quite clearly preferred the towelling-covered surrogate. If they had a choice, they would spend their whole time clinging closely to it, only moving across to the wire model to feed, and then returning quickly. Moreover, even when they had got a bit older and were starting to explore more, when Harlow introduced novel and alarming stimuli into the cage (a wind-up teddy bear, which marched along beating a drum) they would flee to the towelling surrogate and remain clinging to it for some time, as if for comfort and reassurance. The monkeys that had only the wire surrogate available, however, didn't show any of this attachment behaviour, even though they had been fed from it.

Surrogate mothers for young monkeys

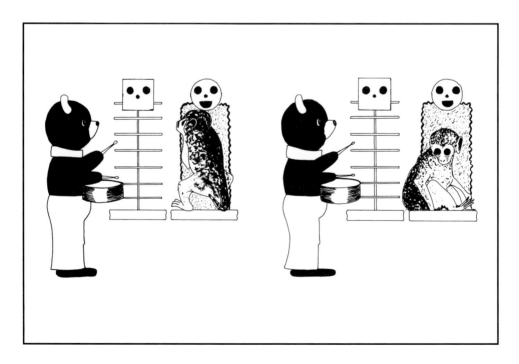

In the long-term, of course, bringing the young monkeys up under these conditions was extremely psychologically damaging. These were the monkeys that became the subjects of Ruppenthal's investigation of maternal behaviour, which we looked at in the last section. It wasn't just their maternal behaviour that was affected, either—they also showed more general social and emotional disturbances. They were unable to interact adequately with other monkeys, and tended to be rejected and bullied by them; and they sometimes engaged in self-mutilation—pulling out their hair, or chewing their limbs. When they matured and came into season, they were often unable to mate because they did not show the appropriate signals to other monkeys.

Harlow and Harlow (1962) compared the long-term development of these isolated infants with two other groups of young monkeys which had also been separated from their mothers, but which had been brought up together, in groups of four at a time. By contrast, the young monkeys in the "together" conditions developed very much more normally, and as adults were able to interact with other monkeys positively, and show adequate maternal behaviour. So it was clear from these studies that the behaviourist account of attachment was far from adequate. Attachments and early interactions, it appeared, set the foundations for later social competence, and interactions with others of their own species seemed to be an essential prerequisite of normal adult behaviour.

That doesn't mean, however, that the social and emotional effects were completely unchangeable. As we saw in the last section, if a monkey mother could be persuaded to keep its infant for 48 hours or more, it tended to become a much more adequate mother on the second occasion that it gave birth. It seemed that it had needed the opportunity to learn from its own experience. Some of the disturbance seemed to be alleviated to a slight extent when a group of the monkeys were placed on a "monkey island" in a zoo with a well-adjusted adult male of the same species. (The researchers had reasoned that contact with a "normal" monkey should help them to learn appropriate behaviour—although one is left wondering just how much influence one "normal" human being would have on a group of severely emotionally disturbed humans.)

In 1973, Suomi, Collins, and Harlow investigated how disturbance resulting from separation from the mother was affected by the timing of that separation—in other words, was the crucial time for development of social competence early in infancy, or later on? In this study, rhesus monkeys were separated from their mothers after different intervals of time: one group after 60 days, one after 90 days, and the third group after 120 days. There were four monkeys—two of each sex—in each group. The timing of these separations had been developed from observational studies, which had seemed to indicate that young monkeys first begin to show evidence of attachment at about 70 or 80 days of age. Around that time, they begin to show distress if separated from their mother, and fear of strangers.

When they were separated from their mothers, one pair from each group was housed together, and one male and one female was housed singly. All of the monkeys became agitated when they were first separated from their mothers, and showed clinging and distress; and those who were kept in isolation showed less exploration and more distress than those kept in pairs. Overall, Suomi et al. found that there did not seem to be qualitative differences between the three groups of monkeys in terms of the effects of the separation—in other words, the effects were pretty well of the same kind for each group—but there were definite quantitative ones. The group that were separated at 90 days showed the effects more severely than either the earlier-separated or the later-separated groups. Suomi et al.'s suggestion was that infant dependency reaches a peak at around this time, and gradually eases off as the youngster becomes more independent—or, as Hinde might say, as the mother promotes greater independence in the infant. Given that it is at this time that the infant is becoming much more independent physically, it makes some evolutionary sense that it should become more timid of strangers at this time.

There is, then, much more to attachment than simply a learned association with food and the presence of the mother; but it isn't just a question of imprinting either. The studies of Harlow and associates showed how important social interaction is to rhesus monkeys, and how attachments develop primarily with members of the same species if they are available. Following on from this work, ethological studies of human infants led to the finding that it is the quality of the interaction between parent and infant which determines the attachment between them: human infants are born with a preparedness to interact socially, through eye-contact, imitation, and other means, with adults (see *Principles of developmental psychology*, this series). It is this interaction that sets the foundation, not only for attachment, but also for social learning in later life. In the next chapter, we will look at some of the many different forms of animal social interaction which may result from social learning.

Summary: Courtship, mating, and reproduction

- Courtship rituals are behavioural exchanges that occur as part of, or as a precursor to, mating. They have been observed in many species, and can sometimes involve the co-operation of more than one individual.
- Courtship has been seen as ensuring appropriate pairing; enhancing survival of the participants; improving the species; displaying fitness; and reinforcing pair-bonding.
- Animal parenting takes many different forms, and parental behaviour may be more or less flexible in different species. Those higher up the phylogenetic scale appear to depend more on learned responses than instinctive ones.
- Imprinting is a rapid form of learning with a strong genetic component, which results in young precocial animals becoming attached to their parent. Neurological studies of imprinting show a number of distinctive brain mechanisms involved in the process.
- Early theories of human and primate attachment assumed that a mechanism similar to imprinting was in operation. Subsequent research, however, showed that the picture was rather more complex.
- Attachments in primates occur as a more interactive, phased process, with a strong element of learning. The opportunity to form attachments with others is extremely important for normal primate development.

4 Social organisation

Extrapolations from animal behaviour to "human nature" have always been popular. Such theories have looked at animal social behaviour, and drawn parallels with human social organisation. Sometimes, this has been done with the intention of inspiring to virtue—many of the Victorian moral educators, for example, exhorted children to emulate the "busy bee" or the "wise old owl". Sometimes it has been done to try to make sense out of human society, like drawing parallels between hive systems and cities, or animal pair-bonding and human partnerships. And sometimes, too, such extrapolations have been used for a far more sinister purpose: the application of Lorenzian ideas of territoriality, dominance, and ritualised aggression in Nazi ideology is a case in point.

Given these issues, then, it is worth looking carefully at what we know about animal social organisation. Researchers live in society too, and they are not immune to the spirit of their times. Forms of explanation that were popular and seemed self-evidently true at one time appear hidebound and biased at a later time. Although we all like to believe that this is only true of the past, and that now we know better, even current theories are not necessarily exempt from these processes. But at the same time, comparative research does accumulate more knowledge about what animals actually do. In this chapter, we will look at some of the findings and theoretical ideas which have come from animal research, and what they can tell us about animal social organisation.

Aggressive behaviour

For most of the 20th century, much of the ethological and laboratory research into animal social organisation centred around the question of aggression. This in turn raised questions about territoriality in animals, and about dominance and dominance hierarchies, which we will be looking at later in this chapter. More recently, researchers have also begun to look at questions of reconciliation and peacemaking: how animals recover from aggressive encounters, and maintain social cohesion among group members.

Models of aggression

In Chapter 2, we looked at Lorenz's theory of ritualised aggression, in which he presented aggression as the outcome of the build-up of an internal action-specific energy, which motivates the animal to perform aggressive acts. These are either released in predatory behaviour—in other words, as acts directed towards other species—or in intraspecies conflicts (conflicts between animals belonging to the same species). In the latter case, Lorenz argued that the conflict would be highly ritualised, involving stylised threat gestures and sequences, and the use of appeasement gestures by the loser to inhibit further aggressive activity.

Other comparative studies looked at different aspects of aggression. For example, in a classic study Calhoun (1962) showed how rats that were allowed to breed freely in a confined space, with a limited food source, became increasingly aggressive, eventually engaging in infanticide and cannibalism—highly untypical behaviours for the species. Calhoun speculated that much intraspecies aggression might be produced by the frustration induced by competition for limited resources.

These two views of aggression encapsulate the two entirely opposing views of aggression that have been influential in comparative psychology. Their conceptual origins can be traced back to 1918, when Craig published a paper attempting to identify the components of motivation. In this he distinguished between *appetitive behaviour*, which is behaviour that involves searching for a specific set of conditions; and *consummatory behaviour*—behaviour which leads directly to the satisfaction of an "appetite". We have already met this distinction in the discussion of Lorenz and Tinbergen's hydraulic model of innate behaviour.

In a later paper, Craig (1928) distinguished between two forms of consummatory behaviour. Some he referred to as "appetites", in which an animal would perform a behaviour which directly consummated an internal state, like eating to reduce hunger. But there were also other types of behaviour, which he referred to as "aversions", in which the animal would act to remove itself from a set of unpleasant conditions.

This distinction lies at the heart of the two opposing views of aggression: it is a question of which kind of behaviour aggression is. Craig identified aggression as an aversion, rather than as an appetite, seeing it as allowing an animal to rid itself of an unpleasant or fear-producing situation. Later researchers (e.g. Archer, 1988) have also taken this view.

Lorenz, on the other hand, viewed aggression as an appetite (Lorenz, 1966). He saw it as an internal energy which was constantly accumulating, and needed to be discharged in aggressive acts. The implication of this theory was that aggression would build up, and if no opportunity was provided to perform aggressive acts, it would be likely to "overflow" into exaggeratedly aggressive responses to relatively innocuous stimuli, or into displacement.

There are a number of arguments against Lorenz's model of aggression. Johnson (1972) showed that empirical investigations of such questions as whether animals directly seek out fights, whether they become more aggressive when they are isolated, and whether they are less likely or more likely to have a fight, show that the appetitive model of aggression isn't supported by the evidence. And Archer (1977) argued that an internal appetitive control of aggression would be of very little evolutionary or functional value to an animal, because it would then happen purely as a result of the animal's internal condition, regardless of whether there was actually someone to fight with, or some reason to fight. This would be unlikely to enhance an animal's survival prospects.

The frustration-aggression approach

Viewing aggression as an aversion, on the other hand, led to an approach that has been very loosely classified as the frustration-aggression approach. This operates from the principle that aggression is primarily a response to environmental circumstances. The model was put forward by Dollard et al. (1939), in an influential book called *Frustration and aggression*. The theory was soon applied widely in social and developmental psychology, as well as in comparative research.

Calhoun, as we have seen, showed that overcrowding in rats led to extreme forms of aggression, including cannibalism and infanticide. Ethological studies of the opposite phenomenon indirectly supported this view, by showing that aggression seemed to be very much less when an animal lived in circumstances where food and other resources were freely available. Geist (1978) discussed how both the wild boar and the reed-buck showed very little aggression, whether it was measured in terms of how often they displayed behaviour that could be interpreted as aggressive, or in terms of the intensity of those actions when they were manifest. Both of these species live in environments that provide them with an abundance of resources. But two comparable species, the warthog and the muntjac, live in dry habitats with few natural resources and show higher levels of aggression.

The frustration-aggression approach also led to a series of laboratory experiments which showed that aggressive behaviour in animals increased if those animals were subjected to pain or discomfort. For example, Ulrich and Azrin (1962) showed that repeated electric shocks applied to the feet could produce fighting between pairs of rats; and many other researchers found similar effects. But Blanchard and Blanchard

(1981) argued that these studies were not really providing much information about aggression as such, because pain-induced fighting should really be seen as defensive, not as aggressive. Defensive behaviour, they argued, is an entirely different type of phenomenon. We will be looking more closely at defensive and anti-predatory behaviour later in this chapter.

Types of aggression

In 1968, Moyer distinguished between eight different types of aggressive behaviour, which are listed in the panel below. However, there are a number of problems with Moyer's classification. Archer (1976) identified three major criticisms. The first is the inclusion of the first category: predatory aggression. Unlike other forms of aggression, this is closely linked with hunger and homeostatic mechanisms. Archer argued that in reality it bears very little similarity to the other types, and shouldn't really be included as the same type of behaviour.

Archer's second criticism concerns the way that the different types of aggression were classified: different criteria were used to identify the different types of aggression, and these were inconsistent with one another. The third criticism concerns the evidence from neuropsychology, which doesn't show any differences in the type of aggression involved in four of the categories: intermale, irritable, territorial, and maternal.

Rose, Kamin, and Lewontin (1984) argued that, in view of the many different ways that the word aggression is actually used, the word has become meaningless, and doesn't represent any one single concept. They argued that to use the same word to describe, say, mouse-killing behav-

Types of aggressive behaviour

---

1. Predatory aggression—in other words, aggressive behaviour that is directed towards some other animal, on which the animal preys.
2. Intermale aggression, in response to the approach or closeness of an unfamiliar male. (Moyer does not appear to have entertained the notion that female animals might behave aggressively towards one another, despite several studies which have shown that this does take place.)
3. Fear-induced aggression, such as the attack behaviour shown by a cornered animal.
4. Irritable aggression, such as responses to pain, frustration, or deprivation.
5. Territorial defence towards an intruder on the animal's territory.
6. Maternal aggression, in response to a threat to the young (again, Moyer does not appear to have noticed that in some animals, like the well-known stickleback, it is the male who defends the young).
7. Instrumental aggression: a learned behaviour which gains the animal some kind of reward.
8. Sex-related aggression, in competitive mating situations.

(Moyer, 1968)

iour in the rat, competitive action on the sports field, and large-scale political-economic events like wars, is simply nonsense, because they are actually very different phenomena. Using the same word obscures the differences and leads to intellectual confusion.

Moreover, Rose argued, the concept of "aggression" itself is questionable. In reality, it is an adjective, not a noun: an animal or person will act "aggressively", in some way, so it is the action that is aggressive. To go from there to argue that there is some quality called "aggression", which an animal has more or less of, is to convert what is essentially a description of how something is done, into a "thing", as if it has an independent existence. The process of converting properties of behaviour into "things" is called *reification*, and Rose argued that it is one which seriously distorts and misleads scientific enquiry. What we should really be doing is not looking for types of "aggression", but addressing questions such as when an animal will perform an aggressive act, and what function the aggressive act serves for the animal.

Archer (1988) proposed that a more useful way of categorising aggression is to look at the processes by which aggressive behaviour has evolved. There are two broad strands in this: first, competition for resources from the animal's environment which would enable it to survive and to maximise its evolutionary fitness; and second, reactions to danger or threat. The second category can also be usefully subdivided, into self-protective reactions to danger, and parental defence of the young. Although these are distinct functions, in evolutionary terms, Archer proposed that the underlying physiological mechanisms that are involved in their manifestation have come to overlap, so they look as though they are similar acts.

Functional explanations for aggression

This type of approach to the study of aggression involves the application of functional arguments, in which aggressive behaviour is considered in relation to its evolutionary contribution—how it helps a species to survive in its environment. Such approaches have tended to reflect the model of evolutionary processes most common in their times. For example, many of the functional explorations of the 1950s and 1960s tended to present "group-survival" explanations for aggression, which emphasised the evolutionary advantage for the species as a whole. Lorenz (1966) suggested that the ritualisation of threat and appeasement gestures had evolved in order to make sure that members of the same species did not kill too many of each other; and Scott and Fredericson (1951) suggested that the purpose of social dominance was to establish a situation in which animals within a group did not have to be continually fighting with one another, which would eventually result in damage to the group as a whole.

Now that times have moved on, and individual models of natural selection have replaced group survival models, functional explanations for aggression tend to emphasise the individual consequences of aggressive encounters. There are two groups of explanations of this kind. The first group concerns explanations which show how such encounters allow the individual to maximise or minimise some aspect of their lives related to either individual survival or likely success in reproduction. So, for example, Hixon, Carpenter, and Paton (1983) predicted that the size of a hummingbird's territory would be related to the area required to guarantee provision of its maximum daily energy intake. An alternative view, but still within the "economic" tradition was suggested by Pyke (1979), who argued that it wasn't so much the energy intake of the bird—in other words, how much it ate—that mattered, as its energy expenditure: the size of a territory would depend on how much energy the bird needed to use in order to defend it successfully. Economic models of evolutionary function, then, are generally directly concerned with the availability of some kind of resource in the environment.

An alternative current functional approach involves attempting to model mathematically what would seem to be a logical individual strategy for survival, and then seeing if there are examples of animal behaviour which conform to this pattern. This approach was developed by the work of Maynard Smith (1972), who used game theory models to analyse fighting strategies. The emphasis of the approach is that it seeks to model behaviour to find an *evolutionary stable strategy* (ESS), in terms of the survival and reproduction of individuals. We will be looking at this approach later in this chapter.

Territoriality

One issue that has interested comparative psychologists for a considerable time is that of territoriality. But territoriality, the more we look into it, is not the single, simple thing that it might appear. The idea of territoriality actually encompasses a number of sub-concepts, and if we are to avoid either confusion or mystification, we need to clarify exactly what these are.

One of the first distinctions that needs to be made is between territory and range. Some animals have a specific territory, which they will defend against all other members of their species, except for an existing or prospective mate, and their own offspring during the period that they are growing up. Having established a territory, they then spend their lives within it, and are fiercely protective of its boundaries and hostile to intruders.

In 1943, Lack performed a study of territoriality in robins, and found that they are fiercely territorial. Robins pair-bond, finding a single mate and staying together, and both partners defend their territory against other robins. During the early part of the spring, while they are establishing their territories, they sing loudly and ensure that they are very visible. If a strange robin should enter the territory despite these signals, the "resident" birds will immediately fly at it, uttering high-pitched calls. If the intruder still remains, the resident robin will perch nearby and perform what appears to be a display of strength: turning from side to side, holding the head and tail up so as to display its red breast, and flicking its wing feathers. If this still isn't enough to rout the intruder (it usually is), then the two birds may fight, flying at one another and pecking, although Lack found that such direct contests were very unusual indeed.

Rowell (1972), on the other hand, observed that strictly territorial behaviour is rare among primates: not many species of primate will actually defend a piece of ground, although it is not unknown for two troops to come into conflict. One of the few exceptions to this is the gibbon, which tends to live in stable pair-bonds, in a defined territory—although even then, Elefson (1968) observed that territorial contests don't actually take place at the boundaries, but in a neutral space between the territories. These contests, too, are rarely more than expressions of excitement—the animals will jump up and down, shriek and chase one another, and then go back to their own areas to feed peacefully.

In some species, then, competition for territories can be very intense—after all, they provide the opportunity to rear young successfully—so it is important that the animal which is trying to maintain a territory is as visible or as audible as possible. Krebs (1976) showed how intense such competition can be, by removing eight territory-holding pairs of great tits from an area of woodland. In three of these areas, he played continuous recordings of the original resident's songs. Three more he left quiet, and in the remaining two he played recordings of other kinds of sounds. Within just a couple of hours, the five control areas had been occupied by new pairs of birds. Only those areas with tape-recordings of the original residents were not occupied, although as the songs didn't change over time, as normal songs do, those areas too were occupied a couple of days later (see Chapter 5).

Seasonal territoriality

Although a rigidly exclusive, all-year round, vigorous defence of territory is something that many of the popular biologists like to imply is the normal state of affairs, in reality it seems to be rather rare, by comparison with other forms. A more common form of territoriality is *seasonal territoriality*:

an animal takes over an area for a specific part of the year, which it then defends against others of the species. During that period, it courts a mate and rears young. When those young have grown to a point where they are able to be independent, the animal ceases its territorial behaviour—in reality, the behaviour has usually ceased before that, as the demands of feeding and rearing young have taken precedence—and for the rest of the year shows little territorial behaviour at all.

Seasonal territoriality, then, is intimately linked with courtship, mating, and rearing young, and it is very difficult to draw hard and fast lines between the two. For example, Catchpole (1981) studied the territorial behaviour of the reed warbler. As these birds live among dense vegetation, a visual defence of territory would be pointless. Instead, they have elaborate songs which they sing very loudly, and which serve as territorial defence. But although the reed warbler's song acts as a territorial claim to other males, Catchpole also found that it is simultaneously a courtship display. The song attracts female reed warblers to the male bird's territory, and so allows the bird to find a mate. This dual function—courtship and territoriality—became very apparent later in the season. By recording songs and playing them back to other reed warblers, Catchpole found that birds who heard an "intruder" would sing in response, even once they had already mated and were no longer singing as a general rule. The apparent presence of another bird into their territory stimulated what appeared to be an almost automatic challenge to the intruder.

Krebs (1976) recorded how birds sing during the course of the day, and found that territorial challenges were most likely to happen in the very early morning. The "dawn chorus" of the springtime, Krebs argued, happens as each bird sings to defend its territory against those who are still looking for a place to nest.

The classic example of seasonal territoriality, of course, is the behaviour of the three-spined stickleback (Tinbergen, 1951). Unlike robins or deer, this territorial behaviour is shown only by the male: as we saw in the last chapter, the female is admitted into the territory solely for the purpose of laying eggs. Once that is over she is chased away. It is the male who cares for the eggs and rears the young, and it is the male who shows the rigid defence of territory. Tinbergen showed how the highly ritualised courtship and fiercely territorial behaviour of the male stickleback only continues for as long as the male remains in the reproductive state. This appears to be controlled, or at least mediated, by a high level of gonadal hormone, and signalled externally by the bright red belly—the fish's visual equivalent of the reed warbler's song. When the hormone level drops, the red breast also fades, as does the male's pugnacious defence of his territory.

This type of territoriality depends on a complex interplay of internal hormones and external stimuli. Sometimes these external stimuli come from other animals: in some species, like pigs, females in oestrus release a pheromone which stimulates courtship behaviour and possibly territorial defence as well. Sometimes, too, the circumstances that stimulate seasonal territoriality are to do with the physical environment, like warming temperature, increasing hours of daylight, and increased availability of vegetation. In reproductive terms, seasonal territoriality and food supply are generally closely linked, so it makes sense for animals which engage in this type of territoriality to ensure that they have exclusive access to an area that will provide enough food for themselves, their mates, and their young ones throughout their period of dependency. One might expect, therefore, to find a correlation between seasonal territoriality and an intensive period of caring for the young, followed by a period of more tolerant behaviour as the young become independent.

Home range

In species where the young remain dependent on their parents for one or more years, like bears, herd animals, and many primate species, we find a different form of territoriality. This doesn't centre on establishing exclusive access to one specific area, so much as on what is known as a *home range*. The home range is the area within which the animal lives and finds its food, and the home range of a given animal or troop often overlaps with that of others of the same species. Because such animals often roam very freely, a range can be very large. Polar bears, for instance, may roam anything up to 600 miles, hunting, mating, and sleeping within that area. Although polar bears for the most part are solitary animals, they do not patrol or defend their range against others unless they come into direct conflict over food or mates, as the range as a whole is big enough to support several individuals.

Like polar bears, orang-utans are solitary animals with very large home ranges, overlapping with several different other individuals. Mackinnon (1974) reported that if they should happen to meet others, for example at a particularly fruitful feeding ground, interactions tended to be peaceful and co-operative. The large adult males, though, took care not to meet, but would yell loudly at one another across large distances, which Mackinnon speculated was a loose kind of territorial display. However, as these animals had ranges that spanned many miles, and as their ranges overlapped considerably, the message wasn't about protecting a specific piece of ground—it seemed to be more of a message to "keep your distance".

Generally, most other primates also operate with home ranges rather than strictly defined territories. Rowell (1972), in a detailed study of

"I SAID, 'KEEP AWAY FROM THE WATERING HOLE'... YOU MANGY OAF!"

baboons which we will look at more closely later in this chapter, found that, despite their pugnacious reputation, baboons simply don't seem to show territorial behaviour. A baboon troop will spend a short period of time in one area, then move on to another and remain there for a few more days before moving on yet again. Both chimpanzee colonies (Reynolds, 1963) and gorillas (Schaller, 1964) seem to operate in similar ways, living nomadic lives within a large home range. During the course of a year, they will move in a large circle around their range, coming to different trees as the fruit ripens, eating their fill and then moving on. Both species build temporary "nests" for sleeping, but abandon these when they move on.

This way of life, however, assumes that the available range remains constant. When it becomes artificially restricted, by human destruction of the forest for farming, the colony comes under considerable strain. Fossey (1980) showed how such restriction stresses the colony's social order, and also produces intergroup hostility between different gorilla troops— something that had not been observed before, despite several years of meticulous observations of gorilla behaviour. Similarly, although Reynolds (1963) reported that for the most part chimpanzee troops can share the same range and show little aggression when they meet, a troop of chimpanzees that had ceased its nomadic life and become settled at the

Gombe Stream Reserve was observed to make "war" on another troop that had also settled in the area (Bygott, 1979).

Nested territories

Some animals, with different forms of social organisation, have a quite different form of territoriality, in which one animal will hold a territory, and others may occupy areas within it. These are known as *nested territories*. Leuze (1980) showed how a male water vole will hold a large territory, and defend it against other males. Within that area, two or three females will establish their own sub-territories, and defend them against other females. Although the male is permitted to enter the territory, other females are not.

A similar territorial structure is maintained by the American jaçana— only this time, it is the female that holds the large territory, and the males that establish smaller territories within it. Jenni (1974) showed how female jaçanas will defend their large territories against other females, and how the males defend their sub-territories against one another, but not against the female. Each male will build a nest in its territory, and the female visits each of the male territories, and lays her eggs in each nest. The males then brood the eggs until they hatch, and rear the young.

Territory in colonies

For the most part, the examples of territory that we have looked at have also been the same as the animal's home range—the area within which the animal forages for its food and brings up its young. But some species, like penguins, seals or gulls, live in large colonies, and for them territory is a very much more restricted phenomenon. Although their range is very large—they may travel or swim for miles to gather food—they nest in large groups, with each group having only a very small area within the colony as a whole. Tinbergen (1951) observed that in such cases the territory consists of just the nest itself and the space immediately around it. This area is vigorously defended against potential intruders, but in a highly ritualised fashion, involving an elaborate set of ritual sequences of threat displays and appeasement gestures, as shown on the page opposite.

This is a form of seasonal territoriality which occurs when members of sea-going, or at least sea-feeding, species come ashore to breed. Because their food supply is obtained elsewhere from their breeding area, there is less evolutionary advantage to defending a large area: it seems to be enough that the young animals are out of the reach of any potentially hostile neighbours. So, again we see an interaction between environmental circumstances, reproductive behaviour, and the form of territoriality that the species displays.

Theories of territoriality

As early as 1962, Wynne-Edwards had observed that the size of the territory in a given species tended to vary from year to year: if food was plentiful that year, territories were smaller, but if it was scarce, they were large. Having an available food supply for raising young ones is important. But attempts to make broad generalisations about such specific aspects of animal behaviour are inevitably doomed to failure: Lea (1984) reported that the highly territorial blackbird will fight off any males that appear to present competition for mating, but will allow other males to feed uninterrupted in their territory if they aren't singing. So a simplistic food-supply explanation for territoriality isn't likely to be adequate.

The traditional idea was that holding and maintaining territories would enhance an individual's opportunity to mate with a suitable member of the other sex, because it would demonstrate that the particular individual holding the territory was "fit" and strong. But the more we look at the diversity of territorial behaviour, and at the factors that distinguish each kind, the more apparent it becomes that this argument, too, is limited. As with just about everything else, this facet of animal behaviour varies according to any number of factors: environmental demands and the ecological niche of the organism, relationships between predators and prey, social organisation, immediate circumstances, and so on.

Marler (1956) speculated that territoriality might have gradually evolved from a self-protective individual distance mechanism. At first, animals would protect themselves by maintaining a distance between themselves and others. Gradually this would have extended to territories which provided a protective function for the individual, such as small caves or holes that prevented attack. As this evolved further, animals occupying areas that provided other resources as well as protection would have an advantage over those having to leave their territories to eat or mate. So, gradually, territory may have evolved from a form of self-protection for the animal into a more complex social arrangement.

The popular biologist Ardrey (1966) used the concept of territoriality to "explain" wars and other social conflicts in human society, arguing that defending a territory was a primeval urge, inherited from animal ancestors, which had to be satisfied, and that this was what wars were all about. But even among animals, strict, all-year-round defence of territory is rare, and those animals closest to us show very little in terms of territorial defence. Even if the parallel were valid (and there is little evidence to suggest that it is), such an argument could only explain things like boundary disputes with neighbours, or conflicts over parking spaces at work—in other words, things that affect the individual's daily experience of resources in an area. To argue from there to the defence of an abstract phenomenon like a nation, which even in physical terms includes vast areas that are not personally known to the individual, is an untenable leap. There are other explanations for human wars, which are social and economic in nature: to treat wars as manifestations of a biological "territorial imperative" may be politically comfortable, but has little scientific evidence behind it.

This applies not only to explanations for wars, but also to the assumptions of male dominance which are so characteristic of the writings of popular biologists. According to these writers, territoriality is largely a male phenomenon. But this again, like so many other forms of animal behaviour, turns out to be much more variable than that. As we have already seen, in some species, like the jaçana, it is the females that hold the territory. Sometimes this fact becomes hidden in the language used to describe the phenomenon: female Belding's ground squirrels, for instance, are described as "sedentary", because it is they who remain in a given area while the males roam away and join other colonies (Sherman, 1981). Effectively, what this boils down to is that it is the females of this species that hold the territory, but the use of the term "sedentary" disguises the observation.

In a study of red deer populations on the Isle of Rhum, it became apparent that the seasonal territories of the rut are held by the female deer, and not the males, as had been previously believed (Lewin, 1978). Throughout most of the year, female deer roam around together in groups, together with their young deer, while the stags roam together in loose-knit male groups. The members of the Rhum Red Deer Project—a long-term, all-year-round study of the deer—found that these groups of hinds all tend to be more or less related to one another, although sometimes fairly distantly. In October, the groups move to traditionally rich pastures, known as rutting grounds, and as the observations continued, it emerged that, without apparent conflict between the females, each hind family has a regular claim on certain areas. These areas differ in the quality of food which they offer, and the quality of the area also correlates with the hinds reproductive success—those in richer areas produce fitter calves. At this time also, the stags become very much less tolerant of one another. They move to the rutting grounds, and begin the series of ritual and sometimes serious conflicts that we looked at in the last chapter.

This example provides another illustration of the dangers that analogies can represent for comparative research. The use of the word "harem" to describe the groups of hinds is an explicit metaphor, comparing this form of social organisation with the traditional harems of Eastern rulers, in which the man was thought to control, and sometimes even "own", the women (closer historical and sociological scrutiny raises some questions with regard to that idea too, but that is beyond the scope of this book). This metaphor led to the implicit assumption that the same thing was happening when a male stag was found with several hinds, and therefore to the assumption that it was the male stag who was defending "his" territory and females. The finding that it is the female groups that "own" the territory, and that the fittest male is admitted into the group on a temporary basis for mating purposes makes us very aware of how powerful metaphors and analogies can be in directing our thinking and assumptions. This is something that we also need to bear in mind as we go on to look at research into animal social organisation.

Game theory explanations of territoriality

One relatively recent approach to explaining territoriality consists of mathematical modelling, in which idealised versions of environmental situations are devised, and behavioural options are explored. First proposed by Maynard Smith (1972), *game theory* analyses are mathematical models which propose different behavioural tactics that animals can use when they are competing with one another. These models aim to show how populations may develop an evolutionary balance, referred to as an *evolutionary stable strategy* (ESS), between different options of behaviour. The ESS, then, is the strategy that will enable an individual animal to maximise its chances of surviving and/or reproducing.

Maynard Smith's original paper dealt with a relatively simplistic situation, concerning the survival prospects of idealised "doves" and "hawks". "Doves" are animals that back down if faced with another animal in competition: they may display when they enter a territory, but they don't fight if they are challenged. "Hawks" are animals that will always fight another animal if it is in competition.

In the game theory model, the costs and benefits of particular forms of behaviour are weighed up by giving numerical values to their possible outcomes. In the straightforward "hawk-dove" game, there are two costs: the cost of a serious injury (C), and the time cost of a long dispute, in terms of the time it takes and the physical drain on an animal in sustaining it (T). But there is also the benefit of the added increase in "evolutionary fitness" which goes to the winner (V).

Although, on first sight, it might seem as though an animal that always attacks has an inherent advantage over one that doesn't, this isn't how it works out. If any animal has an equal chance of meeting any other animal, and there are equal numbers of "hawks" and "doves" in the populations, then in fact either strategy is just as likely to help an animal maximise its chances of survival and/or reproduction. To understand this, we have to look at how the odds work out mathematically.

In this model produced by Maynard Smith (1972), the value of V (the increase in fitness for the winner) is set at 50 units. C (the cost of a serious injury) is set at 100 units, and T (the cost of a prolonged fight) is set at 10 units. As you can see from the panel below, when a dove meets a hawk, there is no question of the outcome. The dove backs down, which doesn't cost it anything but doesn't benefit it either; and the hawk wins, which gains it 50 points. But if there are equal numbers of doves and hawks in the population, then sometimes a hawk will meet a hawk, and sometimes a dove will meet a dove. When this happen, the payoffs are quite different.

If a dove meets another dove, either of them is equally likely to back down, but it is likely to take a little time while the two animals display to one another. So the possible number of points available is V–T, or 50–10, in other words 40. But because these points are equally likely to go to either

Game theory strategies and their payoffs

	Hawk	Dove
Hawk	0.5 (V–C)	V
Dove	0	0.5 (V–T)

	Hawk	Dove
Hawk	–25	+50
Dove	0	20

V = the increase in fitness for the winner   V = 50 points

C = the cost of a serious injury   C = 100 points

T = the cost of a prolonged fight   T = 10 points

animal, the amount is halved. An individual dove, if it meets another dove, will get on average 20 fitness points from the encounter.

If a hawk meets another hawk, the story is quite different. Both animals will fight, and the chances that either of them will be seriously injured will be high. So the total number of points available is V–C, or 50–100, in other words –50. Because, in this model, either animal is equally likely to win, that means that each individual hawk will get an average of –25 points from the encounter.

The way that this works out is that both types of strategy confer some advantages to the individual who uses them, but both have costs too. Maynard Smith (1972) argued that the balance between the two is evolutionarily stable, because neither strategy has an advantage over the other. Moreover, the population will naturally tend to revert to this balanced state. If there were more "doves" than "hawks", for instance, then the chances of the "hawks" being seriously injured in an encounter would be much less, because they would be less likely to meet other "hawks". So the proportion of "hawks" in the population would gradually increase until it was balanced with that of the "doves". Alternatively, if there were more "hawks" than "doves", there would be more chance of any given "hawk" being seriously injured through conflict, and so it would become more advantageous to use the "dove" strategy, in the sense that the animal would be more likely to survive. Consequently, the "dove" population would gradually increase until the two were balanced again.

There have been several modifications to the basic mathematical model, to represent different possible strategies. Caryl (1981) modelled the "prudent hawk" strategy, representing an animal that fights for a time, but withdraws if the fight goes on beyond a certain time. This limits the likelihood of serious injury to the animal, and so maximises its chances of survival. A number of other phenomena have been modelled by changing the numerical values involved. So, for example, it is possible to use game theory to illustrate Lorenz's principle that animals which possess particularly dangerous weapons need to refrain from having damaging intraspecific fights. In this case, a higher numerical value is assigned to C—the cost of a serious injury. This higher disadvantage of getting injured changes the balance of the equation to make a "dove" strategy more advantageous—and therefore predicts that animals which do have dangerous weapons will be more likely to use "dove"-like strategies.

Alternatively, it may be that the rewards for winning will be higher: Clutton-Brock, Guinness, and Albon (1982) showed that red deer are particularly fertile during the first two weeks of October, so it is clearly very advantageous in terms of evolutionary fitness to mate at that time. In a game theory model of this situation, the value for fitness (V) would be given a higher numerical value, so the prediction is that this would increase the likelihood of very aggressive behaviour. Exactly such an increase in aggression is observed during the red deer's rut, at this time of year.

This example, though, illustrates one of the biggest problems of the game theory approach to understanding animal behaviour: that it depends entirely on confirmatory instances. As we have already seen, there is enormous diversity in animal behaviour. So it is open to question whether a research technique that involves developing a logical mathematical argument, finding a species whose behaviour fits it, and then arguing that this proves the principle must work, is at all valid. It doesn't tell us anything about the animals whose behaviour doesn't fit the model, so it doesn't really bring us any nearer to understanding the underlying principles of evolution and development.

This is very clearly illustrated by another modification to game theory, which was proposed by Maynard Smith in 1974, This involved the addition of a factor in the equation where an individual would fight harder if it was already resident, or in possession, of a territory: in other words, it would behave like a hawk to defend its territory, but like a dove if it didn't already have a territory to defend. Maynard Smith referred to this as the "bourgeois" strategy. This looks like a very plausible model, and one that seems to fit what we already know about animal behaviour. But in reality, it only models a very limited number of instances, and doesn't really reflect what we know about ownership and territory. There are three predictions that follow directly from Maynard Smith's model, and looking at them can show us just how limited those instances are.

Prediction 1 is that if Animal A "owns" the territory, then it will always win outright—in other words, that an intruder, Animal B, will always back down and never escalate the fight to increase its own chance of winning. Prediction 2 is that the situation would be reversed of the other one owned the territory: if Animal B was the "owner", then Animal B would inevitably win, and quickly, because Animal A would back down. Prediction 3 is that, because an animal fights if it perceives itself to be the owner of the territory, if both Animal A and Animal B believe they "own" the territory, then they will both fight like "hawks", producing a long drawn-out, escalated fight, with a strong risk of serious injury.

Davies (1978) showed that speckled wood butterflies do seem to conform to this pattern. This behaviour concerns the temporary mating territories of male butterflies, which consist of small patches of sunlit woodland. The first male butterfly to settle in such an area becomes the resident, and if an intruder comes into the area, there is a brief, highly ritualised "fight", and the intruder withdraws. Davies showed that these contests were always resolved in favour of the resident, and that if the same butterflies were exchanged, so that the previous intruder was now the resident, that would be the one that would win. But if the two butterflies were deceived, using screens, so that each of them "believed" that they had been there first, then there would be a very prolonged battle, with neither butterfly willing to give up.

But the speckled wood butterfly is just one species—and, moreover, one that has a very temporary kind of territory. There aren't many other situations where things are that equal. A pair of animals, for instance, may show *correlated asymmetry* (Parker, 1974)—in other words, they may be unequal to one another in ways that correlate with their chances of winning a fight. One animal, for instance, may simply be bigger than another, or may have more experience at fighting. Such correlated asymmetries make one animal intrinsically more likely to win an encounter, regardless of whether they are actually holding the territory or not.

Resource holding power

In view of these correlated asymmetries between animals, it makes sense for an animal to assess what its chances are of winning the fight. This means weighing up potential opponents, in terms of how likely they are to be able to gain, or hold on to, resources—what has become known as their *resource holding power* (RHP).

There are three main dimensions to resource holding power which have been identified by comparative psychologists and related to known practices of animals. The first of these is *size*—bigger animals are more likely to win a fight, and conversely, if the two animals are of equal size, the fights will tend to last longer. This prediction was supported in Clutton-Brock's observations of conflicts between red deer (Clutton-Brock et al., 1982). The second dimension is *weaponry*: Geist (1966) showed that Stone's sheep with larger horns were more likely to win contests than those with smaller horns. The third dimension is *information* about past experience. Thouless and Guinness (1986) report that female deer may resolve a conflict between two stags on the basis of their previous experience with those particular individuals.

Parker (1974) argued that it is to an animal's advantage to weigh up the RHP of a particular opponent before starting an antagonistic encounter—there's not much point getting into a fight that you're only likely to lose! So this model again focuses attention on the role of ritual and threat displays, but this time they are seen as a form of communication, rather than simply ritualised inherited sequences. They represent ways of communicating the resource holding power of the individual to the opponent.

The emphasis on communication presents a very different angle on what is going on between the animals. Rather than the simplistic response to the presence of another individual modelled by game theory, the animal's behaviour becomes a response to an elaborate message, tailored to the specific evolutionary demands of the situation. In the next chapter, we will be looking at some comparable forms of communication between animals, such as those between predator and prey.

Maynard Smith (1982) proposed a new strategy of "assessor" to incorporate RHP into game theory. In this strategy, the animal would behave like a "hawk" if their opponent's RHP was low, but like a "dove" if it was high. A study of the behaviour of female funnel-web spiders by Riechert (1978) showed how initial assessments of the weight of the opponent determined the strategy that the spiders then used: a spider that was heavier than the one it was fighting would escalate the fight directly to a much more intense attack than if it were fighting a more equal opponent.

However, once again, the problem is that these are a few examples set against the huge diversity of animal behaviour. The mathematical models of game theory become ever more complex as variations and additional strategies are added to the model, but they remain a simplification; and enlarging them to include new behaviours can become a never-ending task. Moreover, even if there was an end-product to this process, it would have become almost as complex as life itself, because all it is doing is describing more and more options. It is debatable how far this type of model can actually explain what is going on, rather than just describing events; and it is also questionable how far it represents an improvement on the technique of just developing ever more lengthy lists of "instincts".

Another method of winning disputes, of course, is to get help from others. Some studies have shown how antagonistic encounters in primates often involve teamwork: Packer (1977) showed how male baboons would help each other out in a temporary alliance to fight a rival, and de Waal (1984) reported similar alliances between chimpanzees. This leads us into questions about social organisation and social structuring in animal societies, which we will be looking at later in this chapter.

Anti-predator behaviour and defence

One of the most important tasks for many animals is that of avoiding being eaten by predators. Blanchard et al. (1990) argued that defensive behaviour is subject to particularly strong evolutionary pressures, for two reasons. The first is that mistakes are likely to be fatal to the individual who makes them; and the second is that success in predation also represents an evolutionary advantage for an animal, and so natural selection will also favour successful predatory behaviour in the attacker.

Blanchard et al. (1990) identified four major defensive behaviours which are shown by wild rats in response to predators and stimuli associated with them. The first of these, and generally the dominant response, is *flight*: rats will run away if escape is at all possible. In 1986, Ydenberg and Dill showed that the speed at which rats flee varies directly with the proximity of the predator: not surprisingly, the closer the predator, the faster the animal will run.

If flight is not available, wild rats will *freeze*, remaining immobile facing the predator, and becoming more tense as the predator gets closer. Generally, they adopt a half-crouch when freezing, although this is not always the case: it depends to some extent on what they are doing when the threat is first spotted. Blanchard, Flannelly, and Blanchard (1986) showed that when a wild rat is in a frozen position, a sudden sound or a sudden movement from the predator will cause it to jump, but the amount that it jumps depends on how close the predator is.

If the predator is extremely close—between contact and about half a metre—the rat will often emit a series of shrill calls, facing the predator in a crouching or upright posture and baring its teeth. This is often the preliminary for the fourth kind of defensive behaviour, which Blanchard et al. (1986) referred to as *defensive attack*. The animal jumps suddenly towards the head of the predator, or lunges towards it if it is too close for jumping. This behaviour elicits defensive reactions in the predator, which typically pulls back, giving the rat a chance to flee.

Another very last-ditch anti-predator technique, which seems to be adopted by the rabbit and some forest-living birds, is that of setting predators into competition with one another. Högstedt (1983) argued that the reason why normally silent animals such as rabbits scream when they are caught by a predator is because their screams also attract other predators. By playing tape-recordings of the screams of a captured bird, Högstedt showed that other predators came hurrying to the area, and suggested that this might be a very last-ditch defence: while in the grip of just one predator, there is very little chance that the animal will escape; but if a scuffle develops between two or more predators, it just might manage it.

For social mammals, the key to anti-predator behaviour often consists of developing effective vigilance and warning systems. Belding's ground squirrels give a high-pitched whistle when they see an aerial predator. Sherman (1985) showed that such a call is valuable for the individual who makes it, as well as for the group as a whole, because when the call is heard the whole group dashes for cover, and the one who makes the call becomes part of a mêlée of squirrels, which is likely to confuse any hawk or falcon. But these ground squirrels also give warnings when they encounter ground-based predators, and this has been seen as rather more problem-atic, because callers are distinctly more likely to be caught by the predator than squirrels that keep quiet (Sherman, 1981). On the other hand, the animals that heard the alarm and acted on it were more likely to get away.

Sherman performed a number of observations that involved noting which squirrels gave alarms to ground-based predators, and showed that females with living relatives nearby were most likely to give the alarm, other females were next most likely, and males least likely of all. Sherman linked this with the fact that it is the females who hold the territory in this species: males leave the colonies to join others, while females remain with the group. As a result, the altruistic, potentially self-sacrificing behaviour of the female ground squirrel is more likely to benefit her relatives. This strategy, known as *kin selection*, will be discussed later in this chapter, when we look at some of the evolutionary mechanisms underpinning the theory of sociobiology.

There are some examples of inter-species co-operation in anti-predator behaviour. For example: both mongooses and hornbills tend to be preyed on by the same animals. Mongooses travel in open country in Africa, in large groups, and several animals act as look-outs at the same time, uttering warning cries if a predator is spotted. Rasa (1984) showed how mongoose troops often travel with a pair of hornbills, and that if the hornbills are present, there are fewer mongooses on guard. If a hornbill flies upwards or cries in alarm, all the members of the mongoose troop take cover as well. Rasa found that the hornbills would even give warning cries when they spotted hawks, which were no threat to them personally, but would prey on the mongooses.

Another strategy in anti-predator behaviour is to warn the predator that it has been spotted. For some predator–prey relationships this is important: in the case of a hunting cheetah, for instance, surprise is essential. A cheetah can run faster than a gazelle, but cannot keep this speed up for long: if the element of surprise is lost, a cheetah is very likely to lose its prey, and to use up a lot of valuable energy in the process.

Thompson's gazelles have developed a technique known as "stotting", which they show when they detect a predator. This consists of jumping into the air, stiff-legged, and landing again almost in the same spot. Caro (1986) compared eleven different hypotheses which have been proposed to explain this behaviour, including the idea that it might help a group of gazelles to flee together, like the whistling of the ground squirrel; that it might help the animal to spot an ambush in the long grass; and several others. But close observations of the animal's behaviour eliminated all but one of these hypotheses, which was the idea that stotting communicates to the predator that it has been seen. Caro found that cheetahs were

Stotting in Thompson's gazelles

significantly more likely to abandon pursuit if the gazelles they were pursuing stotted; if they did chase, the pursuit tended to fail. Gazelles that saw a cheetah approaching would generally stott, and if they did the cheetah generally just lay down and gave up stalking that animal entirely. The strong possibility, then, is that stotting represents a communication between prey and predator, whereby the gazelle lets the cheetah know that it has been seen.

Social structures in animal groups

Animal social organisation ranges from that which involves minimal contact—lone individuals who come together with other members of their species purely for mating purposes—to that involving maximal contact—animals that live with myriads of others in highly structured hive systems. In between, we find a number of different types of social system. In the examples we have already looked at, we have seen instances of many kinds of social organisation, because the form of social organisation adopted by an animal is inevitably linked with other aspects of its behaviour, like courtship, mating, and territoriality.

A number of animals live essentially solitary lives, coming together only to mate. Such animals include many species of spider, polar bears, and, in the primate world, orang-utans. Some species live in monogamous pairs, including robins, swans, and, in the primate group, gibbons. Some animals live in polandrous or polygamous groupings: as we have seen, jaçanas live as one female with several males, whereas other species, such as water voles or lions, live in groups that consist of one male with several females. Some species, such as gorillas, chimpanzees, baboons, and mongooses, live in larger groups which consist of several different families, and some species, like herring gulls, penguins, and seals, live in large colonies. Some species, notably termites, ants, and bees, live in hive systems containing enormous numbers of individuals, all of whom are related to one another.

Again, the message we receive when we look at animal social organisation is one of diversity. The size of the group varies enormously, the way in which the members of the group are related to one another varies, and so does the way that they interact with one another. If we look closely enough at studies of animal behaviour, we can find an example of almost any type of social organisation that we could imagine—and probably several that we couldn't!

Among primates in particular, we find many different forms of social organisation, including "loners", and monogamous pairs, although the most common form of organisation seems to be largish social groups comprising several families and kinship lines. Even within that structure, there is still considerable diversity. A study of social structure among rhesus monkeys, conducted by Kawai (1965a) showed how the basic structure is matrilineal, with a large group of monkeys consisting of ten or a dozen kinship groups. Kawai found that it is female relationships that are important in this structure: males tend to wander between groups. The different family groups of a rhesus monkey troop relate to one another according to a clear dominance structure: each family has its own rank, which is enforced by coalitions and family support in aggressive encounters. That the status tradition is a social one is shown by the way juveniles of a high-ranking family will show aggressive behaviour towards lower-ranking adults, but only if their sisters or other relatives are there to support them. If not, they don't initiate aggressive encounters.

The rigid enforcement of the status hierarchy within the families of such groups results in an extremely high level of aggressive encounters. Teas et al. (1982) observed a large troop of free-ranging temple monkeys in Nepal, and found that they averaged roughly 16 aggressive acts in a 10-hour period. Observations of the large colony at the Wisconsin Primate Research Centre showed a similar rate: an average of 18 such encounters in a 10-hour period (de Waal, 1988). But that doesn't mean that rhesus monkeys are simply nasty animals: when placed in a situation where pulling a chain to receive food would also give the monkey in the next cage an electric shock, rhesus monkeys would go without food altogether, several of them even keeping it up for as long as five days (Masserman, Wechkin, & Terris, 1964). Instead, the aggressive behaviour of rhesus monkeys is all about maintaining and defending social status.

By contrast, stump-tailed monkeys also live in large groups with a matrilineal status structure, whereby families show distinct social rank, based around their female relatives. But these monkeys are very much less aggressive than rhesus monkeys, and do not enforce their status so rigidly. Many everyday threats from higher-status monkeys are ignored by their targets, or countered by the individual threatening back—a behaviour that does not occur in the rhesus monkey troops which have been studied. These monkeys make considerable use of symbolic punishments: one monkey might offer its wrist to a higher one for a mock-bite, for instance. They also show a high level of social bonding behaviours such as reconciliation strategies. As a result of all this, only about one in a thousand confrontations ever proceeds to serious biting. The proportion for rhesus monkeys is 18 times higher (De Waal & Ren, 1988).

The outcome of this comparison shows the contrast between two types of monkeys with overtly similar social organisation but very different ways of interacting. Stump-tailed monkeys are peaceable, socially close (they groom each other about one-fifth of the time), and act in an egalitarian fashion across social status boundaries. Rhesus monkeys are belligerent, aggressive, and enforce social status rigidly. In reviewing recent research on the social organisation of over 100 primate species, Hamburg (1991) remarked on the extreme richness and diversity of primate social behaviour. Primates live in groups of many different configurations and patterns of organisation, and they also create subgroups, alliances, and long-term associations. All this combines to present a picture of wide variation. More importantly, it also acts to challenge ideas about one particular form of social behaviour being more "natural" than others.

Dominance

One of the central concepts in social organisation is the idea of dominance. The idea of the *dominance hierarchy* first became popular in research into animal behaviour as a result of an ethological study of farmyard fowl published by Schjelderuppe-Ebbe, in 1922. Schjelderuppe-Ebbe observed that if hens were fed in such a way that only one of them could feed at a time, they showed a definite and regular pattern of precedence. The same bird would always feed first, the second on the first occasion would always be second, and so on right down through the line. As Schjelderuppe-Ebbe observed the behaviour of these animals more closely, it emerged that the same pattern was also apparent in the antagonistic encounters that occurred between the hens. The one that fed first would peck at any of the other hens. The one that fed second would peck at any hen except the first one; the hen that fed third would peck at any others except for the first two; and so on all down the line. The hen at the bottom of the pecking order, in addition to coming last in feeding and being liable to be pecked by any of the others, was also significantly less healthy than the others. Physical fitness, too, seemed to reflect the pecking order: the fittest hens were those at the top of the hierarchy.

Following Schjelderuppe-Ebbe's work, a number of investigations of dominance in other species took place. It rapidly became apparent that, in some species at least, the establishment of dominance depended on previous experiences. Ginsberg and Allee (1942) showed that, in the house mouse, previous success in dominance encounters (fights) with other mice increased the likelihood that the mouse would succeed again: mice that had lost earlier encounters were unlikely to establish themselves as dominant. Scott and Fredericson (1951) examined the work of a number of researchers in this areas, and showed that fighting in both rats and mice—which was interpreted as the behavioural expression of dominance behaviour—could be influenced by a number of variables, including temperature, food deprivation, and castration of males.

In these studies, "dominance" was defined rather differently from the pattern of social organisation defined by Schjelderuppe-Ebbe and taken for granted by many of the ethologists who talked of the functional value of dominance. Comparative investigations of dominance in rats and mice were essentially descriptions of how regularly a given animal won or lost a fight. This was assumed, implicitly, to relate to other variables, such as access to females on the part of males, or priority of access to food. But in reality, there was little evidence for such a correlation—in fact, quite the reverse. As early as 1938, Uhrich compared these different measures of "dominance" in the house mouse, and found that an entirely different pattern of social organisation resulted, depending on which measure was used. An animal that regularly won fights did not also have priority of access to food, or to mating.

Despite this, ethologists and comparative psychologists continued to talk of dominance as if it represented a multiple complex of social qualities which were always found together. As with the concept of imprinting which we looked at in the last chapter, the idea of the dominance hierarchy was applied very widely, and assumed to occur in virtually all types of animal societies. The concept of the dominance hierarchy in primates became particularly significant in the 1960s, both with the general public and with ethologists. On the popular side, this occurred as the writings of Desmond Morris invited the public to see the human being as just a "naked ape" (Morris, 1967), and Lorenz explained human aggression as a biological inevitability (Lorenz, 1966). On the professional side, an increasing number of ethological studies of primate groups appeared to show that dominance hierarchies were an inevitable aspect of primate social organisation.

But, as had also happened with the concept of imprinting, as researchers looked more closely at the concept, it became apparent that its application was more specific, and very much more tied to environmental and adaptational demands for a given species, than had initially been thought. Rather than being characteristic of all social groups, the linear dominance hierarchy turned out to be rather rare. Appleby (1985) showed that the data from many of the ethological studies which had assumed that they were reflecting a dominance hierarchy really showed that dominance was much more flexible.

One particularly common pattern, Appleby found, was a triangular system, in which animal A was dominant over animal B, animal B was dominant over animal C, and animal C was dominant over animal A. In such systems, who is dominant over whom often changes. Hayes (1975), in a study of dominance behaviour in a captive chimpanzee colony, found that over a six-week period, when all the different instances of dominant behaviour were charted according to who did what to whom, the behaviours cancelled out. Animal A might step aside from animal B on one day, but on another day animal B was just as likely to step aside from animal A. So although there clearly are some species that show hierarchical dominance relationships, like farmyard fowl, this doesn't mean that all species do. In fact, Appleby suggested that, as a form of social organisation, the dominance hierarchy may be rather rare!

Studies of dominance in primates

In 1961, Washburn and deVore reported on a series of observations of baboons, in which they undertook a detailed study of behaviours which they claimed were used by baboons to indicate dominance. These behaviours included initiating aggressive encounters by snarling, biting, or shoving; "presenting" the genital region to the other animal, as if in invitation to mate; "precedence", in which an animal would step aside from a trail to allow another one to pass (the assumption was that a subordinate animal would step aside to allow a dominant one to pass); and eye-contact, in which one animal (assumed to be dominant) would stare directly at the other one, until the other moved away.

Washburn and deVore reported that the use of these behavioural criteria indicated that baboons had strong dominance hierarchies. Male baboons comprised two groups: high-ranking alpha males, and lower-ranking beta males. The alpha males, they said, were dominant over both the beta males and the females in the troop, and acted extremely aggressively towards all the other animals.

The Washburn and deVore study attracted considerable attention, and formed the basis for much of Lorenz's theory of human aggression. But many comparative psychologists were less convinced of the validity of the argument. One problem was that the term dominance hierarchy seemed to have shifted its meaning, and was used to refer to general groups being dominant over other groups, rather than the rigid individual pecking order originally described by Schjelderuppe-Ebbe. Another was the problem of being sure that these signals really meant what they seemed to mean.

In 1972, Rowell reported that dominance relationships within baboon troops were actually much more variable than the Washburn and deVore study had suggested. Moreover, these variances were systematic, not random, and seemed to have everything to do with the nature of the environment in which the baboons lived. Rowell studied three large troops of baboons. One was a captive troop that lived on a large rock in a zoo; the second was a troop living on the African savannah, as had the baboons studied by Washburn and deVore; and the third was a troop that lived in the African forest.

Rowell found that the type of environment seemed to exert considerable influence on the animals' social organisation. The troop that lived on the "monkey island" in London Zoo showed a rigid dominance hierarchy—a classic pecking order, in which each baboon had its "place", was bullied by those above it and was able to bully those below it in the hierarchy. The troop that lived on the savannah showed a more flexible social structure. There were clearly some males that were dominant over other males, and some females that were dominant over other females, but an individualised dominance hierarchy was not apparent. Alpha males and alpha females were dominant over beta males and beta females, but, as Washburn and deVore had found, dominance occurred through general groups rather than through individual rank-orderings. The third group, however, despite being of the same species as the other two, did not seem to show any dominance systems at all. Although they sometimes showed behaviour of the type that had been identified as "dominant" or "submissive", there was no detectable consistency or regularity to it.

Rowell interpreted this finding in terms of how antagonistic encounters between individuals were resolved. In the forest, two individuals who had come into conflict would be quickly out of sight again, and in an enriched environment with plenty of opportunities for distraction. This made it likely that the next time they met the episode would be more or less forgotten. In the zoo, on the other hand, there was no opportunity for getting out of sight, and virtually no scope for distraction: the two animals would remain aware of one another, with the result that antagonistic encounters would be more likely to be fought out. This had led to the emergence of a dominance hierarchy based on size and strength, as animals learned which others they could defeat, and which they should avoid provoking. The savannah provided an environment that was midway between these two extremes, and this seemed to be reflected in the looser dominance structure that the savannah baboons showed.

The idea that dominance structures might link with environment was supported by Jay (1963), who observed that arboreal monkeys and ground-living monkeys seem to differ systematically in their social organisation. In particular, arboreal monkeys rarely showed dominance-style interactions, whereas ground-living monkeys were more likely to. But whether this relates to being in the trees, to differences in the richness of the environment, or to other environmental factors is harder to distinguish. Reynolds (1963) found that free-ranging chimpanzee troops, too, showed little evidence for dominance structures in their social organisation; whereas Goodall (1974), in describing a chimpanzee colony which had become settled in one spot as a result of daily handouts of free bananas, referred to them as having a clear dominance hierarchy.

There were two important differences between these two studies. The first, as has been mentioned, is that the two chimpanzee troops differed: the chimpanzees studied by Reynolds were free-ranging, often travelling for a two or three kilometres a day, over a large range. Those studied by Goodall, on the other hand, were static: as a result of the daily handouts of free bananas emerging from the research centre, the troop had settled in one place, and did not range freely as the others. It is possible, therefore, that the fact of remaining in one place had led to a change in the nature of the social relationships between the groups. It is also the case that the only documented cases of chimpanzee troops making "war" on one another also occurred at Gombe (Bygott, 1979). Two chimpanzee groups were fed by the Gombe researchers, generally referred to as the Northern and Southern troop. Both of these had settled down to a static life, as opposed to ranging freely around a large territory, and it was these chimpanzees that were observed attacking, and even killing, members of the other group.

Another important difference between the Reynolds and Goodall studies concerned whether dominance itself was a focus of interest for the researcher. Reynolds looked explicitly for signs of dominance, expressed by the established criteria derived from earlier studies with baboons. These behaviours were carefully counted and assessed for signs of dominance. Goodall, on the other hand, was concerned with different facets of the chimpanzees' behaviour, particularly mother–infant and kinship interactions. Because dominance was not the focus of interest, it formed a general background to the observations of the troop, rather than being the subject of rigorous investigation. And it is generally those interpretations that we are not consciously investigating which are most susceptible to influence from our unconscious assumptions.

This is not to say that there had been no attempts to assess dominance behaviour. In 1968, Goodall reported that roughly 600 instances of dominance behaviour had been observed in a period of six years of study. This actually seems a very low figure, given the sort of dominance hierarchy that seems to be assumed in the accounts: it works out as far fewer than one incident in three days. In a study of a captive chimpanzee troop, Hayes (1975) counted over 120 such incidents during a 10-week period. There is some occasion for doubt, therefore, as to how much of a dominance hierarchy—or even dominance structure—was really manifested by the

Gombe stream chimpanzees, at least in the early years. What does seem apparent from these studies, though, is that the existence or otherwise of dominance in primates is much more related to environmental demands than the "biological inevitability" of dominance, as some researchers argue.

Peacemaking and reconciliation

As we have seen, a major problem with studies of dominance, territoriality, and aggression in comparative psychology is that these studies are often influenced by implicit social assumptions about which bits of animal behaviour count as important. De Waal (1989) pointed out that although there has been a tremendous amount of research into aggressive, antagonistic encounters between animals, if social species were really as aggressive and competitive as all that, their social groups would simply fragment. What is really important for social animals isn't the fact that they have aggressive encounters, but the way those encounters are resolved—in other words, the process of peacemaking.

Rowell's (1972) study of baboons, and the way in which aggressive encounters were resolved, brought out the importance of reconciliation after two animals have experienced an antagonistic encounter. De Waal argued that these reconciliation strategies are essential in maintaining the social unity of the group, so strategies for peacemaking and reconciliation are a valid subject of study in their own right.

One of the difficulties of studying any form of primate social behaviour is that of moving from anecdotal accounts of particular events to scientific evidence from the systematic collection of data about similar events. So one of the first steps that needed to be taken was to show whether reconciliation behaviour really did take place. In order to test this, de Waal and Yosihara (1983) performed a study which involved recording the behaviour involved in and after nearly 600 aggressive encounters between pairs of rhesus monkeys. The encounters were limited to those that involved actual chasing and biting—simple threats were not included. Each incident was carefully matched with a control observation, generally taken the next day, of the same pair of animals. The control was therefore a recording of the same individuals, at the same time of day and season of the year, and for the same period of time; the only difference was that there was no aggressive incident between the two individuals beforehand.

There were three hypotheses that de Waal and Yosihara were testing. The first was the null hypothesis: that the types of interactions they had observed following aggressive encounters were just as likely to happen without the aggressive acts, and that therefore no reconciliation was taking place. The second was the traditional aggression hypothesis: that aggression maintains social control by causing animals to disperse, avoiding one another. And the third was that the behaviours observed following aggressive encounters really did represent attempts at reconciliation.

The null hypothesis was rejected: 21% of the pairs engaged in friendly physical contacts after conflicts, as compared with only 12% of such pairs in the control condition—a difference that was highly significant. In addition, the pairs that did not actually make physical contact sat near each other more often than they did in the control periods. The dispersal hypothesis was also rejected, because it was clear from the data that the increased contact specifically involved those particular individuals who had had aggressive encounters. The data showed that rhesus monkeys were attracted to the individuals with whom they had just had an aggressive encounter.

De Waal (1989) argued that the study of reconciliation illustrates a fundamental change in the way we understand animal social behaviour. The behaviourist view represented animals as simply mechanical recipients of stimulus and emitters of response, being bounced around by their environment. This was reflected in attitudes towards their capacity for understanding: Zuckerman (1932) stated bluntly that "subhuman primates have no real apprehension of the social situations of which they themselves form a part". But reconciliation behaviour, de Waal argued, requires a much more sophisticated level of cognition. At the very least, it involves individual recognition, memory, and reasoning; so the inference to be drawn from the outcomes of studies of reconciliation is that the animal's awareness of social situations is very much more sophisticated than it was previously thought to be.

Detailed comparisons between the peacemaking strategies of rhesus monkeys and stump-tailed macaques (de Waal & Ren, 1988) highlighted differences between types of reconciliation. We saw earlier in this chapter how the rhesus status structure is very rigidly enforced by a high level of aggression, both in terms of number and intensity of encounters, whereas the stump-tails' attitudes to their social structure seem to be much more relaxed, involving fewer such encounters of very low intensity. The reconciliation behaviour of the two species is different too.

De Waal and Ren (1988) drew a contrast between *implicit* reconciliation signals—acts that break the tension between the two individuals as if by accident—and *explicit* ones, which involve specific actions that appear to be based on both animals recognising that the encounter occurred, and trying to make up for it. Implicit reconciliation signals included developing what seemed to be "excuses" to approach the other closely—like drinking together from the same small bowl, brushing lightly against the other while going past, or "accidentally" coming close to the other while apparently concentrating on catching flies. Explicit reconciliation signals, on the other hand, included kissing, embracing, and grooming.

Although both species used both types of signal, rhesus monkeys were much more inclined to use implicit reconciliation signals than explicit ones; whereas stump-tailed macaques tended to use explicit signals. It is possible that what de Waal described as the more relaxed attitude towards social status shown by stump-tailed macaques is also manifest in their readiness to acknowledge and make up for conflict. De Waal (1989) speculated that this might result from a high emphasis placed on social unity in this species, because they are ground-dwellers and fend off attacks by banding together, with the stronger males on the outside of the group. It would be important, therefore, that some degree of trust between the animals existed in such situations.

Chimpanzees show a number of different reconciliation gestures. Often, one chimpanzee will approach another with whom it has just had an aggressive encounter, holding out its hand as if begging for food. Another option is for one chimpanzee to approach the other and begin to groom it, usually fairly hesitantly while waiting to see how the gesture will be received. The most common mutual reconciliation signal, however, is kissing, which is quite a common action between two chimpanzees who have just been in conflict. Hugging, however, is more common between an individual who has been in conflict and one who was uninvolved in the original fight. De Waal and van Roosmalen (1979) suggested that the

Reconciliation gestures among chimpanzees

uninvolved individual offers consolation to the other through hugging—kissing is a reconciliation gesture, but hugging is a consolation gesture.

These gestures are often used very rapidly, in cases where the individuals want to end the conflict quickly. De Waal (1989) observed young chimpanzees hastily making up quarrels in this way with younger siblings if they saw their mother approaching. Adult females, too, were observed quickly making up quarrels by kissing and embracing when they saw the keeper approaching with food.

"...AND FURTHERMORE....OOPSY!...ER,... HELLO MUM...A-HA-HA."

Sometimes, however, more elaborate strategies are required before a conflict can be adequately reconciled. De Waal observed that it was not at all uncommon for two males to stay close to one another after a fight, glancing covertly at one another yet apparently unable to initiate peaceable interaction. In such cases, a third party often becomes involved. A female from the group, typically, will approach one of the males and briefly glance at him or touch him. Then she walks over to the other, followed by the male who was first approached, and sits down between them. Both of the chimpanzees then groom her, and as they become more and more involved with the activity they approach each other more closely. Presently the female moves off, leaving the two males grooming one another.

Another elaborate strategy, which seems to be used when two chimpanzees, usually male, have been in a conflict and neither wants to appear to be backing down, is the "collective lie". In these cases, one of the chimpanzees would pretend to be very interested in some small object, and would hoot loudly as if it had just been discovered. The other males, including his previous opponent, would rush over and all pretend to be examining the object. Quickly, however, those who had not been involved would drift away, leaving the two erstwhile protagonists meticulously examining whatever it was, making excited sounds about it, and incidentally touching head and shoulders in the process. After a few minutes, the pair would calm down and begin to groom one another.

In the other ape species which is often confused with the chimpanzee, the bonobo, sexual contact is often used as a method of reconciliation. Bonobos engage in a considerable amount of sexual activity between pairs of the same sex, as well as between opposite pairs. On examining those situations where sexual activity occurred, it was very clear that the majority of mounts and matings occurred in tense situations, and served to reduce the tension and promote social harmony. De Waal (1987) conducted a series of observations on the bonobo (pygmy chimpanzee) colony at San Diego Zoo, and found that aggressive encounters tended to be very brief, and to be followed very quickly by physical contact between the animals concerned, which frequently involved genital massage or copulation. These observations were supported by studies of bonobos in the wild (e.g. Badrian & Badrian, 1984).

Studies of reconciliation remain under-researched by comparison with aggression, but they carry some very different messages. One of these is about the diversity of social behaviours: even within a similar general social structure, as maintained by rhesus and stump-tailed monkeys, social behaviour may take very different forms. Another is about the function of peacemaking in maintaining the social group. To focus only on aggressive encounters is to distort the picture: a full analysis of what is happening when two social animals have an aggressive encounter needs to involve the complete episode, which means it must also look at how those two animals become reconciled again. De Waal is in no doubt that studies of primate reconciliation, and particularly of reconciliation in chimpanzees and bonobos, can also throw light on mechanisms of human reconciliation, but points out that this, if anything, is even more under-researched than peacemaking in primates.

De Waal's findings also tie in with Bateson's observation that the communication of social animals is likely to be primarily about relationships, rather than about phenomena or objects (Bateson, 1973). Bateson suggested that this should be the first step in any attempts to understand, for example, the language of whales or dolphins; but argued that it applied just as much to the communication patterns of any other social animals. We will go on to look at animal communication in the next chapter.

Summary: Social organisation

- Explanations for aggressive behaviour include the idea of aggression as a ritualised expression of instinctive drive, and the frustration-aggression hypothesis. However, the same word is often used to refer to several different phenomena.
- Territoriality is generally seasonal, and is often closely linked with courtship and mating. There are several different forms of territoriality, including home range, nested territories, and territory in colonies.
- Game theory explanations of territoriality approach the issue using mathematical models to evaluate the advantages of particular strategies. They may be applicable in some cases, but present problems for explaining diversity.
- Studies of anti-predator behaviour include vigilance and behavioural responses to different types of threat. They encompass many different strategies, including inter-species co-operation and prey–predator communication.
- There is a wide diversity of social structure apparent in animal groupings, which encompasses tightly defined hierarchies, loose social gatherings, monogamous pairs, and solitary individuals.
- Studies of dominance in primate societies show it to be closely linked to environmental factors, and not necessarily an inevitable consequence of social living.
- De Waal argued that one of the most important aspects of social behaviour is reconciliation, or peacemaking, after aggressive episodes. Primate observations show that this can involve many different strategies.

Communication and information 5

The ability to receive information and to transmit it to the outside world also provides animals with the mechanisms of communication. But what is communication? Defining what we mean by communication isn't very easy, not only because communication can take so many forms, but also because it may be entirely unintentional on the part of the communicator. If a bird sings to advertise its ownership of territory to other potential rivals, but also incidentally informs a prowling cat of its whereabouts, has it communicated with the cat? The simplest definition of communication, that it involves information passing from one animal to another, would imply that it has.

Some researchers, however, take a different view. Slater (1983) argued that an essential feature of communication is that the receiver should benefit from it, at least on average. In evolutionary terms, Slater argued, communication has evolved because it contributes somehow to the animal's *inclusive fitness*. That doesn't mean that it always benefits the animal—as just described, there may be occasions where it is disadvantageous to a particular individual on a particular occasion. But on average, it will be more of an evolutionary advantage to the animal than not communicating would be.

Another view of communication focuses on the effect that the communication has on the recipient. Krebs and Davies (1978) argued that the reason why communication benefits the animal that is sending the information is because it allows that animal to influence, or manipulate, the behaviour of the animal that receives it. This manipulation of others confers an evolutionary advantage on the sender. The bird sings because the behaviour of its potential rivals is different as a result of its singing.

Marler (1984) argued that communication is a much more interactive process than either of these two models suggest. Both sender and receiver, Marler argued, benefit from an act of communication: the important element in communication is that it is mutual, and involves both of them. To the bird singing the song, there is an advantage in sending information because that influences the behaviour of potential rivals; but there is also an advantage to the receiver of the message, because it can use that information to maximise its own survival as well. It is the *transaction*, Marler argued, which is important in the act of communication.

The question of deception

One of the arguments of the sociobiologists, particularly emphasised in Dawkins (1976), is that communication provides the opportunity to deceive, by giving false signals; and that because this is possible, it will be an evolutionary advantage to an organism to use that potential. As Dawkins (1976, p.70) said:

> We must expect lies and deceit and selfish exploitation of communication to arise whenever the interests of the genes of different individual diverge. This will include individuals of the same species... we must even expect that children will deceive their parents, that husbands will cheat on wives, and that brother will lie to brother.

Marler, however, argues that this is a very short-term view of the advantages of deception. If deception were the normal strategy, as this argument suggests it would become, then it would become evolutionarily worthless, because communication mechanisms would then cease to have any further function. For example, Munn (1986) described two species of insect-eating birds which have learned to give alarm calls when there are no other predators present. The rest of the group then flies off and they are able to eat. In the short term, this benefits those birds. In the long term, however, evolution would favour the members of the flock who learned to ignore alarms given by those individuals.

There are some forms of deception, of course, that are clearly an evolutionary advantage—the hover-fly mimics the colours of the wasp, and by doing so protects itself from predation, because it deceives potential predators into perceiving it as poisonous, or at least aversive. But intra-species deception of the type that Dawkins was describing would, in the long run, be pointless if it were as common as was suggested by his argument.

Of course, it is possible to point to several examples of deception used by animals. But it is equally possible to point to many more instances of very straightforward communication. Deceit involves breaking rules, but if deceit were the norm, there would be no rules to break: as Marler pointed out, most communication must take place within the rules in order for any deception to be convincing. So the norm for communication is that it should be a straightforward passing on of accurate information; some animals may have been able to capitalise on that by deception, but these instances must be, by definition, far less common than instances in which the signals are used in a straightforward manner.

Voluntary and involuntary communication

Although communication is not necessarily about making oneself vulnerable, that can sometimes happen as a side-effect. Tuttle and Ryan (1981) investigated the two-part call of the rainforest mud-puddle frog. The first part of this call is an "aow" sound, and this is followed by a set of short calls that sound a bit like "chuck-chuck-chuck". Sometimes a male frog will make the full call, and at other times it will limit itself to the first part. By playing back tape-recordings of different calls, Tuttle and Ryan showed that female frogs preferred partners who made the full call.

So why did the frogs sometimes make the shorter version? The answer turned out to be that the short call was a defence against predatory bats. Because the calls are broadcast, they can be picked up by other animals too; and bats are the main predators of this species of frog. Tuttle and Ryan had observed that the frogs would fall silent if a bat flew overhead on a clear night; but on cloudy nights they would continue to call, and were often caught by the bats.

The two parts of their calls, though, varied in terms of how easy they were to track down. The first part gave a general sound that was hard to pinpoint, but the second part made it very easy for a predator to home in on the calling animal. When they tried playing tape-recordings of these sounds to bats, they found that the animals would instantly home in on the "chuck-chuck" part of the call, sometimes even ripping at the cloth of the playback speaker in order to find the frog underneath. They were much less influenced, however, by the "aow" part of the call.

So it seemed that the frogs were engaging in some kind of evolutionary trade-off: giving the full call was more likely to attract a female, and so increased the frog's chances of reproduction. But it also increased the probability of the animal being caught and eaten. By varying when they would give the full call and when they would give the short one, the animals were balancing the two types of communication in order to maximise their inclusive fitness.

Receiving information

In order to communicate, we need to be able to receive information. Animals are capable of receiving a wide range of information, and it is worth beginning our exploration of animal communication by looking at some of the different sensory modes that animals are known to use.

Light and electromagnetic radiation

For human beings, the primary sense is vision. Our eyes are specialised receptors for light, which is the name that we give to electromagnetic radiation within a defined wavelength range—the visible spectrum. Visible light consists of light with wavelengths that fall between 420 and 670 nanometres (a nanometre is a billionth of a metre). Many animals, as well as humans, have eyes that respond to light in this waveband, and can detect variations in wavelength (colour) and in the intensity of the signal (brightness).

Colour and brightness are used by animals to signal to one another. Not all animals can perceive colour, but among those that can, it often forms an important signal. In Chapter 3, we looked at courtship displays, and the way that coloured visual signals are used by some animals to indicate readiness to mate, or to signal competition (like the red belly of the male three-spined stickleback). The ability to perceive colour is closely related to the usefulness of colour in the animal's environment: ground-based mammals rarely seem to have the retinal cone cells that are receptors used for colour vision, but instead have a high degree of visual acuity, produced by the highly sensitive rod cells in the retina. Arboreal animals, on the other hand, such as fruit bats and monkeys, do have colour vision, as do many birds. This may be related to the need to detect ripe fruits or to distinguish poisonous from edible prey.

Some visual signals are used by social animals to give warnings to the other members of their herd or colony. For example, rabbits and some species of deer have distinctive white tails and rump areas, which become particularly visible when the animal is fleeing from danger. The visual contrast produced by these signals can be seen over quite long distances, and acts as a warning signal to the rest of the group. Colour signals may also be used to give warnings to some predators: the yellow and black colours of the wasp, for example, act as a deterrent to birds that prey on the insect; and the vivid colours of poisonous South American tree frogs seem to serve the same purpose.

Posture and gesture act as important signalling devices in many species. Hinde and Rowell (1962) listed 22 different signals which rhesus monkeys use to communicate with one another. In a different study of the same type of monkey, Altmann (1962) described 50 communication signals. The difference between these two observations illustrates the different definitions of communication; Altmann took a very broad definition, and included any action from which another animal could gain information; whereas Hinde and Rowell were concerned with identifying only communicatory signals that seemed to have evolved specially.

Visual forms of communication are important for human beings as well as for animals, and some visual non-verbal signals that are used by human beings appear to have their origins in our evolutionary past. Eibl-Eiblesfeldt (1972) showed how the rapid "eyebrow flash", signalling recognition, seems to be shown by all human beings, regardless of their culture or upbringing, and is therefore likely to have been inherited. As early as 1872, Charles Darwin suggested that emotional expressions in human beings had evolved from comparable signals shown by animals. Following this idea, Andrew (1965) showed how the evolutionary origins of frowns, grins, and smiles could be traced in the actions and facial expressions of primates and other mammals. These visual signals are important: although we human beings like to think that language is our main mode of communication, researchers have shown that we pay far more attention to visual messages, such as posture and facial expression, than we do to the words that are actually spoken to us (Argyle, Alkema, & Gilmour, 1971).

Evolutionary origins of facial expressions

A special use of posture can be seen in the play behaviour of mammals. Cats of all species, and dogs as well, often play with one another, and in doing so they chase, tumble, and play-bite. Although these actions resemble the ones that the animal would use to hunt its prey, they are carefully restrained so as not to hurt the other. When they are attempting to initiate a bout of play, members of these species give a postural signal which states, explicitly, "what I am about to do is not serious", by crouching down with their forelegs and looking intently at the other animal. This type of signal is referred to as *metacommunication*, because it is communication that describes the interaction which will follow— communication about communication, as it were.

Light itself is also used by some animals to communicate with one another. Fireflies, for example, signal to one another during the mating season by making light, using photochemical equipment at the tips of their abdomens. They flash to one another at night, using a complex sequence of signalling which indicates their particular species as well as whether they are male or female (Lloyd, 1966). One species of firefly has even learned to manipulate this signal to their advantage, by imitating the flash patterns of smaller females from a different species. When the males arrive to investigate the signal, they are set upon and eaten (Lloyd, 1975)—one example of Dawkins' deceptive communication.

Some animals also respond to electromagnetic radiation from beyond the visible spectrum. Bees, for instance, respond to patterns on the petals of flowers which reflect *ultraviolet light*. To human beings, these patterns are invisible, but to bees, whose eyes are sensitive to a different range of electromagnetic radiation, they are very clear (see opposite). The patterns form lines, guiding the bee to the source of nectar in the flower—and incidentally, allowing the flower to deposit pollen on the bee's fur or to receive pollen that the bee is already carrying from another flower.

When the sky is overcast with cloud, it seems as if the whole sky is of a general brightness, and the sun is invisible. This is because the light that is arriving at our eyes is scattered, and arrives from all directions, so it isn't possible to detect the whereabouts of the sun—the source of the light. There is some evidence that the ancient Norse navigators used special pieces of quartz to locate the sun on such days. These pieces, some of which still survive, have a polarising effect: they only allow the passage of light rays that are travelling in the same direction. Using a polarising filter cuts out the scattered rays, and so means that it becomes possible to locate the sun in the sky. Bees, too, can detect polarised light, which is an important ability, because when a bee is communicating the location of food to other members of its hive (a process that we will look at later in this chapter) it uses the sun as a reference point.

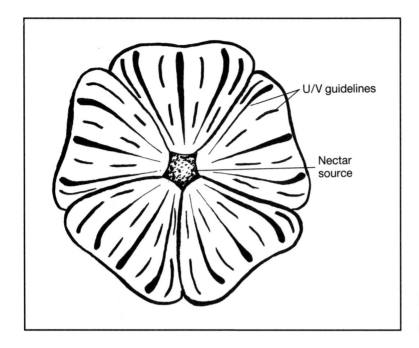

U/V guidelines

Nectar source

Electromagnetic patterns on flowers

Sound waves and pressure changes

A great deal of animal communication takes place using sound. Bright (1984) argued that this is because it has several advantages over other modes of communicating information: the signal is over quickly and doesn't stay around, but it also permeates most environments, and can pass over or through many things that would obscure visual information.

Different animals respond to different frequencies and patterns of sound. Narins and Capranica (1980) found that sound can serve more than one function in the frog. They studied a species of Puerto Rican tree frog in which the male has a two-tone call that sounds a bit like "ko-kee". By playing back tape-recordings of the calls and observing the frogs' behaviour, Narins and Capranica found that the first part of the call acted as a territorial warning to other male frogs, whereas the second part was the bit that attracted female frogs. So, during the first part of the night, when they were establishing their territory, they would make the "ko" sound more often, and then later they would add the second note.

In studying the receptivity of the frogs' auditory systems, Narins and Capranica found that the frogs were selectively receptive to these particular sounds. In physiological investigations, it emerged that the hearing of male frogs was selectively tuned to the "ko" note of the call. Females would ignore this call entirely, because their hearing was tuned to the frequency of the "kee" call.

The experience of sound results from systematic changes in air pressure, arriving in regular waves. The more rapidly a set of waves arrive at a receptor (in other words, the shorter the wavelength), the higher the pitch of the sound. Sound waves are measured in hertz (Hz), which denote the number of cycles per second—so a high value on this scale means a high-pitched sound. In a comparison of the way that sound travels through different habitats, Morton (1975) found that only a relatively narrow range of sound travels through dense forest—sounds between 1,585Hz and 2,500Hz. Birds that live in the forest canopy have songs with an average frequency of 2,200Hz. By comparing forest, forest-edge, and grassland environments Morton showed that the animals living in them had calls that were well adapted to those environments.

Human beings can hear sounds with frequencies from about 20Hz to about 20,000Hz. But many animals can hear a much greater range. Dogs, for example, can hear sounds in the same range as human beings, but they can also hear *ultrasounds*: sounds which are too high for human beings to detect. Ultrasonic dog whistles have been sold to people who don't want to disturb others when they are calling their dogs—the dogs have no trouble detecting the sound of the whistle, but most human beings (there are always individual differences) can't hear them.

Ultrasonic communication is also used by other animals. White and Barfield (1987) discussed how both male and female rats emit ultrasound while they are mating, which may act as a kind of "stand-off" signal for other rats. Rats also emit ultrasound when they are defending themselves against attack by predators, and Blanchard et al. (1990) suggested that these messages may function as alarm signals to warn other rats in the vicinity.

Detecting things that are making noises is not the only way of using sound to get information. Bats, for example, use sound to locate insects flying in the air through a process known as *echolocation*. The bat, as it flies, emits a series of shrill ultrasonic squeaks. If the sound wave hits an obstacle, it is reflected back in exactly the same way as happens with a radar signal. By listening to the echoes of these squeaks as they travel, the bats are able to locate the small insects that form their food, and to home in on them.

Bats use more than one form of echolocation to hunt down their food. Pye (1980) showed that the small European pipstrelle bat uses a wide-range system a bit like "Doppler" radar when it is cruising high in the air, but then changes to a tight, narrow-band signal when it has located its prey. The wide-band system allows it to scan large volumes of air, but is not very precise; the narrow-band system allows the bat to home in on its prey accurately.

Although echolocation is mostly used for hunting, Barclay and Fenton (1983) found that some bats do seem to use it for communication as well. By playing back recordings of little brown bats to members of the same species, they showed that the bats responded to one anothers' signals, and that they often used the calls of others to help them in finding food. But it is difficult to tell whether this form of communication is deliberate or accidental on the part of the bat.

A similar process, with sound passing through water, is known as *sonar*, and this is used by dolphins when they are hunting. Dolphins produce a series of pulsed sounds, usually as a series of clicks or rattles. They emit a burst of these sounds, and then listen as they travel through the water and are reflected by any small objects. This system of echolocation means that dolphins can home in on their prey even in waters where vision would be impossible.

Some animals, too, can hear *infrasound*—sounds that are so low that they are below the threshold of perception for human hearing. The world contains a great range of sounds of all wavelengths, and research into infrasound has shown that there are some sounds so low that they are almost unimaginable. Large mountain ranges, such as the Rockies or the Alps, for example, emit infrasounds that are so low that a beat of the sound arrives only once in four or five minutes. We couldn't begin to hear something like that—but pigeons can. Moreover, infrasound may travel slowly, but it travels a very long way. Blakemore (1984) described how pigeons are so sensitive to infrasound that a pigeon in California would be able to hear the low notes made by the sonic boom of Concorde crossing the Atlantic!

Sound involves rhythmic changes in pressure which are detected by ears; but there are other kinds of pressure detector as well. Most fish, for example, have a sensitive area along the side of the body known as the *lateral line*, and this is extremely responsive to slight changes in the pressure of the water. Through these changes in vibration, the fish can detect the presence of other animals, and the amount of the vibration gives an idea of the size and speed of their approach—helpful in detecting possible predators as well as potential prey.

Tactile, olfactory, and gustatory information

The three direct senses that human beings are most aware of are touch, smell, and taste. Vision and hearing are indirect senses—they can be used to detect things while they are still at a distance. But touch, smell, and taste are more immediate. Tactile information, in particular, is one of the most direct ways that we have of learning about the world around us. For example, we learn very rapidly to avoid bumping into things that are hard and uncomfortable. As we become more sophisticated in our use of touch, we may even recognise emotional states, for instance, that someone is in a tense or nervous state by feeling the tension in their muscles.

Animals use touch as well: a male spider, when approaching a female to mate (a hazardous undertaking, as there is a very high risk of being eaten) may use touch to calm the female and inform her of his intention. One species approaches the female from behind and strokes her back and legs in a rhythmic fashion, which seems to calm the female and encourages her to be receptive. In another species, the male shakes the female's web, again in a particular rhythmic pattern, so that the female becomes sexually receptive and allows him to approach her.

Both human beings and many other animals respond powerfully to smells. The human sense of smell is nowhere near as sensitive as that of the dog, but it is still much more sophisticated than many people realise. Schleidt (1980) showed that, generally, people can distinguish a shirt which had been worn just once by their partner from one worn by someone else by smell alone. But for many animals, of course, the sense of smell is even more sensitive, and the part of the brain involved with the interpretation of odour is much more highly developed.

Smell is often used as a direct method of communication. Animals frequently use scent-marking to identify their territories or ranges, and have special scent glands for the purpose. Dogs mark out their extended ranges by scent-marking, and often develop communal locations for these signals: several dogs will urinate at the same spot, signalling to others that they have been there. Olfaction may also be an important signal for kinship: a ewe learns to identify her lamb partly by scent, and Greenberg (1979) found that sweat bees appear to be able to detect the degree of relatedness between themselves and other bees by scent.

In addition to the detection and interpretation of everyday smells, the olfactory senses are also sensitive to the presence of particular chemicals known as *pheromones*. Pheromones were first detected in 1959, by Karlson and Lüscher, who noticed that a certain kind of chemical seemed to have a direct link with the hormones of the body, and could therefore produce hormone-linked responses—particularly in sexual activity. Further research showed that pheromones seem to be of two kinds: releasing pheromones, which signal immediate messages, such as readiness to mate; and primer pheromones, which act in a more long-term manner, such as to accelerate puberty (Wilson & Bossert, 1963).

For example, when sows that are in oestrus detect a particular phero-mone, they immediately become sexually receptive, and adopt a stiff-legged position ready for mating (Melrose, Reed, & Patterson, 1971). The pheromone is produced in the saliva of boars, and one of the responses of a boar to the presence of a female in oestrus is to champ its jaws, working its saliva up into a foam, which helps to release the pheromone into the atmosphere. Sows that are not in oestrus, however, are not affected by the pheromone. This pheromone, and a similar one for cattle, are used exten-sively in farming to aid artificial insemination.

Some animals also use taste to receive information about the world, and in such cases, it isn't always possible to draw a hard and fast line between taste and smell. For mammals, and particularly humans, gusta-tory information seems to be mostly concerned with detecting whether something is good to eat; but snakes, for example, explore their worlds by flicking their tongues in and out and tasting the air. Their extremely sensitive tongues detect tiny chemical molecules carried in the air from nearby animals and other objects, and allow the snake to build up a picture of its world accordingly.

Electrical and magnetic information

Some animals are capable of detecting and using electricity as a source of information. Neural activity occurs by means of minute bursts of electrical activity, so all animals that have a nervous system use electricity in some way, even if it is only in very minute amounts. The duck-billed platypus has sensors around the edge of its bill that allow it to detect the tiny electrical field produced by a crayfish or freshwater shrimp. Scheich et al. (1986) showed that a free-swimming platypus would turn stones over to uncover even very weak electrical sources placed in its pool. The electrical fields in the study were designed to be of about the same magnitude as that produced by a fresh-water shrimp.

There are two groups of fishes, in Africa and South America, which also use electricity to detect their prey, but this time by generating a small electrical field around their bodies. When another animal comes near, its own electricity distorts the field, and the change is detected by special receptors in the skin. In this way, the fish can become aware of the presence of other fish, and even very small sources of potential food (Hopkins, 1974). Some fish, like the electric eel, take this even further, and can generate not just a general electrical field, but a sudden burst of high-volt-age electricity (high-voltage in animal terms, that is), which stuns the animal that forms its immediate prey or threat.

Even magnetic information can be detected by some animals. Walcott, Gould, and Kirschvink (1979) showed that homing pigeons have a structure in between the brain and the skull which includes bits of a magneti-cally sensitive substance known as *magnetite*. This means that the pigeon can still find its way on overcast days, when directional cues provided by the sun are not present. When the operation of this structure was inter-fered with by fitting a small electromagnetic coil to the bird's head, the homing pigeons were able to get home on sunny days, but not on overcast ones (Lednor & Walcott, 1983). In another study, Walker, Kirschvinck, Chang, and Dizon (1984) showed that yellow-fin tuna, which migrate for long distances, also possess magnetite particles in the brain, which they seem to use for navigation. Many other migratory species seem also to possess such a sense.

Gould, Kirschvink, and Defeyes (1978) showed that some bees have magnetite in their abdomens, which allows them to identify compass points. If the comb on which they dance to inform the others of the location of food is turned round, so that its surface is horizontal, the bees are no longer able to use vertical angles to indicate the orientation of food in respect to the sun, which is their usual practice. Gould et al. showed that, after a period of confusion, these bees gradually reorient, and use the points of the compass for this purpose.

Species-specific communication

There have been several examples of animal communication which have attracted the attention of researchers. One of these is the complex signalling system used by honey bees, as they inform their co-workers of sources of food. Another is birdsong. In other chapters, we have already seen several examples of the way that birds use song to communicate with one another, and this is a phenomenon that has amply repaid detailed research. A third area of research into animal communication has been concerned with communication in the "higher" mammals, particularly cetaceans such as dolphins, as well as chimpanzees. We will look at each of these in turn.

Communication in honey bees

The honey bee is one of the most interesting and well-documented examples of animal communication. The source of this is threefold. First, it is because the information that the bees use is visual in nature, and therefore is something that we can decode: olfactory signals may be equally complex, but human beings would find it very hard indeed to catch on to those kinds of messages. Second, it is because the information that is exchanged is much more complex than just describing the immediate situation—bee communication is about things that are not physically present. Third, it is because bees use a very clear and well-defined form of *symbolism*—a capacity once thought to be unique to human beings—to convey their messages.

Honey bees are a classic example of what is known as a *eusocial* insect. They live in large colonies, with three castes: a queen bee; some male drones; and worker bees, which are sterile females. All members of the colony except the drones are genetically related to one another. The colony begins when the drones join a new queen on her mating flight, and then settle with her in a suitable place, such as a hive. The queen then lays eggs more or less continually, and these hatch into the sterile female worker bees. The worker bees gather nectar and look after the new clutches of eggs. As E.O. Wilson (1975) pointed out, because the new young are their full siblings, it is genetically in the worker bee's interest to look after them.

Worker bees forage across very long distances to bring nectar back to the hive, where it is turned into honey. By analysing over 6,000 cases of the actions of bees returning to the hive, von Frisch (1950) was able to show that bees which have found a particularly rich source of nectar will return to the hive and attempt to recruit other bees, to help them to collect the nectar. They do this by communicating the location of the source, very precisely, using a system of dance symbols to indicate the direction and the distance of the food.

Von Frisch performed a number of studies which involved providing bees with lavender-scented sugar water at particular locations, observing the bees' dances when they returned to the hive, and counting the number of bees that subsequently arrived at the original source, and at similar sources placed at varying distances along the route. There was a surprising amount of accuracy on the part of the bees in terms of the distances they travelled: over 60% of the bees that were counted arriving at the feeding boards came to the ones that were closest to the original site. It was clear that they had somehow "learned", from the original bees, where the source of the food was.

Bees usually dance on a vertical surface, usually the side of the honey comb, although some bees may perform the dance on a horizontal one instead. If the food is close by—within a hundred metres—then the bee simply moves round in a circle, and the other bees leave the hive and fly around until they spot it. But if the food is more distant, the bee performs a kind of "waggling dance", in which it moves first in a straight line, then runs round and crosses its previous path, and turns again, so as to form a kind of figure-of-eight, around a central line, as shown at the top of the next page.

It is the angle of this central line that indicates the direction of the source. If the dance is being performed on a horizontal surface, then the

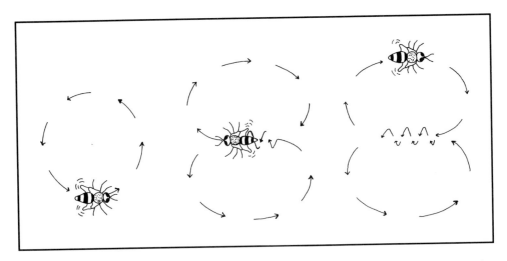

The bee dance line will point directly at the food source. If it is on a vertical surface, the line represents the angle between the hive, the position of the sun, and the food.

The distance to the food is indicated by the speed of the bee's dance. A distant source will produce a slower dance than a near one. By timing the dances, von Frisch found that a food source 10,000 metres away will produce dancing at the rate of two figure-of-eight patterns in 15 seconds, but one that is only 500 metres away will produce six such patterns in the

"IF WE HAD A MAP, WE COULD AT LEAST GET TO THE FLOWER BEFORE IT DIES...."

same time. It has been suggested this represents a coding of the flight-time required to reach the source.

Although researchers have identified the main features of the bees' communication, there are other aspects of it which are still not yet fully understood. For example, Wenner (1964) noticed that bees make small sounds as they dance, and that these sounds only occur during the "straight run" part of the dance. Esch (1967) showed that these sounds do seem to form an important component, because bees ignored dancers that were silent; but it is not clear what meaning the sounds actually have.

Birdsong

Human beings have always been fascinated by the songs of birds. Just about every culture has legends which explain the origins of the songs of particular species of birds, and in many languages, the idea of "singing like a bird" has become synonymous with singing particularly beautifully. Perhaps as a result of this interest, there has been a considerable amount of research into birdsong.

As we saw in Chapter 1, Tinbergen (1963) identified four areas of research into animal behaviour: development, mechanisms, function, and evolution. The first of these is concerned with *ontogeny*—how the behaviour develops in the individual. The second is concerned with *mechanisms*—what causes the behaviour to happen, how it is triggered off and what internal systems are involved. The third is concerned with *function*—the purpose that the behaviour serves for that animal; and the fourth is concerned with *phylogeny*—the evolutionary contexts and implications of the behaviour. In the case of birdsong, researchers have investigated each one of these four areas, and it is worth looking at some of the main outcomes of research in each.

The ontogeny of birdsong. In 1981, Slater reported a study of 40 chaffinches on one of the Orkney Islands—the total population on that particular island. Recordings showed that the colony of birds as a whole had 17 different song types, and that each individual bird on the island had up to five different songs which it would sing.

This finding posed a number of questions. The fact that there were fewer types of songs than there were chaffinches showed that it wasn't simply a question of each bird having its own song. Nor was it a question of the whole group knowing all the songs, as any given bird only sang five or so. Obviously there was some sharing, but the sharing had to be distributed in some way. By analysing the birdsongs in different areas of the island, Slater found that the distribution was geographical: the birds in one area would sing a slightly different song from those in the next area, and the ones in the area further on would be slightly different again. As it moved across the island, the birdsong changed so much, just a little bit at a time, that it became quite different.

Some of the birdsongs that Slater recorded were also sung, in exactly the same way, by other chaffinches. Others were sung in an almost identical manner, except for just one or two notes—possibly a "copying error". But some songs seemed to be purely individual, sung only by that bird and no other. The implication seemed to be that the song was partly learned from other birds, and partly inherited.

By hand-rearing chaffinches and not letting them hear any wild birds, Slater found that they produced a very different type of call. In fact, the young birds seemed to be very powerfully inclined to copy from any other birds: when one of the hand-reared birds heard a wild sparrow outside the window of the laboratory, it imitated the sparrow's "cheep", although that isn't a sound that chaffinches normally make.

Slater's findings are congruent with those of Marler and Tamura (1964), in their investigations of the American white-crowned sparrow, which we looked at in Chapter 2. These birds have a distinctive song with a number of regional "dialects": they inherit the basic song, and will produce it as adults whether or not they have ever heard any other birds. But it is a very spartan outline, and doesn't have any of the additional trills and warbles that form the dialects of the wild birds. Those, Marler and Tamura found, have to be learned during a critical period in the bird's youth, and just hearing an adult bird will be enough. Both Slater (1981) and Marler (1970) concluded that, although birdsong in these instances is partly learned, there is a powerful genetic predisposition for that learning to take place.

Marler (1991) showed that different species vary in the degree to which their song development is influenced by environmental factors. Some species, like the alder flycatcher, will produce the full adult song even if they are reared in isolation (Kroodsma, 1984); whereas others, like the swamp sparrow or the chaffinches mentioned earlier, produce only a simplified, very basic version unless they have been able to learn the full version from adults.

Swamp sparrow song passes through three stages as it matures (Marler, 1991). The first stage is *subsong*, in which the young bird makes its first efforts at singing behaviour. This bears very little relationship to the final adult song, consisting of discontinuous notes and erratic timing. It seems to be mainly to do with developing the bird's motor control and its ability to refine its song through auditory feedback. Birds that seem to inherit the full song, like the alder flycatcher, don't have this period of subsong—instead, the first stages of singing consist of recognisable sequences of the final adult version.

When the young swamp sparrow is about 170 days old, it begins the second stage of *plastic song*, in which it rehearses song patterns that it memorised when it was much younger. Plastic song consists of large numbers of trilled sequences, which are often put together in a much more complex form than will appear in the final version. The bird also uses far more different themes in its song at this stage than it does in the final version, implying that it has memorised much more than it shows in its adult behaviour.

The third stage is that of *crystallised song*. This develops as the young bird gradually adopts the adult form, a single string of one trilled syllable, rather than the multiple trills that it produced when in the second stage. It also narrows down its repertoire to about three different songs. When producing its adult song, the bird will sing one of the songs repetitively about 50 or so times before moving on to the next one. But although its song pattern has crystallised, there are still very minor variations, and the bird may shift its preference for some items, or even drop some altogether. But effectively, the overall pattern of the song has become established, including recognisable similarities with the songs of other birds that the animal has heard.

Mechanisms of birdsong. We have already seen that there is a powerful genetic influence which constrains the learning of song patterns in species like the white-crowned sparrow or the swamp sparrow. This produces a critical period in the bird's early life, during which it is extremely receptive to the stimulus of other bird's songs. There is variation between species in this too: in one study (Marler & Peters, 1980) swamp sparrows and song sparrows were both reared in isolation, but exposed to identical sets of synthetic songs consisting of two trills. The swamp sparrows showed a significant increase in the number of two-trilled songs in their repertoire, but the song sparrows were much less affected. Song sparrows do learn their songs from adults as swamp sparrows do, but it seems that swamp sparrow behaviour is more flexible within those constraints.

This illustrates the action of more direct genetic influences on the song, which may contribute to the overall state of "preparedness to learn" shown by the bird. For example, the mature song of swamp sparrows is different from that of song sparrows, and one of those differences is that the notes tend to be shorter. Comparisons of subsong in these species showed that even from the very beginning, song sparrows are more likely to produce sustained notes in their subsong than swamp sparrows. Even though the subsong isn't anything like the adult song, it still contains some of the basic units.

When we contrast these two species, and compare them with the alder flycatcher, we begin to see what looks like a continuum between species with regard to the amount of flexibility in the genetic and learned components of birdsong. It is important to realise, though, that all of these findings are probabilistic—there are variations between individual birds of the same species as well as between species. However, it seems likely that the various degrees of flexibility carry significant implications for our understanding of evolution and adaptation. We will be returning to this question in the next chapter.

Apart from genetic factors and external environmental stimuli, there are also internal learning processes which are necessary in the acquisition of adult birdsong. Konishi (1964) showed that if white-crowned sparrows were deafened from an early age, so that they did not receive any feedback from the sounds they produced, their song developed abnormally—even if they had received the appropriate external stimuli at the right time. The suggestion is that the external stimulus of the adult bird's song gives the young bird a kind of *auditory template*, which it uses to perfect its own singing by making comparisons. If it can't hear its own singing, then this auditory template won't work. The songs produced by these birds are much more variable and less highly structured than those produced by normal adults.

Again, there are species-specific variations in the amount to which deprivation of auditory feedback affects the bird. Marler and Waser (1977) showed that young canaries that were hatched and reared in high-level white noise loud enough to drown out their own voices and those of their parents, still showed far more features of their species-specific song than young white-crowned sparrows. So these birds must be able to generate quite sophisticated motor programmes for their singing behaviour, as well as using auditory song templates for matching their songs to ones that they have heard.

Nottebohm (1981) showed that some species may even grow new brain cells during the singing season. Male canaries produce increased amounts of testosterone in the spring, and this seems to have two effects: first, increasing their repertoire of songs, and second, enlarging a region of the brain known as the hyperstriatum ventrale (see p.104). In a later study, when testosterone was injected into female canaries, they too burst into song, although they did not show the same enlargement of the hyperstriatum ventrale. Radioactive labelling, however, showed that they too were growing new brain cells in that region as a result of the testosterone (Nottebohm & Goldman, 1983).

The implication, then, is that the mechanisms underlying the emergence of birdsong are varied and complex, involving a range of different elements and a high degree of variation in the ways that these different elements operate from one species to another. What is very clear is that there is an interactive relationship between the inherited components and the environmental and learning experiences of the bird, and Marler (1991) proposed that a deeper understanding of these may help us to understand how genetic variation and learning abilities combine in evolutionary adaptation.

Functions of birdsong.   Birdsong serves a number of different functions. As we saw from Catchpole's (1981) study in Chapter 4, it can be simultaneously a territorial warning and a call to attract a mate. Marler (1984) suggested that it may be possible to range the function of song in different bird species along a continuum, from territoriality at one end to mate attraction at the other. Some birds use songs purely for territorial purposes, and some use it purely for attracting a mate. But many, as Catchpole showed, use it for both reasons.

Birdsong can also serve to identify specific individuals: Thorpe (1961) showed that gannets returning to the colony would drift on the air thermals and call to their mates, using the mate's reply to show them whereabouts they should land. And birdsong can also be a warning: blackbirds make a "pink pink" sound when they see a predator, which warns other birds in the neighbourhood that there is danger.

Bright (1984) listed 16 different examples of chaffinch songs, and their different meanings. These are listed in the panel overleaf. As you can see, for a basic message like alarm, the sound may vary at different stages in the bird's life-cycle. So each individual bird has a range of signals with which it can communicate, and these change over time. Every species is different, of course, but the range of possible meanings is much larger than many early researchers realised.

Communication, of course, isn't just a one-way event: there is the question of the effect it has on the listener. Krebs (1976) showed that birds listen attentively to one another's songs. When pairs of territory-holding birds were removed from a patch of woodland and replaced with recordings of their songs, other birds stayed away from the area for about two and a half days, although they moved into empty areas within the same day. So it was apparent that the recorded song was acting as a "keep-out" signal.

But after a couple of days, other birds would move in and occupy the territory, and part of the reason for this seemed to be the way that the recorded song was static—it didn't change. In recordings of real territorial singing "contests", Krebs found that the songs varied. The challenger would listen to the song of the resident, and then sing it over again,

Alarm 1	'Tew'	Common in young birds, but also used by adults
Alarm 2	'Seee'	Extreme alarm in breeding male
Alarm 3	'Huit' or 'Whiit'	Moderate danger, used by males in spring
Courtship 1	'Kseep' 'Tsit' 'Tzit' 'Chwit'	Used by males during early courtship
Courtship 2	'Tchirp' or 'Chirri'	Used by males later in courtship season
Courtship 3	'Seeep'	Used by female during breeding season
Begging 1	'Cheep'	Quiet sound made by nestlings
Begging 2	'Chirrup'	Penetrating call of fledglings
Flight	'Tsupe' or 'Tupe'	Flight or preparation for flight
Social	'chink' or 'spink'	Helps reunite separated birds
Escape	'cheenk'	Used during courtship in new pairs
Aggression	'Zzzzzz' or 'Zh-zh-zh'	Used during fighting by captive males
Injury	'Tseee'	Made by birds hurt during fighting
Intermediates	'Huit/Seee', 'Huit/Chink'	Links between alarm and social calls
Sub-song	'Chrrps chrrps, chrrps'	Used by birds in first phase of summer
Song	'Tchip-tchip-tchip-Cherry-erry-erry-Tchip-Tcheweeoo'	Song

matching it exactly. Then the resident would go on to another song, similar to the first but slightly different in one or two respects, and the challenger would match that. This would continue for some time. The tape-recordings, however, did not respond as they should, and Krebs suggested that this was why the other birds eventually felt able to ignore them and move in anyway.

Birdsong and evolution.   As we saw earlier, Marler (1991) argued that a detailed analysis of the various characteristics of the mechanisms and features of birdsong could be useful in helping us to understand how genetic and environmental factors have influenced evolutionary adaptation. The degree of inter-species variation suggests how these mechanisms may have evolved gradually, in such a way as to produce all kinds of variations in development of the behaviour, ranging from relatively fixed inherited templates which produce the behaviour regardless of post-hatching experience, to the limited flexibility of the critical period, to behaviours that seem to be entirely learned. We will be looking at how these findings may contribute to a progressive model of evolutionary adaptation in the next chapter.

Marler (1991) also proposed that the study of birdsong may help to throw light on the way that human abilities have evolved. In 1970, he identified a number of parallels between birdsong and human speech. One of these is the powerful genetic predisposition to imitate: both young humans and young birds imitate the sounds made by adults of their species much more readily than any other kind of sound stimulation. A second parallel is the way that both birdsong and speech are most readily learned when the animal is extremely young. A third parallel is the way that dialects are transmitted from one generation to another, purely through imitation, and a fourth is the way that both chaffinches and humans have a dominant side of the brain for language.

These similarities raise interesting questions about the evolution of bird vocalisation and the way that speech may have developed out of other kinds of vocalisation. If we are to explore this idea further, we need first to look at what is known about communication in the "higher" mammals, and then go on to consider whether we can find any evidence for half-way stages between the kinds of vocalisation shown by birds, and the symbolic representations involved in human language.

Communication in "higher" mammals

The study of the development and neuroethology of birdsong may help us to understand a great deal more about how such forms of communication have evolved, or coevolved, with their environment. But in many respects, of course, birds are very different from us. Their brains, for instance, do not have a cerebrum, although there is a parallel kind of structure which, evolutionarily speaking, is related. If we are to learn about communication in such a way as to be able to apply any of that knowledge to human beings, we need to look at the communication of animals that are much closer to us, at least in respect to brain development.

Human beings have a very highly developed cerebrum, with a deeply convoluted cerebral cortex (see *Principles of Biopsychology*, in this series, for more detail). As most of what we understand as the "higher" mental functions, including language, are mediated by the cerebral cortex, it seems appropriate that we should look at communication in species that have brains which have developed in a similar kind of way. There are two groups of animals that come into this category. One of them includes our closest relatives in genetic and evolutionary terms: the apes, and in particular chimpanzees. The other is the group of animals known as cetaceans.

Cetaceans

Cetaceans—dolphins and whales—have developed a large brain, with an extremely large cerebrum. The cerebral cortex of the dolphin brain is extremely convoluted, representing a large amount of cortex relative to the mass of the cerebrum. That these animals are also highly intelligent is clear to those who have worked with them; although it is much less clear whether we would ever have a basis for communicating with them fully, because the nature of their experience is so very different from ours.

Our consciousness and knowledge of the world is based, almost from the very beginning, on transactions and interactions with the world: we learn to manipulate things, literally, with our hands: to change our world by our actions. Dolphins, by contrast, have a far more experiential mode of existence: the fact that they don't have hands means that they don't actively manipulate objects in the same way. That isn't to say that they are unable to influence their environments—as I said, their experience is very different from ours, and such things may be possible. But the manipulation would be unlikely to occur in a form that we would directly recognise. Bateson (1973) argued that it seems likely that the communication of dolphins, and of many other social animals, will be primarily about relationships rather than about manipulating things, and that we should use that as a starting point for investigation. But at the moment, we are still in the early stages of identifying the modes of communication that these animals use.

Most cetacean communication, as far as we can tell, takes place through sound. Sound travels for extremely long distances through water, which makes it an effective mode of communication for animals that are not only spread out over very long distances, but also may be in an environment where other signals, such as visual ones, are obscured.

Humbback whales. One of the most important modes of communication for whales seems to be through the construction of elaborate "songs", which can be anything up to half an hour long, and which are then repeated, sometimes for very long stretches of time. The whale co-ordinates its breathing with natural breaks in the song, so that the themes themselves are not interrupted. The longest recorded continuous singing session was 22 hours, but it was the researchers who had to cease their observations at the end of the period, so nobody knows how long the whale continued to sing after that.

A whale song itself has a number of themes—anything from four to ten, although the average seems to be round about six. Each theme consists of a group of melodic phrases, each of which is similar but slightly different from the previous one. The notes of the song are long and drawn-out, and the sound has a haunting, echoing quality which many people find both beautiful and fascinating. The song travels long distances through the water: Payne and McVay (1971), reporting a study of humpback whales, suggested that their song could be picked up by other whales several hundred miles away.

The same songs are sung by the whole group of humpbacks in an area, and change gradually, over time. New phrases are added or old ones are dropped, so that in the end the song is recognisably different from its form at the beginning of the season. In this way too, a new song evolves each year, building on and elaborating the elements present in the previous year's song.

When Tyack (1983) played tape-recordings of whale songs to a group of excited whales, the group would disperse, which again suggests that it is primarily a communication about individuals interacting, rather than the sort of sound that is made when the animals are participating in group action. However, there was often an exchange of singing between individuals. A singing whale would be swimming alone, several hundred yards away from any of the other whales, when it would be approached by another whale, which wasn't singing. The two would swim together, silently, for a while, before the previous singer would depart and the newcomer would remain in place and take up the song. Tyack interpreted this as a kind of courtship behaviour, although it's always difficult to work out exactly what is going on in such situations.

From time to time, Tyack (1981) would observe a singing whale approaching a female with a young calf. If the cow and calf continued to swim in the same direction as before, the singer would swim in the same direction, and would sometimes be allowed to join them. If that happened, the singer would stop singing, and from time to time it and the female whale would leave the calf at the surface and dive deeply for 15 minutes or more—possibly to mate. If the female wasn't receptive, however, she would begin to swim away as soon as the other whale approached.

Sometimes such a group would swim into the path of another singing whale, and a competition between the two males would develop. Tyack observed that, in such situations, the trio would often try to swim away, but the strange singing whale would approach them and try to displace the escort. Other whales would also gather around them, and they would often act very excitedly, making a range of different calls and ramming into one another, or slapping one another with their flukes. The calls that the whales make at times like this are a mixture of high-pitched trumpetings, low grunts, and fragments of songs. When Tyack (1983) re-played a tape-recording of these noises to a group of singing whales, they instantly became very excited, and he was quickly surrounded by whales diving around the boat as if looking for the group that was making the noise.

Although whales only seem to sing during their breeding season, the social noises that Tyack recorded from the whales when they were engaging in group activity like this are similar to the sounds that have been recorded from humpback whales in their feeding grounds in the Arctic and Antarctic. While they are feeding, they don't sing, but they do make a variety of noises, including, as before, fragments or phrases from songs, taken out of context. Observers have shown that these calls are particularly likely when a group of whales either come together or split up, or when they are engaged in some kind of co-operative activity like "bubble-net" fishing, in which the whales "herd" fish into a small area by creating a ring of bubbles which becomes smaller and smaller—see opposite. So it seems clear that the noises are social signals, and have meaning for the whales; but, so far, decoding specific signals or identifying what sort of information they are exchanging has not been possible.

Dolphins. Free-ranging dolphins are generally seen in fairly large groups, sometimes containing 50 or more individuals. Wells, Irvine, and Scott (1980) showed that these are often subsets of much larger populations, which can include several hundred animals, so the composition of the immediate group often changes from day to day. The communication that has been observed within these groups also varies: for example, Norris and Dohl (1980) showed that for most of the day, Hawaiian spinner dolphins spend their time resting, or in quiet play. But towards the evening, they begin to gather together and show a mounting excitement before the whole group moves out into the sea to hunt. At such times they engage in vigorous play and a great deal of whistling and calling to one another. Norris and Dohl suggested that the vocalisation is an important

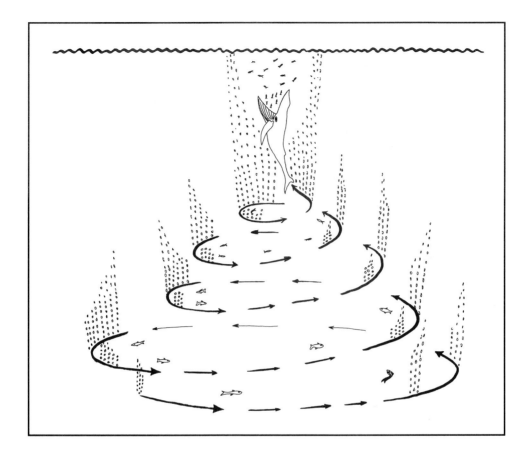

co-ordinator for the social group, and as its range and intensity increases, so too does the involvement of members of the group.

Like whales, dolphins seem to communicate with one another primarily by sound. There are two groups of sounds that dolphins make: pulsed sounds, like sequences of clicks and rattles; and unpulsed sounds, like whistles, chirps, squeaks, and groans. They also make a large number of sounds in the ultrasonic range, which can only be detected by human beings through the use of special equipment. The pulsed sounds, for the most part, seem to be mostly to do with echolocation when hunting fish; although there are some instances of dolphins using pulsed sounds to communicate with one another.

Richards (1986) observed that when a dolphin, called Akeakamai, was originally captured and her vocalisation recorded, she initially made a repeated, stereotyped, and characteristic whistle, in a variety of different circumstances. Observers interpreted this as a signature whistle. At the same time, there was obviously a considerable amount of communication going on using graded pulsed vocalisations between the dolphin and her companion in the tank. There are any number of ways of interpreting this observation, although it is worth noting in passing that human beings, if they find themselves in a strange place and not knowing the local language, also tend to limit themselves to just one or two phrases, frequently repeated.

In the wild, dolphins whistle to one another frequently, in a number of situations: when feeding, when investigating something unusual, or when calling to others. Graycar (1976) showed that dolphins appear to have regional "dialects", with dolphins from one area having slightly different patterns to their whistling from those from other areas; but they are also extremely good mimics. Gish (1979) showed that if two strange dolphins were kept in adjacent tanks, they would sometimes imitate one another's whistles. Gish speculated that the ability to mimic one another's calls would be a helpful adaptation for an animal with a fluid social group, because it would mean that a dolphin could join up with a new group more easily.

Dolphins also whistle when they are in distress, such as is caused by being captured, harpooned, or stranded. Bright (1984) described one occasion when the whistles recorded during the capture of a male dolphin were played back to other members of its group. Immediately, each of the animals turned and fled. But when the same tape was played to dolphins from a different area, they registered only curiosity, not fear. Some people believe that the implication of this is that different dolphin groups may have developed quite different "language codes" for their whistles.

Dolphins also seem to be able to exchange quite complex information using sound. Bastion (1967) reported a study in which two dolphins were kept in adjacent tanks, in such a way as to be able to hear, but not see, one another. One dolphin learned to press a paddle to receive a reward, and as soon as the other was tested with the same apparatus, it showed that it too could do the task correctly. The only way that the animal could have known the solution was if it had been transmitted through the various clicks, whistles, and squeaks that the animals frequently exchanged, and which were kept up by the first animal as it was being trained.

There has been a considerable amount of research into how dolphins learn to communicate with human beings, and we will look at some of this in the next chapter. But it's clear that communication, for the dolphin, serves a range of purposes: it doesn't just warn of danger or distress, but is also used for social co-ordination, and sometimes to communicate quite complex information between individual animals.

Chimpanzee communication

Darwin (1872) argued that the evolutionary origins of human facial expressions could be identified by looking at the facial expressions of other mammals, and particularly primates. Human beings have a number of ways of expressing emotions: facial expression seems to be the most important, as human beings are such very visual animals, but we also use posture (another visual cue) and tone of voice. When we look at the communication signals of our closest genetic relatives, the chimpanzees, we find that they, too, use very similar kinds of signals.

Chimpanzee faces are not as mobile as those of human beings, but are still used to express a range of expressions. When the animal is relaxed and playful, it often shows an expression which is referred to as the "play-face"—a relaxed, open-mouthed expression in which the teeth are covered by the lips. If it is alarmed or startled, on the other hand, a chimpanzee shows an exaggerated "fear-grin", in which the lips are pulled fully back, baring the teeth. Andrew (1965) argued that the human smile had probably evolved from just such a "fear-grin", given in response to surprising or startling stimuli, which then turned out to be pleasurable rather than threatening.

There are intermediate expressions too: a nervous chimpanzee may show a closed grin, keeping the jaws closed but exposing the teeth; or an animal that is gradually calming down may relax its fear-grin into a half-grin, in which the top row of teeth is covered by the lips but the bottom row remains exposed. These expressions, too, have their parallels in human beings.

Even more similar is the use of eye-contact. Chimpanzees use brief eye-contact for reassurance and reconciliation, and they will avoid eye-contact with another if they are still recovering from an antagonistic encounter. When they are threatening another chimpanzee, they use a direct and prolonged stare—which is an act that seems to represent a threat gesture, incidentally, for almost all mammals. This is usually accompanied by a threatening posture: standing upright, muscles tense, and fur on end—as if to make the animal seem as large and intimidating as possible.

Such a threat display is also accompanied by a set of intimidating sounds, which begin with a series of hoots, becoming louder and more rapid until they end in a screech. A milder, but similar vocalisation is known as the "pant-hoot", in which the chimpanzee makes a series of "hoo" sounds with audible breathing in between. These again gradually increase in volume and rapidity, until they end in a series of loud "waa" sounds. The "pant-hoot" seems to be a social signal, in that it takes place at times of great excitement (like arriving at a new fruit-laden tree), and often several chimpanzees will join in together with the call.

Each chimpanzee has its own distinctive pant-hoot, and Marler and Hobbett (1975) suggested that this is a unique identifying call for the various members of the troop, enabling other chimpanzees to recognise that individual. Goodall (1974) also suggested that pant-hoots are used to identify the location of the group, as it is not unknown for a troop resting peacefully to begin a call, which is then answered by a similar call from another troop some distance away.

When they are simply playing, feeding, or resting, chimpanzees also grunt to one another, and the tone and durations of these grunts can vary, seeming to express different emotions. A chimpanzee being groomed, for example, may utter a few soft grunts from time to time, as if expressing its contentment; one that is passing near another may utter a fairly quick series of soft grunts which appear to act as a greeting. These can quickly turn into squeaking or screaming if the other animal seems aggressively inclined. Young chimpanzees also squeak or whimper, and will sometimes bark or scream if they become excited.

Types of chimpanzee communication.   Communication in chimpanzees, then, appears to be through a combination of visual and auditory signals. But making sense of these signals is a complex task. Menzel (1984) suggested that there are three possible routes for exploring chimpanzee communication. The first of these is to observe and describe social interactions between chimpanzees as meticulously as possible. In doing so, one would need to take into account the animals pre-existing concerns: foraging for food, Menzel suggested, might be a good way to study complex forms of communication. The second would be to look at the group as a whole in an attempt to identify what they might be communicating about and to link it with the signalling; and the third, to try to teach a chimpanzee to communicate using human language.

We will be looking at the third type of research in the next chapter; but there have been several studies of spontaneous communication conducted with chimpanzees in captivity. Menzel and Halperin (1975) investigated whether members of a stable group of half a dozen young chimpanzees could communicate about objects that were not immediately present. One chimpanzee would be taken out of the cage, and taken, by a circuitous route, to a place where some food was hidden. It would be shown the food and returned to the enclosure. Then the whole group would be released.

Typically, in these studies, the chimpanzee that was aware of the food became an instant "leader", taking the others straight to the food. But often, other members of the group would run ahead of the leader as it went to the food, searching in any possible hiding places. It seemed as if they knew what they were looking for. In order to test this, Menzel and Halperin hid a small snake, rather than food, on some occasions. When this happened, the group also acted as if they "knew": the leader would stop about 10m from the place where the snake was hidden, and one of the other chimpanzees would pick up a stick and very carefully poke around with it—a cautious action which they didn't perform if it was food that had been hidden. If the snake was no longer there, the animals would search for it, climbing on trees and fences, and scanning the ground.

It was clear, though, that the presence of the leader was required. If the leader wasn't released with the others, they would simply mill around the cage and not go to the food. So although we can conclude from this that chimpanzees can communicate something to one another about objects that are not immediately present, there are limits to this ability: actually describing where food is seems to be something that they don't do as readily. And this type of communication also seems to be limited to chimpanzees that know each other well. This group had been living together for over a year; but when Menzel and Halperin used strange chimpanzees in the "leader" role, the others completely ignored them.

There are two possible conclusions to be drawn from this. One is that chimpanzee communication—and cognition—is very limited: more sophisticated than the behaviourists would have allowed, but still limited. The other way of looking at it ties in with Bateson's (1973) argument that the communication of social animals is likely to be mainly about relationships. It is a very human thing to manipulate one's environment to the degree manifest in that study: most of the time, if a chimpanzee comes across food, the other chimpanzees of its troop will be in the immediate vicinity and a series of direct pant-hoots will tell them that here is something worth investigating. So it is unlikely that the ability to communicate about food sources that are not present would have been a part of the animal's natural repertoire—unlike in the honey bee, where it is essential. A study of chimpanzee communication which investigated relationships and social nuances might reveal a far higher degree of sophistication.

Symbolic communication

One of the most intriguing questions to arise as we study animal communication is whether animals have "words". It is apparent that there is considerable use of symbolism of one sort or another in animal communication, ranging from the ritualised feeding gestures of grebe courtship behaviour, to visual threat displays and appeasement gestures. But these are in many ways direct analogues of a particular form of behaviour, which have become adapted through evolutionary pressures. One can speculate, as Lorenz did, that they probably evolved gradually: the behaviour patterns were already part of the animal's behavioural repertoire, and the situational demands on the animal meant that it became advantageous to use them in a slightly different context.

Words, however, are symbolism of a different kind, in the sense that they are specific conceptual signals, dependent on conjuring up a mental representation, in such a way that the receiver of the message can respond as if that thing were present. Early comparative research took the view that animal communication was simply a signalling of emotional or motivational states. But more recently, researchers have been questioning the idea. As it becomes more acceptable to consider questions of animal cognition, the idea that animals may use forms of symbolic representation to communicate with one another has been more carefully investigated.

Language involves grammar as well as words. Words are not strung together randomly, but according to particular meaningful sequences. It is possible that we can identify some potential evolutionary antecedents for grammar in the behaviour of some animals. For example, Smith, Smith, Oppenheimer, and de Villa (1977) showed how prairie dogs regulate the intervals between their barking vocalisations, according to a number of different forms, which have meaning for the other members of the colony.

Prairie dog "grammar" is based around simple barks. Barks that come at regular intervals signal to the others that there is something present, and that the signaller is continuing to pay attention to it. Barks that become quicker and quicker signal that the animal is very likely to break off and escape, and the troop members respond by showing increasing tension themselves. Barks that come irregularly at lengthening intervals indicate that the signalling animal is paying less attention to the object, and may break off and do something else entirely.

We have already seen how some animals can communicate highly complex messages between themselves. Bastion's (1967) study of dolphin communication showed that a dolphin could communicate all of the essential requirements of a lever-pressing task to another dolphin, using sound. The implication of this is that these dolphins were able to use a mutual system of symbolic representation, to describe and understand the objects and environmental conditions involved in the task.

Investigations of animal "words" in the wild have mostly been concerned with danger signalling. Robinson (1980) identified two types of signal used by Belding's ground squirrels in response to two groups of predators. Avian predators led to an animal giving the alarm call and running for cover, but ground-based predators involved an animal giving the alarm call and then standing upright, scanning the ground before escaping. Although these behaviours are clearly analogues, and it may be that they simply demonstrate the appropriate behaviour to the others, the fact that other squirrels modify their behaviour on the basis of the different signals without having seen the predator itself, implies that some sort of cognitive representation is taking place.

Seyfarth and Cheyney (1980) showed that African vervet monkeys have gone one step further. The monkeys have three main types of predators: eagles, leopards, and pythons. Different behaviour is required to escape from each type of predator, so it is vitally important for a vervet monkey to know just what it is being threatened by. As a result, these monkeys have three different alarm calls, not one or two.

By tape-recording some of these calls and playing them back, Seyfarth and Cheyney (1980) were able to demonstrate that there was a systematic relationship between the alarm call given and an animal's subsequent behaviour. When the "eagle" call was given, the monkeys would look up into the sky and run for cover. When the "leopard" alarm was given, they would climb into nearby trees. When the "snake" alarm was given, the monkeys would scan the ground near the troop very carefully, and if they saw a python, they would run away.

Seyfarth and Cheyney found that young monkeys belonging to the troop would often give false alarm calls, which were clearly a mistake. They might, for example, give the "leopard" alarm when they saw a warthog, or give the "eagle" alarm to another kind of bird. As they gained

"SO, RUN IT BY ME AGAIN, DAD... HOW MANY HOOTS FOR A LEOPARD...? TWO? OH, THREE! HOW MANY FOR A SNAKE THEN..?"

more in experience, and in particular as they observed the adults, they made fewer such mistakes. Seyfarth and Cheyney observed that, if a young monkey gives an alarm, adult members of the group will look, and if it is correct, give the alarm as well. If it isn't correct, they resume what they were doing. So the young monkeys seem to learn to give appropriate alarms through observational learning.

Natural categories.   A second interesting aspect of the way that young monkeys learn to give alarms was discussed by Seyfarth and Cheyney in 1982. They showed that, even though the young monkeys sometimes make mistakes, the mistakes they make always fall into the same rough category: they don't mix up threats that require entirely different behavioural responses. A "leopard" alarm, for instance, would only be given in response to a ground-based mammal, not a bird. Seyfarth and Cheyney proposed that the young monkeys may have inherited a genetic predisposition to respond in certain ways to certain *natural categories*, and that this is then refined by experience as the young animal gains in knowledge of the world.

Seyfarth, Cheyney, and Marler (1980) also suggested that the natural categories identified in field studies of vervet monkeys form an evolutionary precursor to the development of more complex language. This observation raises an interesting parallel, because Rosch (1973) argued that human concept-formation, too, was based on natural categories. For Rosch, the fundamental basis of a concept or group of concepts is action: what you actually do with or in response to things belonging to that concept. Higher or lower levels of categorisation are simply more sophisticated or more selective groupings to do with that concept, but these are always refinements or generalisations of the original action basis. So human conceptualisation and primate "words" may have more in common than appears on the surface.

Marler (1982) suggested that the process of language evolution would have to begin with the way that innate predispositions are refined through experience. Factors like the basic song of the white-crowned sparrow, or the basic type of stimulus to which a vervet monkey alarm should be given are innate; but these are developed and made more appropriate to the immediate circumstances by the interactions of the young animal with members of its species and by its experience.

The innate predispositions, Marler argued, also mean that any evolving language would be species-specific, building on the basic discrimination and learning aptitudes of members of that species. Zoloth and Green (1979) showed how the natural vocal range of a primate species strongly affects what they can learn easily and what they find difficult. They showed that Japanese macaques found it easy to make subtle distinctions between two "coo-calls" which sounded similar except that one set of calls had a frequency peak occurring near the beginning, and the other had it near the end. The Japanese macaques who were tested managed this discrimination quickly and easily. However, tests with two other species of macaques and some vervet monkeys showed that they found it very difficult. The other macaques, though, found it relatively easy to discriminate between calls of different pitches, which the Japanese macaques found difficult.

So although all of the monkeys could learn to solve all of the tasks, eventually, there were considerable differences in the ease with which they managed it. It was this sort of difference, argued Marler, which would mean that the evolution of language would have to be specific to a particular species; and which might explain why, as we have seen in this chapter, some animals seem to have developed more sophistication in their modes of communication than others.

In the next chapter, we will be looking at some of the attempts that have been made to teach animals human-based language, and also at some of the other evidence concerning animal cognition.

Summary: Communication and information

- Definitions of communication have emphasised, variously, the benefits of communication, manipulation, interaction between animals, and the possibility of deception.
- Information can be received and transmitted by animals in a number of forms, including light and electromagnetic radiation, sound and pressure waves, tactile, olfactory, and gustatory information, and electrical and magnetic information.
- Honey bees communicate the locations of sources of food to other members of the hive by performing a coded dance, in which different elements convey different bits of information.
- Studies of birdsong have encompassed its development, the mechanisms involved, its function for the individual, and aspects of its evolution. It involves the interaction of both learned and innate components, but to different degrees in different species.
- Studies of cetacean communication have shown that it serves several distinct functions. Some whale song appears to be associated with courtship, while dolphins emit distinctive sounds for communal hunting, and for escape. Dolphins appear to have regional dialects.
- Chimpanzee communication consists of a combination of visual and auditory signals. Chimpanzees who know one another appear to be able to communicate about distant objects, but it is unclear whether this is possible between strangers.
- Several animal species appear to have "words", or at least their evolutionary precursors. They are often used to represent different types of threat, and may link with research into natural categories.

Animal cognition 6

As we saw in Chapter 1, one of the oldest ideas in comparative psychology is that animals act in a machine-like fashion, with nothing other than the most basic kinds of associative memory—without thinking or other forms of cognitive processing. But the more we find out about what animals do, and what they are capable of doing, the more this idea is gradually disappearing. In Chapter 2 we found that the idea that animals act in a purely mechanistic fashion has even been seriously challenged by those researching into classical and operant conditioning: the areas once thought to represent the essence of mechanistic learning.

Over the past few decades, the evidence has been building up that animals have far more cognitive abilities than has traditionally been believed. This evidence comes from all branches of comparative psychology. We have seen in the preceding chapters how cognitive appraisals may be involved in parent–infant relationships, social organisation, and various aspects of communication. Some of the other evidence has come from explicit research into animal cognitive abilities, including the cognitive types of learning, like imitation or the formation of cognitive maps, and also including research into other cognitive abilities of animals. Some evidence, too, has come from attempts to teach animals language. In this chapter we will look at some of the evidence for animal cognitive abilities, before going on to consider how these findings may make sense, in terms of our knowledge of evolutionary processes.

Imitation

Imitation is a form of learning which, of necessity, involves some degree of cognitive input. By copying the behaviour of another, an animal needs to maintain some kind of representation of that behaviour and some rudimentary concept of self-and-other, to allow it to make the shift from a behaviour that is simply witnessed to one that is directly performed.

The physiological mechanisms underlying imitative learning are not very well understood—indeed, imitation itself seems to be a relatively under-researched area in comparative psychology. There is, though, some evidence that it involves the formation of an internal representation, to which behaviour is then matched. As Marler and Tamura (1964) showed, white-crowned sparrows acquire the distinctive regional accent of their song through being exposed to the sound of adults singing at an early age. But Konishi (1964) showed that if they were deafened, such that they could not hear themselves sing, they would not be able to produce the accent. Konishi speculated that the experience of hearing adult song during the sensitive period produces an auditory template—a kind of internal representation—for the finished song. As the young bird begins to sing, it practises the phrases and trills required by this model, until eventually it can match its song with the template. It may be that this is a more general model for how imitation takes place; but a great deal more research is needed before we can be sure of that.

Gould and Marler (1987) emphasised the way that imitative learning often works hand in hand with innate behaviours. For example: Curio, Ernst, and Vieth (1978) investigated the innate mobbing response that birds like chaffinches or blackbirds show to potential predators during the nesting period. In one study, they kept European blackbirds in separate, but facing, cages, so that the birds could see one another easily. Between the birds was a rotatable box, divided into four sections. As shown in the figure on the facing page, the birds could only see into the part of the box that was directly facing their own cage—they couldn't see into the section of the box that faced the bird opposite.

In the first part of the study, a stuffed Australian honeycreeper was positioned each side of the box, and shown to the birds. They didn't respond to this. Then one of the stuffed honeycreepers was replaced with a stuffed owl. The bird that could see the owl immediately gave the mobbing call, and tried to attack the model. The second bird, which could only see the honeycreeper, watched the first bird for a moment, and then began giving the mobbing call as well, and trying to attack the stuffed honeycreeper. When the owl was replaced by another stuffed honeycreeper, the first bird observed the second showing mobbing behaviour, and imitated that.

On subsequent occasions, each of the pairs of birds that had been part of this experiment would try to mob honeycreepers if they saw them—even though they had never seen a bird of this species attack a nest. Moreover, they passed this response on to the second generation—the young birds learned to mob honeycreepers by watching their parents. In the case of mobbing, then, it seems that the environmental conditions under which this innate behavioural response will be produced are acquired through imitating older members of the species.

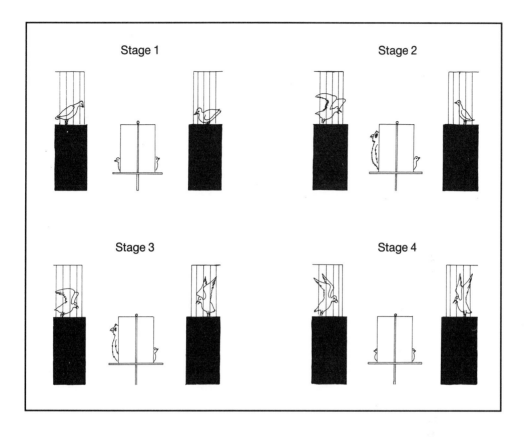

Stage 1   Stage 2

Stage 3   Stage 4

Pepperberg (1983) trained an African grey parrot to use spoken English words. When the parrot, Alex, was being introduced to a new word, one researcher would hold up an object and ask another researcher what it was. The second researcher, imitating the role of parrot, would answer correctly, whereupon she or he would be praised and given the object to play with. Alex would watch these interactions, and then the same routine would be conducted with him. If he named the object correctly, he was allowed to play with it or eat it. Alex was eventually able to identify, categorise, and request over 50 items using this training method. However Pepperberg (1986) emphasised that the social aspect of the second trainer acting as model was also accompanied by competition for the researcher's attention. This, too, seemed to represent an important motivation for the parrot.

In a project that ultimately aimed to teach dolphins to use English, Lilly (1965) used a combination of imitation, reinforcement, and behaviour shaping to teach the dolphins. The dolphin would be reinforced for

Studying learned "mobbing" behaviour

matching its own sounds to those uttered by a trainer, and these rewards were gradually adjusted so that, in the end, the sounds had to be matched syllable by syllable. The dolphins, incidentally, learned what was required of them very quickly indeed, needing much less training and reinforcement than would normally be expected of any other animal. Despite their proficient imitation, however, Lilly's dolphins didn't make the transition from imitation to spontaneous generation of language. Later on in this chapter we will looking more closely at a different method of training dolphins in language use.

Imitation and social organisation

Imitation is also implicated in the social organisation of some animals. Kroodsma (1979) showed how marsh wrens are particularly flexible in the songs they can acquire, and how they learn their song through imitation of others. There also seems to be what looks very like a social organisation based on a dominance structure within a group. A submissive male marsh wren, Kroodsma found, will match its song themes precisely with the dominant individuals in the group—possibly as a message about social acceptability.

The use of imitation for social cohesion has also been observed in other species. Bertram (1970) investigated the highly sophisticated form of imitation shown by Indian hill mynah birds. These birds are sometimes kept as pets, and much of their attraction for their owners lies in the way that they are able to mimic such an extremely wide range of sounds. Bertram showed that, in the wild, this ability seems to be used by mynah birds for mimicking the individual birds in neighbouring territories, and so reinforcing social relationships.

Richards (1986) speculated that the dolphin's highly sophisticated imitative abilities might be a response to its very fluid social organisation. Gish (1979) showed that captive dolphins in adjacent tanks would imitate each others' whistles, and Graycar (1976) showed that wild dolphins have definite regional dialects, which they acquire through imitation. Moreover, unlike the white-crowned sparrow, dolphins remain able to change to other dialects—in fact, a whole group will often change its dialect, possibly in response to the way that different members of the group come and go. It would make adaptive sense for an animal that was likely to join a new group more than once during the course of its life to be able to adjust to the traditions or customs of that group.

Imitation in primates

In primates, imitation is also a very important source of learning—although it seems too often to have been taken for granted and not researched explicitly. Ethological descriptions of the interactions of primate groups incorporate the importance of imitation as part of their day to day descriptions: for example Goodall (1974) described how young chimpanzees learn everyday behaviour from imitating their mothers and the actions of other members of the troop, and both Schaller (1964) and Fossey (1980) described the same sort of observational learning in young gorillas.

Explicit investigations of observational learning, however, have tended to take place only when researchers have been interested in some other facet of the animal's behaviour. For example, Hamburg (1971) pointed out the importance of observational learning of aggressive behaviours among non-human primates, and Hamburg and Goodall (1974) noted that young infants seemed to observe aggressive interactions with particular interest. De Waal (1989) described how members of a captive chimpanzee group which had observed a traumatic conflict involving the mutilation and killing of one of the males had shown new fighting tactics, which had evidently been learned by observing the fight.

Imitation and cognitive capacity

Among the studies that originally raised the question of the importance of imitation was Lilly's pioneering research with dolphins (Lilly, 1962). Lilly linked mimicry in dolphins with cognitive capacity, arguing that there was a close connection between the dolphin's intelligence and its ability to mimic the vocalisations of both other dolphins and also, to some extent, human beings.

This idea was challenged by Andrew (1962), who pointed to the existence of vocal mimicry in birds like Indian hill mynahs and parrots—not species that were well known for their intelligence. But Richards (1986) pointed out that Andrew had oversimplified the dichotomy between call elicitation in birds and vocal mimicry. As we have already seen, bird species vary in the extent to which their song is influenced by learning and environmental factors. Richards proposed that some kind of motor flexibility is necessary before any behaviour can be successfully imitated, and that species like parrots or mynah birds are simply showing extreme motor flexibility. This, Richards argued, is quite different from the generalised concept of mimicry demonstrated by dolphins, in which they will apparently comprehend an instruction to imitate whatever follows.

We can see, then, that although research into animal imitation has been relatively limited, at least by comparison with research into other areas, it is an important feature of animal learning. By definition, imitative learning involves some kind of internal representation of the behaviour that is to be learned, so the ability to form such internal representations may be more widespread among animals than was previously thought. There are variations, too, in the scope of imitative learning, and it is possible that this indicates some relationship between imitation and animal intelligence.

Cognitive motivation: exploration and curiosity

For several decades now, curiosity has been recognised as a significant motivator for animal behaviour. Montgomery (1954) was among the first to demonstrate that rats would learn to perform a task purely in order to obtain the opportunity to explore an unfamiliar area—without any additional food reward. Researches with other animals showed that even a limited visual exploration of the environment seemed to be intrinsically rewarding. For example, Butler (1954) showed that rhesus monkeys would prefer to look at anything new than to look at scenes which were familiar to them, and that most of all they were interested in viewing and hearing other monkeys.

The drive theory of motivation which was current in the 1940s and 1950s assumed that there are primary drives, essential to maintain the animal's survival, such as hunger and thirst, and that there are also secondary drives, such as the drive for companionship with others, which become important for the animal because they are associated with primary drives. As we saw in Chapter 3, Harlow's research on attachment in infant monkeys, using "surrogate mother" models, showed that infant attachment was more complex than a simple association with the primary drive of hunger. Research into exploration and curiosity in animals produced another challenge for this theory.

Harlow and colleagues investigated tactile exploration in rhesus monkeys (Harlow, Harlow, & Meyer, 1950). They found that monkeys would learn tasks for the reward of receiving opportunities to touch and manipulate objects. In view of the strength of the monkeys' drive to investigate new things, whether visually or through tactile exploration, and in view of the fact that it did not seem to be associated with any of the established primary drives, Harlow proposed that curiosity was a primary drive in itself.

One argument that was raised against Harlow's ideas was the question of the animal's early history. It was possible, critics said, that early associations between, say, feeding and exploration had established the drive. Investigating this, Miles (1958) brought kittens up in such a way as to make sure that, from the very beginning, their experience of feeding or pain avoidance (primary drives) was dissociated from any opportunities that they had to explore their environments. When the kittens were eight weeks old, Miles showed that they nonetheless had an active tendency to explore their environments, and that providing opportunities to explore could be used as a reward in training them to solve a maze. The evidence, therefore, pointed strongly to curiosity as a "natural" drive, which encourages the animal to explore its environment.

In evolutionary terms, of course, the development of curiosity can be very clearly seen as advantageous. An animal that is curious about its environment is more likely to locate safe places in which to hide itself or its young from predators, and also more likely to find hidden or non-obvious sources of food. But this also assumes that the animal is in some way able to store what it has learned: the existence of a drive to explore would have no evolutionary value unless the information gained during that exploration was somehow represented internally, so that it could be used later. Curiosity is a cognitive drive, not a behavioural one.

Cognitive maps

One way that information learned from exploring the environment is represented internally is through the *cognitive map*. Cognitive mapping seems to be a very fundamental part of animal cognition. Most animals need to be able to orient themselves, in terms of where they are and how they can get home; and any territory-holding or -ranging animal needs to have some kind of representation of their own range or territory.

Evidence that animals use cognitive maps has existed for a long time. In 1932, Tolman showed that rats exploring a maze appeared to develop a cognitive map of that maze, which they would only use when it became advantageous to do so. Tolman developed a complicated maze and tested different groups of rats in it, timing how long it took each rat to reach the goal box at the end, from the point where they were placed at the start.

One group of rats received a food reward when they reached the goal box, and over successive trials, these rats steadily reduced the time that it took them to reach the goal. When plotted on a graph, their times formed a classic learning curve (see Chapter 2, p.64). A second group of rats were not rewarded at all, and they continued to take a long time to meander through the maze—by the end of the study they took almost as long to reach the goal as they had at the beginning. A behaviourist explanation for this would be that they had not learned anything, because they had not been reinforced for making any particular stimulus–response associations. The third group of rats that Tolman used spent the first 10 days without reward, like the second group; and like the second group they took just as long to reach the goal by the tenth day as they had at the beginning. But from the tenth day onwards, they were given rewards for reaching the goal box, and their behaviour showed a dramatic change. Within just a couple of days, they were performing as efficiently at running the maze as the group who had been rewarded from the start (see the graph below).

The implication, then, is that this third group of rats had not needed to go through the trial and error process of learning experienced by the first group. Instead, they acted as though they already knew the way to the goal, and were using that knowledge when it was advantageous for them to do so. Tolman argued that this was, in fact, the case: their explorations had allowed them to build up a *mental representation* of the maze—a cognitive map—which they could call on when the situation seemed to demand it. But, rather than simply appearing as a change in behaviour, as the behaviourists insisted, the learning had remained latent, not apparent to an observer, until it was needed.

In 1979, Olton performed a study which also showed that rats can use cognitive maps in a complex maze. Olton's maze was a multiple one with radiating arms from a central point and a goal box at the end of each arm. When food was placed in each of the goal boxes, the rats would visit the different arms, in random sequence but never visiting the same arm twice.

Tolman's maze-running study

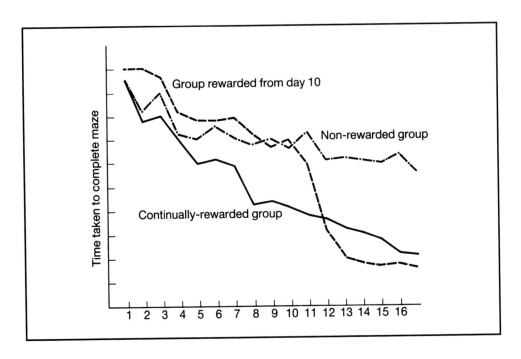

188   PRINCIPLES OF COMPARATIVE PSYCHOLOGY

Olton argued that this indicated that they remembered where they had been, which in turn implied that they had a cognitive map of the maze.

Even honey bees, it seems, may have some kind of cognitive map. As we saw in Chapter 5, honey bees communicate the location of sources of nectar to the other bees in their hive by performing a special dance. Gould (1986) described a study in which honey bees were fed from a boat in the middle of a lake. When they returned to the hive and danced to indicate the location of the nectar, the other bees ignored them. But when the boat was moored at the lakeside, and the bees' dance indicated that, the other bees would go off in search of honey. It was as if the bees were somehow aware that the lake was in the location that the dance was indicating, and that the middle of the lake was a pointless place to look for food.

Being able to use cognitive maps in selecting appropriate behaviour can be an important survival trait. Blanchard, Fukanaga, and Blanchard (1976) performed a study in which rats were placed in a box at the same time as a cat: the two were divided by a clear Plexiglas screen. One group of rats tested in this way had been placed in the same box for two minutes just beforehand; the other group had not. Blanchard et al. found a clear difference in the way that the two groups reacted to the presence of the cat. Those with prior experience of the box "froze", but those rats that had not explored the box beforehand attempted to flee. The researchers argued that this finding requires a cognitive explanation: the rats that had explored the box were aware that it was not possible to escape from it, and so made the most appropriate response to the threat. The others had no prior experience to tell them that escape was not possible, and so they acted in a way that would normally maximise the possibility of escaping.

Research into cognitive mapping is difficult, if not impossible, to interpret in purely behaviourist terms. Tolman's researches showed that it is necessary to invoke some degree of cognition in order to make sense out of what is happening. Moreover, there are sound evolutionary reasons for this: the implication of studies of cognitive mapping in animals is that being able to locate oneself in the environment spatially has considerable survival value.

Homing

Cognitive maps are concerned with established and familiar territories. Some animals, however, manage to orient themselves across territories that they have never encountered before. Homing pigeons, for example, are able to find their way back to their roost from completely unknown and unvisited areas, over hundreds of miles.

Pigeons are not the only animals to show impressive abilities to find their homes. Matthews (1955) described how a Manx shearwater flew from Boston, Massachusetts, to its home in Wales; and Kenyon and Rice (1958) reported on an albatross which was shown to travel over 4000 miles to return home. There have always been anecdotal accounts, too, of cats and dogs finding their way across long and unfamiliar distances to return to their original homes. But most, if not all, of the experimental studies that have been conducted into homing have, for understandable reasons, been concerned with homing pigeons.

The question, then, is how do they do it? An early suggestion was the idea that the pigeon somehow manages to identify and remember the country that it covers while it is travelling away from its loft, and that it returns by re-tracing that route. But Walcott and Schmidt-Koenig (1973) showed that pigeons can still return home effectively even if they were anaesthetised while they were travelling outwards, so that explanation doesn't really hold up.

Pigeon breeders have always known that allowing the pigeons to explore the area around their base seems to help them to develop their homing abilities, and another early explanation for pigeon homing was the idea that they navigated using familiar landmarks to guide them. But this was challenged by Schlichte and Schmidt-Koenig (1971), who fitted homing pigeons with translucent lenses before releasing them 80 miles away from their bases. Even though they couldn't make out any of the details of the landscape unless they were very close to it, some of the pigeons found their way home, and others were observed to set off in the right direction, even though they didn't actually arrive. Obviously navigating by visual landmarks wasn't the answer.

It is possible, however, that pigeons do navigate by different kinds of landmarks. As we saw in Chapter 5, pigeons have an ability to detect infrasound. Yodlowski, Kreithen, and Keeton (1977), in a classical conditioning study, showed that pigeons could detect a sound with a frequency as low as 0.1Hz—well below anything that a human being could possibly detect. Infrasound travels very long distances without distorting: Balachandran, Dunn, and Rind (1977) recorded the sonic boom of Concorde crossing the Atlantic from over 1,000 kilometres away. Given what we know about the pigeon's capacity for detecting infrasound, the implication is that a pigeon in California would be able to detect Concorde crossing the Atlantic!

Detecting aeroplanes is unlikely to be a skill that has specifically evolved in pigeons, although one can see how the process of natural selection might currently be at work along those lines. But infrasound is also emitted by some geological features, like large mountain ranges. Blakemore (1984) suggested that it is possible that pigeons are able to detect the "signatures" of such geological features, and to use them in aiding their navigation. If that were true, it still wouldn't be the whole answer to the question of how pigeons home, of course, but it might form part of the solution.

Finding the right direction

Another part of the solution may lie in the question of magnetic sensitivity. As we saw in the last chapter, some animals, including pigeons, have structures containing magnetite in their brains, which act as a kind of "compass", allowing the animal to orient itself with reference to North and South. Gould (1982) showed that pigeons do not home as well when there is a magnetic storm, and Walcott (1978) showed that the same effect applies when they are in an anomalous part of the Earth's magnetic field. Walcott, Gould, and Kirschvink (1979) showed that interfering directly with the pigeon's magnetic sense by fitting a small electromagnetic coil to the head also limited the bird's ability to navigate, resulting in them only being able to home successfully on sunny days, not overcast ones.

This is turn suggests that the location of the sun is also important for the pigeon's homing ability. Von Frisch (1950) showed that bees can use polarised light to locate the sun on cloudy days. But although Kreithen (1978) suggested that pigeons are sensitive to polarised light, in the sense that they can be conditioned to recognise it as signalling an impending electric shock, they do not appear to use this ability for navigation. The experimental evidence concerning pigeon direction-finding suggests that pigeons use two ways of finding the right direction: one magnetic and the other by direct reference to the position of the sun. When one becomes unusable, they rely on the other. If both are unusable, as they were on the overcast days during the Walcott et al. study, then the pigeons become confused.

Using the sun to navigate also assumes that the animal knows what time of day it is. Keeton (1969) showed that pigeons have a strong internal clock, which they use in computing the direction of flight. By keeping pigeons in an artificial environment, Keeton managed to shift their internal clocks by six hours. If the pigeons were using their internal clocks to co-ordinate with the position of the sun, the implication of this was that these pigeons should have their directional sense out of phase by 90°. Keeton's studies showed that this did indeed seem to happen.

Other sources of information have also been suggested as possible factors in homing. Yeagley (1951) suggested that pigeons can detect lines of coriolis force across the Earth's surface, produced by the spin of the Earth. Papi et al. (1978) suggested that the pigeon's acute sense of smell might also be a factor. It is also possible that pigeons combine information from several different sources of information, using information from two or more different sources to "triangulate" on the location of their home (Gould, 1982). But whether we accept these speculations or not, the abilities that we know about—such as the ability to compute direction from time of day and sun location—are impressive. The homing pigeon may not be the intellectual equivalent of an academic philosopher, but it clearly has a set of abilities which (possibly unlike the philosopher) it is able to apply to the ever-changing, real-life problems with which it is faced.

Concept formation

One of the striking features of human cognition is the way that we categorise our experience. Objects, events, and situations are classified into groups, or "types", and are used as the basis for the concepts that we use in our thinking. In Chapter 2, we saw how Harlow's (1949) research into learning sets suggested that monkeys are able to learn to solve a type of problem, rather than just one problem itself. These experiments, and others of their kind, strongly suggest that animals are able to form basic concepts.

Further experiments into animal concept-formation also support this view. Herrnstein, Loveland, and Cable (1976) showed pigeons a series of 80 different slides. Some of these were of scenes containing trees, and the pigeons were rewarded for pecking a response key if such a picture was shown. Other pictures contained no trees, and responses to these were not reinforced. Later, when they were tested with a new set of slides, the pigeons reliably picked out the ones with trees (even though they were different kinds of trees) from the rest. They did not make many mistakes, but the ones they did make were interesting, because they tended to contain tree-like items such as telegraph poles or television aerials.

The implication was that the pigeons had been able to form a concept of "tree", which they were then applying to the task. Herrnstein et al. also reported that the pigeons had been able to respond similarly to water, or to pictures of one specific person, but that they took much longer to learn "unnatural" concepts, like chairs or wheeled vehicles. They did, however, manage to learn to distinguish between underwater pictures containing fish and those without (Herrnstein, 1984).

Ethological evidence for the idea that animals also use concepts comes from the study by Seyfarth and Cheyney (1980) on the alarm calls given by young vervet monkeys. As we saw in the last chapter, these monkeys have different alarm calls for different types of predators. While the young monkeys are learning to give these calls, they often give an alarm call when they see a harmless animal. But these calls, although incorrect, are not random: the call they give is always the correct call for that type of animal: a leopard call, for instance, will only be given to a ground-based mammal; a python alarm will only be given when a snake is seen; and a martial eagle alarm will only be given in response to a bird.

The Seyfarth and Cheyney study strongly suggests that a predisposition to categorise their experience—at least the experience of danger—exists among vervet monkeys. Gould and Marler (1987) propose that the drive to categorise is innate in some species, and that, as with other forms of learning, the most powerful categorising predispositions—those that are most easily learned—would be those which have most direct relevance for the animal's evolutionary fitness. The suggestion of an evolutionary framework for categorisation may also help to make sense out of Herrnstein's (1984) findings, which showed that pigeons learn categories that are "natural" to them more readily than artificial ones.

Herrnstein's finding that pigeons could learn to distinguish fish from non-fish underwater scenes is more problematic, because this is not likely to be a category that pigeons would use directly. One possibility is that such predispositions were quite an early evolutionary development in birds. Many species of birds live by fishing, and it may be that different species of bird share a common evolutionary predisposition towards certain concepts. Another possibility may concern the notable adaptability of the pigeon, as a forager and omnivore: perhaps it is genetically prepared to exploit pretty well any kind of food source. Alternatively, to a pigeon eye, fish swimming underwater may resemble birds flying above ground.

There is, of course, an entirely different kind of explanation, which is that pigeons are just acquiring a sophisticated form of pattern recognition, which develops from stimulus generalisation through operant or classical conditioning. In other words, they are not really forming concepts at all. That type of explanation conforms to Lloyd Morgan's canon, which we looked at in Chapter 1, and which states that we should always seek to explain animal behaviour using the lowest possible level of explanation. But if we were to stick rigidly to that argument, we would also need to be able to state very clearly how a concept differed from the kind of learning set that we looked at in Chapter 2, which also comes about from stimulus generalisation. It may be that the two are entirely different, and certainly some researchers believe that they are. Other researchers, however, believe that learning sets may be precursors to concepts, so the two may not be as different as all that.

Self-concept

Another form of concept is the sense of self. It is long been generally believed that human beings are the only animals that are capable of having a sense of self: that this is one of the mental characteristics which distinguishes human beings from animals. Many animals, including parakeets and Siamese fighting fish, will treat their image in the mirror as if it were another animal—Siamese fighting fish will attack their images ferociously, and can even do themselves quite serious damage. There is no evidence that they recognise themselves at all. But dogs, cats, and monkeys will lose interest in their image after a while, and Fox (1982) suggested that this is because they have the beginnings of self-awareness.

When chimpanzees are first shown their own image in a mirror, they also treat it as if it were another animal at first: displaying to the mirror, and trying to look behind it. Very quickly, though, they seem to learn that the image is somehow related to themselves. At that point, they will often make faces in the mirror, or decorate themselves by placing vegetables on their heads (de Waal, 1989), or use the mirror to look at hidden parts of their bodies. In a more systematic investigation of this behaviour, Gallup (1979) anaesthetised chimpanzees who were familiar with mirrors, and placed a non-irritating spot of dye on their foreheads and ears. When they saw their reflections in the mirror, the chimpanzees showed considerable interest and touched the dye spots on their own bodies while looking in the mirror.

Suarez and Gallup (1981) showed that orang-utans, too, were able to recognise their own images in a mirror, although gorillas did not. Anderson (1983) reported that monkeys could not do this either—a generalisation supported by de Waal (1989), who nonetheless pointed out that there do seem to be individual variations. Fox (1982) suggested that it may be not so much that these animals are incapable of recognising themselves, as that they are not as continually fascinated by themselves as are chimpanzees, orang-utans, and humans. Being less narcissistic, they are simply less interested!

Fox's views are a far cry from the mechanistic behaviourist approach to understanding animals; but increasingly, research into animal cognition is suggesting that animals are capable of far more sophisticated comprehension than was hitherto believed. Where such views might have been dismissed out of hand in the 1950s, the evidence is building up to such a point that they are now treated as potentially viable explanations, if rather on the extreme end of the spectrum.

Novelty

As early as 1948, Tolman showed that rats can synthesise the outcomes of two different sets of training. In one study, Tolman placed rats in a maze which had two goal boxes, one white and one black. They both contained food, and the rats were equally likely to choose either box. In another study, the same rats were taken to a different room, and shown a black box and a white box side by side. When they entered the black box, they were given an electric shock. The next day, the rats were released into the original maze. Without fail, they entered the white box. Tolman concluded that the rats were applying their previously learned experience to plan novel forms of behaviour. This was one of the first demonstrations of animal ability to show entirely novel behaviour.

A problem with this, of course, is what we mean by novel behaviour. Tolman was taking this idea very literally: if an animal was showing behaviour that it had not directly acquired through stimulus-response learning, then the behaviour was novel. But we could equally well interpret these results as showing simply that the animals had learned to avoid black boxes—which wouldn't be a particularly astounding result. Other studies of novelty, however, show more intriguing results.

A particularly striking demonstration of novelty in animal behaviour came from a study by Pryor, Haag, and O'Reilly (1969), which described in detail the training of a rough-toothed porpoise, Hou, to produce novel behaviour. The idea had come from a set of five demonstrations with another porpoise, Malia, who had been reinforced during public displays to produce novel behaviour. Within just five days, Malia was performing aerial flips, "skidding" on the tank floor, and gliding with her tail out of the water—all hitherto unknown behaviours.

Pryor et al. conducted a more systematic set of training sessions, in which Hou, a quiet and undemonstrative porpoise, was systematically reinforced if she showed a new type of response in each training session. Hou appeared to catch on to the idea that some new behaviour was necessary by the third session. Over the first seven sessions, a pattern emerged. She would begin each training session by showing the response that had been reinforced the previous time; if it was not rewarded, she would run through the repertoire of responses that had been rewarded in previous training sessions, and then, if none of these was rewarded, she would produce a novel behaviour.

Because the behaviours that Hou showed were very limited, the researchers then devoted a few sessions to training some new behaviours (tailwalking and the "tail wave") using shaping techniques, before resuming the reinforcement of novel actions. This appeared to produce a powerful effect, as Hou began to include more responses in her training sessions, until by session 16, she produced eight different types of behaviour, including four entirely novel ones (see the picture below). By session 31, she appeared to have grasped the concept of novelty: she began the session with a novel behaviour, and once it was clearly reinforced, performed only that behaviour over and over again. Some of her behaviours became so inventive that the observers found it difficult to describe them.

Novelty in porpoise behaviour

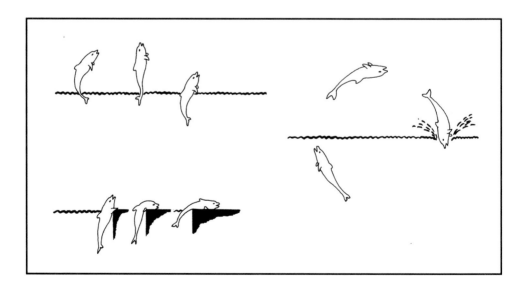

Porpoises and dolphins are not the only animals who can invent new games. De Waal (1989) described the behaviour of Aziut, a long-tailed macaque kept at the Identity Research Institute in India, who played repeatedly with mirrors. As well as demonstrating that he recognised his own image, Azuit learned to use mirrors to see what humans or dogs were doing behind his back, and would often turn his head to compare the image in the mirror with a direct look at the scene. Azuit also learned to guide his own hand in reaching for food by using the mirror, and to explore the images resulting from facing two mirrors towards one another by holding one mirror on the ground with his foot and the other above his head with his hand. The inventive games demonstrated by this animal were rigorously observed, and suggest a highly developed capacity for synthesis and novelty.

Kawai (1965b) reported the acquisition of novel behaviour by a group of red-faced macaques on Koshima Islet, Japan. A juvenile female named Imo discovered that it was possible to wash the sand off sweet potatoes by rinsing them in the sea. Very quickly, the other monkeys in the troop adopted this behaviour as well, until it became completely routine for macaques on that particular island to wash their food, and was taught to members of the new generation as well. Kawai described this behaviour as "pre-cultural", arguing that the transmission of the behaviour to the new generation showed how learning through novelty and imitation could form the basis for long-standing "cultural" practices, transmitted down the generations until the animal that originated them was no longer alive, but the behaviour was still maintained by the group as a whole.

Other cognitive abilities

There have been a number of other investigations of cognitive abilities in different species. The panel overleaf compares the performances of six species in seven different areas which are considered to represent "higher" cognitive abilities or characteristics. The species concerned are: elephants, Californian sealions, macaques, green vervet monkeys, chimpanzees, and dolphins. The tasks are: the ability to manipulate objects to solve puzzles; the ability to use numbers as concepts, memory for concepts; the diversity of the behaviour repertoire in situations like courtship; the ability to use symbols referentially, vocal mimicry, and dependency on social tradition.

Animals and language

One of the ultimate tests of animal cognition would be if animals could learn to communicate with us, using a human language. There has been a large body of research into animal cognition which focused on attempts

	object manipu-lation	numbers	concept memory	repertoire diversity	referentia	vocal mimicry	social tradition
Elephant Rensch & Altevogt, 1953	3	2	3	4	—	2	4
Sealion Schusterman & Krieger, 1984	4	—	3	4	2	—	2
Macaque Rumbaugh, 1975	4	—	3	4	2	1	3
Vervet Marler, 1983	4	—	3	4	2	1	3
Chimpanzee Rumbaugh, 1975	4	3	4	4	4	1	4
Dolphin Herman, 1986	4	—	3	4	4	2	3

Key: — = unknown; 1   2   3   4

← little developed   highly developed →

Some social and cognitive attributes of "higher" mammals (adapted from Eisenberg, 1986)

to train animals to use human languages of one sort or another. In this section, we will begin by listing briefly some of the studies in which researchers have attempted to teach human languages to animals, and then go on to use the evidence from these studies to examine whether there are grounds for supposing that these animals are really using language as a human being might do.

Earlier in this chapter we looked at the study by Pepperberg (1983), who used a combination of modelling and reinforcement in training an African grey parrot, Alex, to use over 50 English words appropriately. Most of the studies in this area, however, have been undertaken with apes—usually chimpanzees, but also gorillas and orang-utans.

One of the earliest attempts to teach chimpanzees human language was conducted by Kellogg and Kellogg (1933). A young chimpanzee, Gua, was brought up with their own infant. The Kelloggs kept careful notes of her development, and found that in many respects she was as quick to learn as a human child, and sometimes even quicker, particularly with respect to practical problems. But Gua only ever learned to say three words. Similarly, Hayes (1950) brought up a young chimpanzee, Vicki, and attempted to teach her to learn to speak, but all she ever managed were the four words "papa", "mama", "cup" and "up"—which she used correctly. Although it was obvious that these chimpanzees were much brighter than their language ability suggested, their vocal apparatus was simply inadequate for spoken language. A study by Laidler (1980), attempting to teach a young orang-utan, Cody, to speak was similarly unsuccessful: like Vicki, Cody only learned four words altogether.

In the late 1960s, three different projects to teach chimpanzees language were started. One project involved the use of a special language code using shapes placed on a magnetic board. Premack and Premack (1972) used this system to teach a chimpanzee, Sarah, to communicate using symbols. The training was conducted using food reinforcements and praise.

Rumbaugh (1977) developed a different method of training. This involved a large computer keyboard containing several different symbols, or *lexigrams*. These not only provided a wide number of possible referents, but also needed to be used according to a simplified grammar known as Yerkish. A chimpanzee, Lana, would type in her answers to questions, or her own requests, and the computer would provide her with a variety of outcomes: films, pictures, music, food, and liquids.

In a subsequent study, Savage-Rumbaugh, Rumbaugh, and Boysen (1978) used the same training system on two chimpanzees together: Austin and Sherman. The two experienced a training system similar to that of Lana's, but with some crucial differences, in particular, a much closer link between the object named and the reinforcement. In Lana's training scheme, naming, say, a piece of fruit correctly had allowed her free choice of possible rewards. Austin and Sherman, though, would only be rewarded with that fruit. Like Lana, though, they still had to produce grammatically correct sentences before they could get a reward. A pair of bonobos (pygmy chimpanzees) were also trained in the Yerkish system, under the same type of training system as Austin and Sherman, and rapidly proved to be even more adept at using the system (Savage-Rumbaugh et al., 1986).

The third training approach concerned teaching chimpanzees the American sign language Ameslan, used by deaf people. The first of these studies was conducted by Gardner and Gardner (1969), who trained a young female chimpanzee, Washoe, using a combination of modelling, manually shaping her hands into the correct position, and reinforcement. Following this study, the Gardners also initiated a group training pro-

gramme, in which several young chimpanzees were trained in Ameslan
together, by native Ameslan speakers. This became known as the Oklahoma colony (Fouts, 1972).

Terrace (1979) trained another chimpanzee, Nim Chimpsky, to use
Ameslan. His training was very similar to that of other chimpanzees in
this type of study, although unlike the other Ameslan chimps, Nim had
many changes of trainers, which was a deliberate strategy aimed at
preventing him from developing a close relationship with any one particular individual.

Patterson (1978) reported a study which involved training a young
gorilla, Koko, to use Ameslan. Koko was also trained using a combination
of modelling and reinforcement. A year after her training began, another
young gorilla, Michael, was added to the project (Patterson, 1979), and

also taught Ameslan. As had been found in the studies with chimpanzees, the interaction between the two animals seemed to enhance the training programme.

Not having hands, it would be somewhat difficult for dolphins to use Ameslan. But Herman, Richards, and Wolz (1984) reported on a programme in which a dolphin, Akeakamai, was trained to respond to a special visual language, in which symbols would be expressed using gestures by a trainer standing at the side of their tank. The language included grammatical constructions as well as a large number of arbitrary symbols: word order was particularly important. Another dolphin, Phoenix, was trained using a comparable language which was expressed as short noises generated by a computer. During the training sessions, the dolphins were rewarded when they responded correctly to these signals. It was not possible, though, to use this technique to demonstrate whether the animals could have used such a language themselves, but only whether they comprehended it.

Since these studies were initiated, psychologists and others have argued about whether the animals concerned have really been using language. The debate has been heated: some people are insistent that these animals' skills should not be considered language, others consider that the performances shown by these animals are obviously perfectly adequate as examples of language. Although the contention really rests on underlying beliefs about the uniqueness of the human being, one scientific way of addressing this issue is to look at some of the criteria for human language that have been developed, and to see how far the abilities of these animals conform to these criteria.

Hockett's design features

Hockett's design features of human language were published in 1959—before any of the recent studies on animal language took place—so they are unlikely to have been influenced by views on this question, one way or another. The full set of design features is given overleaf. Here, we will look at each one of them in turn, drawing relevant information from the studies that have been mentioned, before going on to consider the debate on whether animals can use language in more detail.

1. Vocal/Auditory and 2. Broadcast/directional.   This doesn't apply to language as it has been taught to animals, but then it doesn't apply to several other forms of human language either, most notably Ameslan itself. Ameslan, and some of the other signing languages, are recognised as full human languages despite the fact that they do not conform to these criteria.

Hockett's design
features of human
language
(adapted from
Hockett, 1959)

1.	Vocal/Auditory	Transmitted by sound from one person to another.
2.	Broadcast/ directional	The sound is broadcast, but the receiver can tell the direction that it is coming from.
3.	Rapid fading	The signal fades quickly.
4.	Total feedback	The speaker can hear what she is saying.
5.	Interchangeability	The same person can both send and receive information.
6.	Specialisation	Speech functioning is purely for communication, and not a by-product of some other behaviour.
7.	Semanticity	Language has meaning.
8.	Arbitrariness	Language does not resemble its meaning.
9.	Traditional transmission	Language can be passed on from one generation to the next.
10.	Learnability	New forms of language can be learnt.
11.	Discreteness	Language is organised into discrete, separate units, and information is coded by the way in which these are combined.
12.	Duality of patterning	Language patterns operate on more than one level: at the level of the organisation of phonemes into words, and at the level of the organisation of words into sentences.
13.	Displacement	Language enables a speaker to refer to things that are not immediately present in space and time.
14.	Openness/ productivity	Language can be used to generate novel utterances, which have new meanings.
15.	Prevarication	Language allows the speaker to talk about things that have not happened, or which are impossible. In short, to lie.
16.	Reflexiveness	Language can be used to talk about itself, as is happening here.

3. Rapid fading and 4. Total feedback. All the languages taught to apes conform to these criteria.

5. Interchangeability. This is true of the languages taught to the apes, although not, of course, of the languages taught to the dolphins, because they could only receive, not send, using that language.

6. Specialisation. Both the ape and the dolphin studies were using a specialist language, purely designed for the purpose of communication.

7. Semanticity. For the most part, the evidence strongly suggests that the apes and dolphins were able to understand the meanings of the words being used. Gardner and Gardner (1969) developed a complex series of double-blind tests to establish whether Washoe really understood what was being signed to her. In one of these tests, an observer would be positioned in such a way that they could only see a picture that Washoe was being shown, and not Washoe herself. Another observer would then be placed such that they could see Washoe but not the picture. Each would write down what they saw—the picture, and the sign that Washoe made in response to it, and the whole procedure was videotaped. In 72% of these trials, Washoe signed correctly; and her mistakes were not random either. They were often related in terms of higher-order categories, like signing "cat" when shown a picture of a dog.

Similarly, the study with the dolphins conducted by Herman, Richards, and Wolz (1984) did seem to show that the dolphins had gained a good grasp of the meanings of the words. For example, when Akeakamai was tested by being asked to fetch specific objects, or to take one object to another, all of the objects that she had learned about were in the pool with her during the test, so it was not possible for the dolphin to be unconsciously "cued" by the equipment provided. The task was only marked as having been achieved correctly if she moved immediately to the first named object and no other.

Although it does seem as though the Ameslan chimps and the dolphins understood the meaning of the symbols being used, this was not inevitably the case. For example: Savage-Rumbaugh et al. (1983) showed that there was some doubt, because of the training system that had been used, as to whether Lana had really learned the meaning of words like "fruit", or whether she had just learned to associate a stimulus and a response. The new training system devised for Austen and Sherman was designed to address this weakness, and seemed to be more clear in terms of establishing that the two chimpanzees really did understand the meaning of the symbols they were using.

There is also some question as to whether the chimpanzee Sarah ever actually progressed beyond stimulus-response learning (Premack, 1983). Although she developed quite a sophisticated ability to use the symbols in the right contexts, and could use conditionals like "if... then", she didn't actually seem to see language as something that had meaning in its own right. Unlike the animals in the other studies, for example, she didn't ever initiate any conversations with her trainer. She would respond to a query, but not begin a conversation. This lack of spontaneity is quite different from the other animals in these recent studies, and does raise some questions about whether there is real comparability between Sarah's use of her plastic symbols and a human being's use of language.

Terrace (1979) argued that the acquisition of vocabulary by Nim Chimpsky was not, in fact, meaningful language. Although, during the period of investigation, Nim signed over 19,000 multi-word utterances, of over 5,000 different kinds, and in the correct contexts, Terrace still argued that this was nothing more than finer and finer discrimination in stimulus–response learning. This largely rested on the idea that Nim did not show evidence of grammatical structure in his utterances—a criticism that we will return to later. Terrrace also argued that the other Ameslan chimpanzees were demonstrating nothing more than stimulus-response learning; and that apparently convincing tests like the Gardner's "double-blind" ones could all be explained away by processes like unconscious cueing. These criticisms, however, were based only on a film of Washoe: Terrace did not examine her, despite being invited to do so. There are a number of researchers (e.g. Lieberman, 1984) who argue that Terrace was being unduly rigid in these arguments, and that he was simply determined to oppose the idea that these animals might be using language.

8. Arbitrariness.   Each of the languages that was taught to the apes and dolphins was constructed such that it consisted, for the most part, of arbitrary units which did not physically resemble the concepts they represented. In addition, the languages contained words for relationships, categories, and concepts, as well as words for objects. In one test reported by Savage-Rumbaugh, Rumbaugh, Smith, and Lawson (1980), Austin and Sherman showed that they had some conceptual grasp of the way that the symbols corresponded to objects, as well as of categorisation.

The chimpanzees were presented with a mixed collection of items, and their first task was to sort them into two categories: foods and tools, placing them on two different trays. In the second stage, the trainer would hold up an object, and they were expected to identify its category, by pressing the key on the computer which represented that category, and not the object itself. In the third stage of the study, they were asked to categorise photographs of objects, rather than objects themselves, and then in the fourth stage they were shown the symbol that stood for the object in the "language" they had been taught, and were expected to categorise that. Austin and Sherman achieved each of these tasks successfully, although they had been way beyond Lana's capabilities.

9. Traditional transmission.   There is some evidence that language has been passed from one animal to another: in the Oklahoma colony, for instance, video films of the group of chimpanzees taken when they were alone show that they were signing to one another and responding to the messages that were being sent (Fouts, 1972). The implication is that it may therefore have become a pre-cultural behaviour, much like sweet potato-washing among Japanese macaques, and would be likely to be transmitted to another generation. Washoe herself appears to have taught at least one young chimpanzee to sign. She was observed teaching signs to a young chimpanzee, Loulis, who she seemed to have "adopted".

10. Learnability.   This criterion has only been investigated implicitly, for the most part. As a general rule, once one form of language has been taught to an animal, researchers do not seem to have investigated whether a new form of language can be learnt later. But throughout these studies, there have certainly been explorations of new combinations in the elements of these languages, and the animals seem to have responded to these adequately. For example, in one test, Herman, Richards, and Wolz (1984) gave the dolphin Akeakamai 193 completely new sentences, and she responded accurately to each of them. These sentences involved careful use of word order in describing combinations of action which she had not hitherto performed, so the implication was that the dolphin was able to understand and learn new uses of language as long as they followed the existing rules that had been learned.

Lucy, a chimpanzee in the Oklahoma colony, not only tended to coin new combinations of words to describe something, but would also use these combinations in preference to the established words (Fouts, 1972). She knew, for instance, the sign for watermelon perfectly well, and would sometimes use it. But more often she preferred to refer to it as "fruit-drink" or "candy-drink"—word combinations that she herself had invented. The implication is that, for Lucy at least, language was a flexible system, open to the learning of new combinations or elements.

11. Discreteness.   Each of the languages that has been taught to animals in these studies comprises discrete, separate units. Some of these animals have shown an ability to acquire and to use quite a large number of these units: Washoe, for example, at four years old could sign 132 different words, including pronouns, adjectives, and verbs, as well as nouns, and Koko, the gorilla, learned 400 different signs during her training period. Almost all the animals studied have shown an ability to combine signs to create meanings: Washoe formed her first two-word sentences at 20 months old, and even Sarah and Lana were able to create simple two- and three-word sentences composed of separate units.

Of course, these abilities are nothing like those of a human infant. A child of four, for example, generally has a vocabulary of over 3,000 words; and some say an innate grasp of syntax (although others believe this may have been overstated). In a direct comparison, the vocabularies and competences of these animals may not look so wonderful—but language is a species-specific behaviour for humans, not for apes or dolphins. We have already seen (in Chapter 2), how learning is to some extent shaped by innate predispositions to engage in certain forms of learning in preference to others. It is much harder, therefore, for an animal to learn a behaviour for which it is not innately predisposed. Given that these animals are learning a task which is as a general rule outside of the range of behaviour shown by their species, the fact that they can acquire such vocabularies is striking, and says a great deal about the flexibility of their behaviour.

12. Duality of patterning. Effectively, this question concerns grammar. It has been claimed (e.g. Noam Chomsky, 1959) that human beings possess an innate sense of grammar, and that this is what makes human language special. In terms of its translation into operational terms, the debates have hinged on the question of word order, and whether it has been used appropriately. In English, "Sally hit Jane" has an entirely different meaning to "Jane hit Sally", and structural linguists such as Chomsky claimed that all human languages have similar "deep structures", in which meaning is predicated on basic grammatical features. The fact that this is a highly contentious claim, which is not supported by modern linguistic evidence—for example, the Finnish language does not use word order—has not stopped critics of animal language studies from using it as an absolute criterion.

For example, Terrace (1979) insisted that Nim Chimpsky, the chimpanzee trained in Ameslan, was not doing any more than expressing a basic stimulus-response learning—despite Nim's demonstration of several thousand types of multi-word utterances, described earlier. This argument rested entirely on the fact that Nim did not appear to have an innate sense of grammar. On the occasions when he might have been demonstrating something of the sort, it was dismissed. For example, Nim always, correctly, placed the word "more" first in a two-word sentence; but

Terrace dismissed this by arguing that "more" was the only word for recurrence that the chimpanzee knew, and so placing it first could just be a habit. The fact that the chimpanzee tended to use relatively short sentences—his mean length of utterance (mlu) remained at 1.5 words—was also taken by Terrace as evidence that he had not developed a sense of grammar: the argument here was that an ability to use grammar would have inevitably meant that the chimpanzee's sentences would have increased in length—simply because it would have become more possible for that to happen.

In more complex sentences, when the chimpanzee used the correct grammatical structure, Terrace dismissed it on the grounds that it could have been acquired through imitation. This is a slightly obscure criticism: the only way that this could be a "wrong" way to learn would be if Terrace believed that grammatical use should be an expression of some innate grammatical sense, but it is entirely unclear why Terrace should have supposed that a chimpanzee should have an innate sense of grammar. From Terrace's accounts, one is also left wondering how much real experience he had with small human children: in the author's own experience, grammatical errors actually seem to be quite common while children are learning language, linguistic orthodoxy notwithstanding.

It is obvious that, to critics like Terrace, animals will never be considered to be using language. More impartial observers, however, might judge that there is more evidence than Terrace had accepted. If we bear in mind, also, that as Gould and Marler (1987) showed, learning is to a large extent shaped by inherited predispositions, we can perhaps take the achievements of these animals at their face value. These studies are not attempting to turn animals into human beings: rather, they are attempting to investigate whether animals can learn to use a language in communicating with human beings.

On that level, we can see that there is indeed some evidence that animals can use word order as part of ascribing meaning. Rumbaugh (1977) reported that Lana had been able to learn semantic differences from word order alone. She understood, for instance, the difference between "Tim give Lana apple", and "Lana give Tim apple". She would also sometimes correct her word order as she typed in her statements or responses. Not all chimpanzees have grasped word order, though. Despite managing to learn to use quite complex vocabularies, including conditional "if...then" relationships , Sarah did not seem to grasp the idea of word order or syntax at all (Premack, 1983).

The dolphins trained by Herman, Richards, and Wolz (1984) seem to have caught on to the idea of syntax quite quickly. In both the visual language which was taught to Akeakamai and the auditory language taught to Phoenix, word order was essential for meaning. Both dolphins showed very little difficulty dealing with it, and even responded appropriately when they were suddenly presented with four-word sentences for the first time. Herman, Richards, and Wolz argued that this showed that the dolphins were clearly grammatically competent to some degree, as otherwise they would have found that test much more difficult.

13. Displacement.   Savage-Rumbaugh et al. (1983) reported a test in which Austin and Sherman were required to communicate about objects that were not actually there while they were doing the communicating. In this test, a chimpanzee would be presented with a table covered with different food items. In order to request one of the items, the animal would have to go round a partition and to a keyboard, away from the table, and key in a grammatical request for one of the items. Then it would go back to the table to collect the food item and take it to the trainer. Both Austin and Sherman were able to do this successfully.

Fouts (1972) performed some tests with the Oklahoma chimpanzees which were similar to those of Menzel, which we looked at in the last chapter. They were different, however, in that they did not involve the presence of the original chimpanzee in finding the food: the idea was that the chimpanzees would have to use signing to communicate. In these tests, one chimpanzee would be taken away from the group and shown where something was hidden. Then it would be put back with the others and left for a while. After that, a different chimpanzee would be allowed out, and observed to see if it found the food—which it generally did. Video recordings of the group strongly suggested that they were using signs to communicate the whereabouts of the food.

The dolphins also showed that they could understand language which referred to items that were not present. In several tests, they were asked to go and find objects that had been hidden, which they managed successfully—in fact, relatively easily, it appears. These requests were also sometimes given when the item wasn't in the tank at all, and both dolphins also learned, successfully, to press a paddle to signal when that was the case.

14. Openness/productivity.   There have been several examples of animals spontaneously combining words to produce novel utterances. Although Terrace (1979) dismissed these on the grounds that they might have simply been the chimpanzees describing two different features of the situation, most researchers in this field agree that the sheer number of examples, and the salience of the combinations, do illustrate a productive use of language. Lana, for example, the first time she saw a ring referred to it as a "finger-bracelet". Washoe called a swan a "water-bird" when asked what it was by her trainer, and Lucy, one of the Oklahoma chimps, described a radish as a "hurt-cry fruit". Patterson (1979) reported that Koko the gorilla had developed 20 of her own sign-combinations for words that she did not know.

Washoe often spontaneously initiated conversations, and sometimes these too involved novel utterances. On one occasion, when she was out with her trainer, Washoe saw a plane flying overhead, turned to her trainer and signed "you, me ride plane". Another time, when a small doll was placed in her cup, Washoe signed "baby in my drink"—not a combination of words that she had ever encountered before. Terrace (1979) claimed that Washoe had been cued to make this statement by an unconscious gesture of the trainer in pointing first to the doll and then to the cup, but this is a contentious argument: other researchers do not find the same evidence in their scrutiny of the relevant videotape (Lieberman, 1984). (Terrace had based his criticisms on a very limited amount of film of Washoe, and refused to look at the more rigorous scientific evidence which had been collected by the Gardners, and which other researchers had found convincing).

15. Prevarication.   Interestingly, the best-documented evidence for non-literal uses of language—or even for direct lying—comes from work with gorillas rather than chimpanzees. Patterson (1979) reported that Koko, and to a lesser extent Michael, even seemed to have developed a sense of humour, and would "tease" Patterson by deliberately using the

"...MY *WHAT* IS UNDONE....?...OH! HA·HA!...SO IT IS...."

signs inappropriately. Patterson was careful to ensure that this was not simply a case of mistaken meaning, but the examples were such that it was obvious that the use of language was deliberate. For example, when she was asked to "tell me something you think is funny", Koko responded by pointing to a green toy frog, and signing "that red". Given the well-known playfulness of dolphins, it seems a pity that Akeakamai and Phoenix were not also in a position to use their "language" for themselves.

Other not-quite-literal uses of language include what appears very like the spontaneous emergence of "swear words". Washoe, for instance, spontaneously began to sign "dirty" before someone's name if she was displeased with them. Koko, too, would call someone "you dirty toilet" if she was annoyed with them. These words were used correctly in their usual contexts, but both animals seemed to have made the connection with expressions of disgust and to have used them outside of their literal meaning—although, of course, it could be that they were simply associating the attitude of disgust with these words in a stimulus-response fashion, without considering their literal meaning.

16. Reflexiveness.   To some extent, even asking an animal to name something involves using language to talk about language; and all of the chimpanzees were successfully able to do that. Premack (1983) showed that Sarah could also respond successfully to a specific symbol which meant "give the name of", implying that the chimpanzee was able, to some extent, to think abstractly about the communication system. But that is perhaps one of the more basic levels of reflexiveness in language use.

A more complex example came from the two gorillas, Koko and Michael. On one occasion, Michael was shut out of the caravan where they lived, and Patterson refused to let him in until he gave the correct signal. Koko, who was inside, demonstrated the sign to him through the window. Michael then made the sign correctly and was allowed in. At this point, Koko signed "good sign, Michael" to the younger gorilla—a clear example of using language to talk about language.

Is it really language?

The debates about whether what these animals are doing is "really" language have relied on increasingly arbitrary criteria. Savage-Rumbaugh and Hopkins (1986) argue that these arbitrary distinctions between animal and human language have been exaggerated, and made more arbitrary than they really are. As each hurdle has been surmounted, another has been raised, until, as we have already been seen, many of the criticisms rest on linguistic assumptions about language which are based entirely on human skills (Seuren, 1976) and may not even be universally true of human language either. For example, one of the increasing findings about how children acquire language concerns the importance of human relationships in the process (e.g. de Villiers & de Villiers, 1978). The Chomskyan model of language acquisition, on which Terrace's criticisms were based, takes no account of that, and nor did his own research. Lieberman (1984) pointed out that Nim Chimpsky had suffered continual disruption of relationships while he was training.

But, of course, these debates are to a large extent expressions of faith and belief about qualitative distinctions between human beings and other animals. Some have said that they are about the uniqueness of the human being, but human beings are no less unique if some animals learn to use a simplified version of their language: it is, after all, a distinctive species-specific skill, which we manage with great ease. What we are looking at in these studies may partly represent our own language's evolutionary past: as Savage-Rumbaugh and Hopkins (1986) argue, we can trace some of the underlying cognitive capacity for our use of language in other animals, and by so doing we can come to understand how language itself developed, and how other cognitive features and abilities present in animal species may have contributed to its evolution. Using Hockett's design features, we can see that there is some evidence for the essential components of language being present in—or at least cognitively possible for—the "higher" animals, although obviously not in anything like the sophisticated form in which they are present in human beings.

Speaking of the attempts to draw grammatical distinctions between human language and symbolic communication by apes, Savage-Rumbaugh and Hopkins (1986, pp.305–306) state:

> We believe that in time, these dichotomies will crumble, and we will look back on them as strangely antiquated views, held as the last comfortable bastion of defense against Darwinism. Human language will be recognised for what it is, a special means of conveying information about objects and events which are removed in space and time ... totally contiguous with similar systems found in other species. Grammar will no longer be viewed as a unique property of human language, but will be understood as a temporal processing system. Grammatical units and syntactical rules, far from being determined by an innate language acquisition device will be seen as being derived from the perceptual characteristics of the organism... This interpretation will be accepted when it becomes more apparent that there is a neurological basis for both awareness and intentionality in other life forms.

Attempts to teach animals to use human languages also, of course, hold out another carrot: the speculative promise that we might one day be able to learn what it is like to be a member of a different species, by asking. But that, at present, is a goal that is firmly relegated to the realms of science fiction. Studies of animal language have a great deal further to go before anything like that can become reality.

Evolution, adaptation, instinct, and learning

In this book, we have looked at a number of examples of animal behaviour, of one sort or another. What we find when we do this, more than anything else, is diversity. Different species of animal go about every single aspect of their lives in all sorts of different ways. Species differ in how they spend their days, how they go about finding a mate, how they go about producing a new generation. So far, we have barely begun to chart that diversity, but the more we investigate animal behaviour, the more we become aware of the vast range of possibilities and adaptations in how life can be lived.

Human behaviour, too, is diverse. Across the world, human beings live in vastly different ways, and with vastly different assumptions about very fundamental aspects of living. The nature of the human being's relationship with the world and with other people, what things are of value in life, how one should go about day to day living, are basic assumptions that differ from one group of human beings to another, and so do behavioural practices such as the homes people live in, the social groups and structures they belong to, and how infants and children are reared.

Pitfalls of animal/human comparisons

Comparative psychologists are in no doubt that the study of animals can help to throw light on human behaviour. But we need to be very cautious in this. As we have already seen, it is far too easy to fall into several traps. One of these traps is that of *biological determinism*: the idea that innate biological mechanisms make certain kinds of behaviour inevitable. As we have seen, this isn't even the case for animals, still less for human beings. Another is the trap of *ethnocentrism*: seeking only to explain human behaviour in our own society, and taking no account of human diversity in cultural practices. And a third is the trap of *reductionism*: trying to "explain" human behaviour by looking only at one level of explanation, as if that were enough in itself.

We have seen examples of each of these traps in the attempts to explain the links between animal and human behaviour. We have seen biological determinism, for example, in the theory that Lorenz developed about aggression, and its biological inevitability. We have seen ethnocentrism in the assumptions of Desmond Morris that only practices of Western industrial society have an evolutionary history that needs to be explained. And we have seen reductionism in the work of Richard Dawkins, in which human behaviour is reduced to "nothing but" the action of "selfish genes".

These examples of extrapolations from animal to human behaviour provide vivid illustrations of some of the pitfalls. Nonetheless, those who work or have an interest in this area remain convinced that there is much we can learn about human beings from the study of animal behaviour. So how can we go about this, while still avoiding the pitfalls of determinism, ethnocentricity, and reductionism?

Explaining diversity

The key lies in the need to explain diversity. As we have seen, almost any behaviour imaginable seems to take place in the animal world. So a theory that only focuses on one central group—trying only to define and explain what is "normal"—cannot possibly represent an adequate explanation for what is going on. What we need are theories that can take account of the full range of possible behaviours, not ones that look only at a narrow range, or even one behaviour at a time.

Stephen J. Gould (1981, p.330), commenting on the tendency of socio-biologists to take a single piece of behaviour and "explain" that in terms of the actions of "genes", commented that:

> Sociobiologists work as if Galileo had really mounted the Leaning Tower ... dropped a set of diverse objects over the side, and sought a separate explanation for each behavior—the plunge of the cannonball as a result of something in the nature of cannonballness, the gentle descent of the feather as intrinsic to featherness. We know, instead, that the wide range of different falling behaviours arises from an interaction between two physical rules—gravity and frictional resistance. This interaction can generate a thousand different styles of descent. If we focus on the objects and seek an explanation for the behaviour of each in its own terms, we are lost.

We are already familiar with some of the generative principles that we could use as a starting point for coming to terms with diversity. As Gould and Marler (1987) showed, in many forms of animal behaviour, instinct and learning go hand in hand. Instinctive behaviours are modified by learning; learning is focused and sometimes constrained by instinctive predispositions. Some behaviours are more modifiable than others. A deeper understanding of the operation of, and the nature of variation in, these mechanisms, is likely to help us to understand the range of animal behaviour much better.

But no form of behaviour occurs in a vacuum. We have already seen how different forms of animal behaviour may be modified depending on the environment in which the animal is operating. The environment, too, becomes modified. Animals and humans are not only active *in* their environments, they also act *on* their environments. As Rose (1983) showed, each animal is in a dialectical relationship with its environment— even an amoeba changes the nature of the water that it swims in, as it eats and excretes. Evolution, then, is not a one-way process: adaptation incorporates the processes of coevolution and the interaction between the animal and the environment, not just changes to the physical characteristics of the species.

In these mechanisms of evolution, adaptation, instinct, and learning we may be able to find the material to express theoretically some general ideas about how the diversity of behaviour could have come about. But if we are to make use of our knowledge of animal behaviour in helping us to understand human beings, we also need to look for systematic trends and patterns: to try to make sense out the mass of data. We need to be able to draw connections between animal behaviour and our own in some kind of systematic way—but without falling into the pitfalls we have just discussed.

Finding evolutionary links

One way to do that is to look at animals who may share a common evolutionary history with us, more recently than do other species. But if we are to do that, we need to be very careful indeed. In particular, we need to avoid falling into the trap of seeing all evolution as leading towards an ultimate goal of the evolution of the human being. Evolution is most emphatically not a theory about progress. It is a theory about adaptation to the environment, through the mechanisms of natural selection. That adaptation can—and does—proceed in almost any direction. So although we may look for some evolutionary roots to our behaviour among those animals that share some of our genetic history, we have to avoid seeing it as some kind of evolutionary progression, towards the crowning achievement of the evolution of the human being.

The other thing that we need to be very careful about is to ensure that we are exploring appropriate levels of explanation. Most, if not all, human behaviour is the product of human culture. We are trained in socially acceptable ways of behaving from the cradle, and what counts as socially acceptable in one culture is often very different from that in another. It is unlikely, to say the least, that we would find evolutionary connections at this level of explanation. But there may be fundamental human characteristics that underpin that culture—not specific behaviours, but abilities and propensities—and it is here that we may trace the origins of our distinctive heritage.

Human language, for example, is not only unique as a species-specific behaviour; it also makes culture and cultural transmission possible. We do not find the equivalent of human language in any other species. But we may find capacities or behaviours in animals which link, in evolutionary terms, with our own evolution of the capacity for language. As we have seen, the study of these behaviours may help us to throw light on some of the ways that this ability may have evolved in the human being.

We have other abilities and propensities, too. One of them is the uniquely flexible nature of our behaviour. Human beings, using their culture and ability to learn, can adapt to living in many different types of environment. We learn how to modify our immediate surroundings such as to provide ourselves with shelter and warmth, we adjust to different types of food, and we teach these things to our young ones.

Brain development and learning

We are able to do this as a result of the impressive learning capacity of the human brain. In 1986, I argued that genetic determinists consistently fail to address the question of what the human brain is for (Hayes, 1986), and that the exaggerated development of the cerebral cortex in the human being may provide the key. When we compare different mammalian species, we find something that looks very like a direct relationship between brain development and flexibility of behaviour. In particular, as Hubel (1979) showed, the cerebrum becomes larger and the cerebral cortex becomes more convoluted (see figure overleaf). We know from physiological research that it is in the cerebral cortex—the outer layers of the cerebrum—that complex sensory information processing, attention, voluntary motor control, consciousness, and above all learning, are all co-ordinated and controlled (see *Principles of biopsychology*, in this series). Increasing this surface, initially by expanding the structure that it covers, and then through convolutions and fissures, increases the potential for such complex information-processing.

With the development of learning to a high degree, an animal can come to modify its experience, and it can pass on such modifications to its offspring. Earlier in this chapter we saw how sweet potato-washing

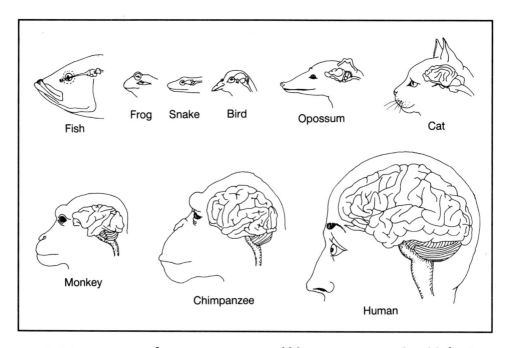

among Japanese macaques could be seen as a pre-cultural behaviour, because it rapidly spread through the group and was passed on to youngsters. A highly developed readiness to learn, coupled with an extensive memory capacity and the ability to negotiate and transmit information symbolically through language, implies an animal that is more than prepared, biologically, to develop cultural practices which will enable it to adapt to whatever demands its environment may place on it. Such an animal is in a position to cope with complex, changing environments much more readily than an animal whose activity depends, to any extent, on specific inherited behaviour patterns.

The phylogenetic development of the cerebral cortex in mammals, then, may represent a fundamental change in the acquisition of behavioural patterns. As we move higher up the "phylogenetic scale" (bearing in mind that this is only one track through evolutionary diversity) we find an increasing dependence on learned, adaptive patterns of behaviour, and a decreasing reliance on specific inherited patterns of behaving. The increased size of the cerebral cortex allows for far greater emphasis on learning in the course of the individual's development. This also seems to go hand in hand with neoteny—the tendency for species higher up the phylogenetic scale to be born at an increasingly early stage in their life cycles, which means that the young have a far longer period of dependency (during which they are learning all the time).

Learning by instinct

That doesn't mean simply that the genes abdicate control, passing everything over to the capacity to learn. As Gould and Marler (1987) showed, genetic constraints and predispositions are fundamental in learning. Nor does it mean that learning is only possible through the cerebral cortex. As we have seen earlier in this chapter, bees can learn, even though their brains are entirely different from that of a mammal. Cerebral development isn't the whole story in understanding learning, but it does seem to provide some significant pointers.

What we seem to be seeing as we move higher up a phylogenetic scale based on cerebral development is a progressive decrease in the genetic control of actual behaviour. A kittiwake or a stickleback inherits its actions, and a sensitivity to the stimuli to which it will respond; but a monkey inherits a readiness to explore its environment, and to interact with other monkeys.

Of course this is purely generalisation. There are examples of specifically inherited behaviour in monkeys, as there are even with human beings—the eyebrow flash for recognition identified by Eibl-Eiblesfelt being a case in point. But these do appear to represent a smaller proportion of the animal's behavioural repertoire in the "higher" mammals. In Chapter 2, we saw that it is actually quite hard to find many examples of behaviours which are either "purely" innate or "purely" learned. As Gould and Marler (1987) showed, learning and instinct work hand in hand: bees are genetically very ready to learn the scents of flowers, slightly less ready to learn their colour, slightly less to learn their shape, and not at all ready to learn by other criteria. Their inherited predisposition shapes what they will learn and how easily.

But that doesn't mean that all behaviour is halfway between instinct and learning. Some behaviours lean more towards one side than another. The pecking of the young gull at its parent's beak may be modifiable by learning, but it is nonetheless a strongly inherited behavioural response. Evolution operates by gradual steps, not large leaps; and it is a large leap from fixed action patterns to adaptation and cultural transmission. So we need to look for intermediate steps between these two.

At the extreme end of the continuum, we find types of behaviour like the one that has just been mentioned: the way that a powerful inherited response like pecking at the red spot on a parent's beak can be modified and improved with practice. The behaviour itself is genetically determined, but the influence of learning is nonetheless present. Moving further along, we might suggest that the genetically determined readiness to learn about certain types of information under certain circumstances which has been demonstrated in bees is another example of an intermediate step. In this case, there is more potential for producing the behaviour in response to different stimuli, but this is still quite strictly constrained.

A third example is the existence of critical and sensitive periods for learning. In these forms of learning, the state of readiness to learn is very powerful, and also genetically determined. The time period when the animal will learn these things is also powerfully influenced by genetic factors. But what is actually learned depends on the environmental situation. In the case of sensitive periods in attachment behaviours, the attachment itself then provides another source of behavioural adaptation for the animal, because so much subsequent behaviour occurs as a result of imitating the object of the attachment. The genetic influences are still there, arguably as powerful as ever, but rather than determining the behaviour patterns themselves, they have taken one step backwards. By doing so, they allow for a greater flexibility in the behaviour that the animal actually performs.

A fourth example, at the extreme other end of the continuum, may be found in the question of human taste and appetite. Across human societies, we find that the human diet comprises a vast range of types of foodstuffs (that we can digest both meat and vegetable food in itself says something biologically significant about the nature of our genetic adaptation to the world). Options of food choice are learned, as is illustrated by cross-cultural studies of diet, which show how what seems "normal" to members of one culture may be regarded with total disgust by members of another.

So human beings can learn to eat many different foods. But even though many people retain some level of adaptability, there is some evidence that food habits learned in childhood not only produce differences in food choice—what tastes "nice" psychologically—but may also produce differences in physiological adaptation. Members of some non-technological societies, for example, express disgust at the idea of eating cheese, regarding it as rotten milk. Although this is a cultural expression, there is also some suggestion that digestive systems adapt to habitual diets, and that such people do experience physiological difficulty in digesting cheese.

That example may be overly speculative, as it is always difficult with human beings to distinguish clearly between physiological and psychological reactions in an example of that kind—one can exert a considerable influence over the other. But there is another, less contentious example of inherited mechanisms in food selection. All human beings, no matter what their cultural background, will avoid a foodstuff that has previously made them vomit. As we have already seen, this is a powerful form of learning which doesn't extinguish easily, and isn't easily overridden by conscious choice. It is also a powerful survival mechanism. In human food preferences, then, we have a widely modifiable set of behaviours, with very little genetic predisposition at all—until it comes to something that might directly threaten our survival. Then the inherited predispositions come into action.

The pattern, then, may be of a gradual abdication of direct genetic control of behaviour through a series of intermediate stages. By the time we come to look at human infants, we find that their most powerful drive seems to be towards sociability: infants are genetically constrained to form relationships with others, and to learn through social transactions with them (see *Principles of developmental psychology*, in this series). The tendency towards social co-operation and the importance of social factors in human behaviour also continues throughout adulthood (see *Principles of social psychology*, in this series). In this way, we are born prepared to learn about our society and culture, and to act in accordance with its norms and expectations. Our biological readiness to be sociable and to learn language, and our impressive capacity for learning and memory makes us perfectly adapted to life as a cultural animal.

The message is still about the interaction of the individual and the environment, but now it has progressed much further than the mechanistic models of inherited behaviours. Fixed, rigid action patterns are only appropriate to a fixed, predictable environment. If changes in behaviour will be needed, inheriting that behaviour is inappropriate. Nonetheless, being ready to learn particular sorts of things is likely to help an individual to survive. It is better to inherit a readiness to learn the particular kinds of behaviour that are most likely to allow adaptation to the demands of the environment—both physical and cultural—into which the individual is born. In mammals, at least, that seems to be the role of the cerebral cortex.

It is worth noting, too, that the human cerebral cortex contains a region, the angular gyrus, which is specifically involved in the processes of reading. The angular gyrus appears to decode the visual symbolic messages, and convert them into the equivalent of an auditory message. But, in terms of human history, it is inconceivable that such an area of the brain could have evolved by direct selection. Literacy is a relatively recent product of human culture, and has never been universally available to all human beings. The fact that we have a region of the brain that is specifically adapted to literacy is a phenomenal message—it tells us more about the potential of the human brain for adapting to new forms of learning and new environmental demands than almost anything else.

The message, then, is not to see either human or animal behaviour as totally genetically determined or as totally learned and plastic. As human beings, we have an evolutionary history which structures and influences our experiences. Part of that history has provided us with the biological potential to learn, to remember, to manipulate our environments, and to transmit information to new generations. Human culture, in all of its diversity, is the result, and human culture cannot simply be "explained" as the product of biological drives or direct evolutionary pressures. It represents, quite simply, an entirely different level of explanation, with its own generative rules, histories, and internal processes. It is no coincidence that many of the criticisms of the genetic reductionism of sociobiology came from anthropologists: they are aware of the diversity of human culture, and the pitfalls of simplistic attempts to "explain" human cultures in terms of biological pressures.

In terms of animal behaviour, too, rather than concentrating our efforts on trying to explain specific examples of behaviour and ignoring others, what we really need to do is to look at the diversity in different kinds and patterns of behaviour, both within and between species, with the aim of uncovering the generative principles by which that diversity is able to occur. Unless we look at the full range of expressed possibilities, we cannot provide a coherent account of why a given behaviour takes place. By exploring diversity and its origins, we are likely to become much better able to explore the relationship between different levels of explanation: between genetic influence, the individual animal, its species, its environment, its evolutionary history, its personal history, and its sociocultural context.

Summary: Animal cognition

- Imitation is a common form of animal learning, which appears to work from mental templates. It seems to be a major factor in primate social learning as well as among dolphins.

- Exploration and curiosity appear to be fundamental sources of motivation in many animals, to the extent that they have been used as a reward in training studies. Exploration may also link with the formation of cognitive maps.

- Homing pigeons appear to use several different abilities, including detection of infrasound, magnetic sensitivity, and the location of the sun.

- A number of animals appear to show basic concept acquisition, and it has been suggested that the ability to use "natural categories" forms an evolutionary precursor to the more sophisticated use of concepts shown by human beings.

- Other research into animal cognition includes studies of novelty, and of the self-concept. Studies of self-concept in apes show that they seem to be able to recognise themselves, and to realise when they are not looking the same as usual.

- Experiments involving teaching animals human languages have taken three forms: those attempting to teach vocal skills, which have generally been unsuccessful; those teaching specialised symbolic languages constructed for research purposes; and studies teaching sign language to apes.

- Whether animals can really learn to use language is a deeply controversial topic, but the application of language criteria developed before the debate began suggests that animals have successfully achieved a great deal in this field.

- One of the more useful ways of conceptualising behavioural diversity in comparative psychology may be in terms of the interaction between genetic and learned influences on behaviour, and the role of genetic preparedness for some kinds of learning to take place, rather than others.

References

Ainsworth, M.D.S., Blehar, M.C., Waters, E., & Wall, S. (1978). *Patterns of attachment.* Hillsdale, NJ: Lawrence Erlbaum Associates Inc.

Altmann, J. (1980). *Baboon mothers and infants.* Cambridge, MA: Harvard University Press.

Altmann, S.A. (1962). A field study of the sociobiology of rhesus monkeys *Macaca mulatta. Annals of the New York Academy of Science, 102,* 338–435.

Anderson, J.R. (1983). Response to mirror image stimulation and assessment of self-recognition in mirror and peer-reared stumptail macaques. *Quarterly Journal of Experimental Psychology, 35,* 210–212.

Andrew, R.J. (1956). Some remarks on behaviour in conflict situations, with special reference to *Emberiza. British Journal of Animal Behaviour, 4,* 41–45.

Andrew, R.J. (1962). Evolution of intelligence and vocal mimicking. *Science, 137,* 585–589.

Andrew, R.J. (1965). The origins of facial expressions. *Scientific American, 213*(4), 88–94.

Appleby, M. (1985). Hawks, doves ... and chickens. *New Scientist* 10 January, 16–18.

Archer, J. (1976). The organisation of aggression and fear in vertebrates. In P.P.G. Bateson & P. Klopfer (Eds.), *Perspectives in ethology 2.* London: Plenum.

Archer, J. (1977). The psychology of violence. *New Society, 42,* 63–66.

Archer, J. (1988). *The behavioural biology of aggression.* London: Cambridge University Press.

Ardrey, R. (1966). *The territorial imperative.* New York: Dell.

Arendt, H. (1863). *Eichmann in Jerusalem: a report on banality of evil.* New York: Viking Press.

Argyle, M., Alkema, F., & Gilmour, R. (1971). The communication of friendly and hostile attitudes by verbal and non-verbal signals. *European Journal of Social Psychology, 1,* 385–402.

Badrian, A., & Badrian, N. (1984). Social organisation of *Pan paniscus* in the Lomako Forest, Zaire. In R. Susman (Ed.), *The pygmy chimpanzee.* New York: Plenum.

Balachandran, N.K., Dunn, W.L., & Rind, D.H. (1977). Concorde sonic booms as an atmospheric probe. *Science, 197,* 47–49.

Barclay, R., & Fenton, B. (1983). Communication through echolocation in little brown bats. *Behavioural Ecology, 10,* 271–275.

Bastion, J. (1967). The transmission of arbitrary environmental information between bottlenose dolphins. In R.G. Busnel (Ed.), *Animal sonar systems vol II.* Jouy-en-Josas, France: Laboratoire de Physiologie Acoustique.

Bastock, M., Morris, D., & Moynihan, M. (1953). Some comments on conflict and thwarting in animals. *Behaviour, 6,* 66–84.

Bateson, G. (1973). *Steps to an ecology of mind: collected essays in anthropology, psychiatry, evolution and epistemology.* London: Paladin.

Bateson, P.P. (1966). The characteristics of content of imprinting. *Biological Review, 41,* 177–211.

Beer, C.G. (1962). The egg-rolling of black-headed gulls *Larus ridibundus*. *Ibis*, *104*, 388–398.

Bertram, B. (1970). The vocal behaviour of the Indian hill mynah *Gracula religiosa*. *Animal Behaviour Monographs, 3*, 80–192.

Blakemore, C. (1984, November). *The sensory worlds of animals and man*. Address given to the Annual Meeting of the Association for the Teaching of Psychology, London.

Blanchard, R.J., & Blanchard, D.C. (1981). The organisation and modelling of animal aggression. In P.F. Brain & D. Benton (Eds.), *The biology of aggression*. Rockville, MD: Sijthoff & Noordhoff.

Blanchard, R.J., Blanchard, D.C., Rodgers, J., & Weiss, S.M. (1990). The characterization and modelling of anti-predator defensive behaviour. *Neuroscience and Biobehavioural Review, 14*, 463–472.

Blanchard, R.J., Flannelly, K.J., & Blanchard, D.C. (1986). Defensive behaviours of laboratory and wild *rattus norvegicus*. *Journal of Comparative Psychology, 100*, 101–107.

Blanchard, R.J., Fukanaga, K.K., & Blanchard, C. (1976). Environmental control of defensive reactions to a cat. *Bulletin of the Psychonomic Society, 8(3)*, 179–181.

Bolk, L. (1926). *Das Problem der Menschwerdung*. Jena: Gustav Fischer.

Bowlby, J. (1951). *Child care and the growth of love*. Harmondsworth: Penguin.

Bowlby, J. (1969). *Attachment and loss 1: Attachment*. London: Hogarth.

Bright, M. (1984). *Animal language*. London: BBC Publications.

Brown, P.L., & Jenkins, H.M. (1968). Autoshaping of the pigeon's keypeck. *Journal of the Experimental Analysis of Behaviour, 11*, 1–8.

Butler, R.A. (1954). Incentive conditions which influence visual exploration. *Journal of Experimental Psychology, 48*, 19–23.

Bygott, J.D. (1979). Agonistic behavior, dominance and social structure in wild chimpanzees of the Gombe National Park. In D.A. Hamburg & E.R. McCown (Eds.), *The great apes*. Manlo Park, CA: Benjamin/Cummings.

Caro, T.M. (1986). The functions of stotting in Thompson's gazelles: some tests of the predictions. *Animal Behaviour, 34*, 663–684.

Calhoun, J.B. (1962). Population density and social pathology. *Scientific American, February* (206).

Carmichael, L. (1956). The development of behaviour in vertebrates experimentally removed from the influence of external stimulation. *Psychological Review, 33*, 51–58.

Caryl, P.G. (1981). Escalated fighting and the war of nerves: games theory and animal combat. In P.G. Bateson & P. Klopfer (Eds.), *Perspectives in ethology 4*. London: Plenum.

Catchpole, C. (1981). Song is a serenade for the warblers. In G. Ferry (Ed.), *The understanding of animals* (1984). Oxford: Basil Blackwell.

Chomsky, N. (1959). Review of Skinner's "Verbal Behaviour". *Language, 35*, 26–58.

Clutton-Brock, T.H., Guinness, F.E., & Albon, S.D. (1982). *Red deer: behaviour and ecology of two sexes*. Edinburgh: University of Edinburgh Press.

Colinvaux, P. (1980). *Why big fierce animals are rare*. Harmondsworth: Penguin.

Craig, W. (1918). Appetites and aversions as constituents of instincts. *Biological Bulletin, 34*, 91–107.

Craig, W. (1928). Why do animals fight? *International Journal of Ethics, 31*, 264–278.

Crook, J.H. (1970). Social organisation and the environment: aspects of contemporary social ethology. *Animal Behaviour, 18*, 197–209.

Crook, J.H., & Gartlan, J.S. (1966). Evolution of primate societies. *Nature, 210*, 1200–1203.

Curio, E., Ernst, V., & Vieth, W. (1978). Cultural transmission of enemy recognition. *Science, 202,* 899–901.

Darwin, C. (1859). *The origin of species.* London: John Murray.

Darwin, C. (1872). *The expression of the emotions in man and the animals.* London: John Murray.

Davies, N.B. (1978). Territorial defence in the speckled wood butterfly *(pararge aegeria)*: the resident always wins. *Animal Behaviour, 26,* 138–147.

Dawkins, R. (1976). *The selfish gene.* Oxford: Oxford University Press.

de Villiers, J., & de Villiers, P. (1978). *Early language.* London: Fontana.

de Waal, F.B.M. (1984). Sex differences in the formation of coalitions among chimpanzees. *Ethology and Sociobiology, 5,* 239–255.

de Waal, F.B.M. (1987). Tension regulation and nonreproductive functions of sex in captive bonobos (*Pan paniscus*). *National Geographical Research, 3,* 318–335.

de Waal, F.B.M. (1989). *Peacemaking among primates.* Cambridge, MA: Harvard University Press.

de Waal, F.B.M., & Ren, R. (1988). Comparison of the reconciliation behaviour of stumptail and rhesus macaques. *Ethology, 78,* 129–142.

de Waal, F.B.M., & van Roosmalen, A. (1979). Reconciliation and consolation among chimpanzees. *Behavioural Ecology and Sociobiology, 5,* 55–66.

de Waal, F.B.M., & Yosihara, D. (1983). Reconciliation and redirected affection in rhesus monkeys. *Behaviour, 85,* 224–241.

Dollard, J., Doob, L.W., Miller, N.E., Mowrer, O.H., & Sears, R.R. (1939). *Frustration and aggression.* New Haven: Yale University Press.

Durrell, G. (1966). *Two in the bush.* London: Fontana/Collins.

Eibl-Eiblesfeldt, I. (1970). *Ethology: the biology of behaviour.* New York: Holt, Rinehart & Winston.

Eibl-Eiblesfeldt, I. (1972). Similarities and differences between cultures in expressive movements. In R.A. Hinde (Ed.), *Nonverbal communication.* London: Cambridge University Press.

Eisenberg, J.F. (1986). Dolphin behaviour and cognition: evolutionary and ecological aspects. In R.J. Schusterman, J.A. Thomas, & F.G. Wood (Eds.), *Dolphin cognition and behaviour: a comparative approach.* Hillsdale, NJ: Lawrence Erlbaum Associates Inc.

Eldredge, N., & Gould, S.J. (1972). Punctuated equilibria: an alternative to phyletic gradualism. In T.J.M. Schopf (Ed.), *Models in paleobiology.* San Francisco: Freeman, Cooper & Co..

Elefson, J.O. (1968). Territorial behaviour in the common white-handed gibbon. In P. Jay (Ed.), *Primates.* New York: Holt, Rinehart & Winston.

Epstein, R., Kirschnitt, C.E., Lanza, R.P., & Rubin, L.C. (1984). "Insight" in the pigeon: antecedents and determinants of an intelligent performance. *Nature, 308,* 61–62.

Esch, H. (1967). The evolution of bee language. *Scientific American, 216*(4), 96–104.

Faaberg, J., & Patterson, C.B. (1981). The characteristics and occurrence of co-operative polyandry. *Ibis, 123,* 477–484.

Fossey, D. (1980). *Gorillas in the mist.* Basingstoke: Macmillan.

Foster, M.S. (1977). Odd couples in manakins: a study of social organisation and co-operative breeding in *chiroxiphia linearis. American Naturalist, 111,* 845–853.

Fouts, R.S. (1972). The use of guidance in teaching sign language to a chimpanzee. *Journal of Comparative and Physiological Psychology, 80,* 515–22.

Fox, M. (1982). Are most animals "mindless auromatons"? A reply to Gordon G. Gallup, Jr. *American Journal of Primatology, 3,* 341–343.

Gallup, G.G.Jr. (1979). Self-awareness in primates. *American Scientist, 67,* 417–421.

Garcia, J., & Koelling, R.A. (1966). The relation of cue to consequence in avoidance learning. *Psychonomic Science, 4,* 123–124.

Gardner, B.T. & Gardner, R.A. (1971). Two-way communication with an infant chimpanzee. In A.M. Schrier, & F. Stollnitz (Eds.), *Behaviour of nonhuman primates (4).* New York: Academic Press.

Gardner, R.A., & Gardner, B.T. (1969). Teaching sign language to a chimpanzee. *Science, 165,* 664–672.

Geist, V. (1966). The evolution of horn-like organs. *Behaviour, 27,* 175–214.

Geist, V. (1978). On weapons, combat and ecology. In L. Krames, P. Pliner, & T. Alloway (Eds.), *Advances in the study of communication and affect 4: Aggression, dominance and individual spacing.* New York: Plenum.

Ginsburg, B., & Allee, W.C. (1942). Some effects of conditioning on social dominance and subordination in inbred strains of mice. *Psychological Zoology, 15,* 485–506.

Gish, S.L. (1979). Quantitative analysis of two-way acoustic communication between captive Atlantic bottlenose dolphins *(Tursiops truncatus Montague).* Unpublished doctoral dissertation, University of California. Cited in R.A. Schusterman, J.A. Thomas, & F.G. Wood (Eds.), *Dolphin cognition and behaviour: a comparative approach.* Hillsdale, NJ: Lawrence Erlbaum Associates Inc.

Goodall, J. van Lawick (1968). The behaviour of free-living chimpanzees in the Gombe stream reserve. *Animal Behaviour Monographs, 1,* 161–311.

Goodall, J. van Lawick (1974). *In the shadow of man.* London: Collins.

Gould, J.L. (1982). The map sense of pigeons. *Nature, 296,* 205–211.

Gould, J.L. (1986). The locale map of honey bees: do insects have a cognitive map? *Science, 232,* 861–863.

Gould, J.L., Kirschvinck, J.L., & Defeyes, K.S. (1978). Bees have magnetic remanence. *Science, 201,* 1026–1028.

Gould, J.L. & Marler, P.J. (1987). Learning by instinct. *Scientific American, 256*(1), 62–74.

Gould, S.J. (1978). *Ever since Darwin: reflections in natural history.* Harmondsworth: Penguin.

Gould, S.J. (1981). *The mismeasure of man.* New York: Norton.

Graycar, P. (1976). Whistle dialects of the Atlantic bottlenosed dolphin *Tursiops truncatus.* Unpublished doctoral dissertation, University of California. Cited in R.A. Schusterman, J.A. Thomas, & F.G. Wood (Eds.), *Dolphin cognition and behaviour: a comparative approach.* Hillsdale, NJ: Lawrence Erlbaum Associates Inc.

Greenberg, L. (1979). Genetic component of kin recognition in primitively social bees. *Science, 206,* 1095–1097.

Grohmann, J. (1939). Modifikation oder Funktionsreifung? Ein Beitrag zur Klärung der wechselzeitigen Beziehungen zwischen Instinkthandlung und Erfahrung. *Zeitschrift für Tierpsychologie, 2,* 132–144.

Guiton, P. (1959). Socialisation and imprinting in Brown Leghorn chicks. *Animal Behaviour, 7,* 26–34.

Guiton, P. (1966). Early experience and sexual object choice in the Brown Leghorn. *Animal Behaviour, 14,* 534–538.

Hailman, J.P. (1969). How an instinct is learned. *Scientific American, 221*(6), 98–106.

Hamburg, D.A. (1971). Psychobiological studies of aggressive behaviour. *Nature, 230,* 19–23.

Hamburg, D.A. (1991). Human aggression. In P. Bateson (Ed.), *The development and integration of behaviour: essays in honour of Robert Hinde.* London: Cambridge University Press.

Hamburg, D.A., & Goodall, J. van Lawick (1974). Factors determining development of aggressive behaviour in chimpanzees and humans. In W.W. Hartup, & J. de Wit (Eds.), *Determinants and origins of aggressive behaviour*. The Hague: Mouton.

Hamilton, W.D. (1964). The genetical evolution of social behaviour I and II. *Journal of Theoretical Biology, 7*, 1–52.

Hamilton, W.D., & Zuk, M. (1984). Heritable true fitness and bright birds: a role for parasites? *Science, 218*, 384–387.

Harlow, H.F. (1949). The formation of learning sets. *Psychological Review, 56*, 51–65.

Harlow, H.F. (1959). Love in infant monkeys. *Scientific American, 200*(6), 64–74.

Harlow, H.F., & Harlow, M.K. (1962). Social deprivation in monkeys. *Scientific American, 207*(5), 136–146.

Harlow, H.F., Harlow, M.K., & Hansen, E.W. (1963). The maternal affectional system of rhesus monkeys. In H.L. Rheingold (Ed.), *Maternal behaviour in mammals*. New York: Wiley.

Harlow, H.F., Harlow, M.K., & Meyer, D.R. (1950). Learning motivated by a manipulation drive. *Journal of Experimental Psychology, 40*, 228–234.

Hayes, K.J. (1950). Vocalisation and speech in chimpanzees. *American Psychologist, 5*, 275–276.

Hayes, N.J. (1975). *Dominance relationships in a captive chimpanzee colony.* Unpublished research, University of Leeds.

Hayes, N.J. (1986). The magic of sociobiology. *Psychology Teaching, 1986* (2), 2–16.

Herman, L.M. (1986). Cognition and language competencies of bottlenosed dolphins. In R.J. Schusterman, J.A. Thomas, & F.G. Wood (Eds.), *Dolphin cognition and behaviour: a comparative approach*. Hillsdale, NJ: Lawrence Erlbaum Associates Inc.

Herman, L.M., Richards, D.G., & Wolz, J.P. (1984). Comprehension of sentences by bottlenosed dolphins. *Cognition, 16*, 129–219.

Herrnstein, R.J. (1984). Objects, categories and discriminative stimuli. In H.T. Roitblat, T.G. Bever, & H.S. Terrace (Eds.), *Animal cognition*. Hillsdale, NJ: Lawrence Erlbaum Associates Inc.

Herrnstein, R.J., Loveland, D.H., & Cable, C. (1976). Natural concepts in pigeons. *Journal of Experimental Psychology: Animal Behaviour Processes, 2*, 285–311.

Hersher, L., Richmond, J.B., & Moore, A.U. (1963). Maternal behaviour in sheep and goats. In H.L. Rheingold (Ed.), *Maternal behaviour in mammals*. New York: John Wiley.

Hess, E.H. (1958). "Imprinting" in animals. *Scientific American, 198*(3), 81–90.

Hess, E.H. (1972). "Imprinting" in a natural laboratory. *Scientific American, 227*(2), 24–31.

Hinde, R.A. (1954). Factors governing the changes in strength of a partially inborn response, as shown by the mobbing behaviour of the chaffinch *(Fringilla coelebs). Proceedings of the Royal Society of London, Series B, 142*, 306–358.

Hinde, R.A. (1970). *Animal behaviour: a synthesis of ethology and comparative psychology*. New York: McGraw Hill.

Hinde, R.A. (1983). Ethology and child development. In P.H. Musson (Ed.), *Handbook of child psychology Vol II* (4th edn). New York: Wiley.

Hinde, R.A. (1987). *Individuals, relationships and culture: links between ethology and the social sciences.* Cambridge, UK: Cambridge University Press.

Hinde, R.A., & Rowell, T.E. (1962). Communication by postures and facial expressions in the rhesus monkey *(Macaca mulatta). Proceedings of the Zoological Society of London, 138*, 1–21.

Hixon, M.A., Carpenter, F.L., & Paton, D.C. (1983). Territory area, slower density and time budgeting in hummingbirds: an experimental and theoretical analysis. *American Naturalist, 122,* 366–391.

Hockett, C.F. (1959). Animal "languages" and human language. *Human Biology, 31,* 32–39.

Hodos, W., & Campbell, C.B.G. (1969). *Scala naturae:* why there is no theory in comparative psychology. *Psychological Review, 76,* 118–130.

Högstedt, G. (1983). Adaptation unto death: the function of fear screams. *American Naturalist, 121,* 562–570.

Hopkins, C.D. (1974). Electric communication in fish. *American Scientist, 62,* 426–437.

Horn, G. (1991). Cerebral function and behaviour investigated through a study of filial imprinting. In P. Bateson (Ed.), *The development and integration of behaviour: essays in honour of Robert Hinde.* Cambridge: Cambridge University Press.

Horn, G., Bradley, P., & McCabe, B.J. (1985). Changes in the structure of synapses associated with learning. *Journal of Neuroscience, 5,* 3161–3168.

Horn, G., & McCabe, B.J. (1984). Predispositions and preferences. Effects on imprinting of lesions to the chick brain. *Animal Behaviour, 32,* 288–292.

Horn, G., McCabe, B.J., & Bateson, P.P.G. (1979). An autoradiographic study of the chick brain after imprinting. *Brain Research, 168,* 361–373.

Huxley, J.S. (1914). The courtship of the great crested grebe. *Proceedings of the Zoological Society of London, 35.*

Huxley, J.S. (1942). *Evolution: the modern synthesis.* London: Allen & Unwin.

Jay, P. (1963). Mother-infant relations in langurs. In H.L. Rheingold (Ed.), *Maternal behaviour in mammals.* New York: Wiley.

Jenni, D.A. (1974). The evolution of polyandry in birds. *American Zoologist, 14,* 129–144.

Johnson, M.H., Bolhuis, J.J., & Horn, G. (1985). Interaction between acquired preferences and developing predispositions during imprinting. *Animal Behaviour, 33,* 1000–1006.

Johnson, M.H., & Horn, G. (1987). The role of a restricted region of the chick forebrain in the recognition of individual conspecifics. *Behaviour and Brain Research, 23,* 269–275.

Johnson, R.N. (1972). *Aggression in man and animals.* Philadelphia: Saunders.

Kamin, L.J. (1969). Selective association and conditioning. In N.J. Mackintosh, & W.K. Honig (Eds.), *Fundamental issues in associative learning.* Halifax: Dalhousie University Press.

Karlson, P., & Lüscher, M. (1959). Pheromones: a new term for a class of biologically active substances. *Nature, 183,* 55–56.

Kawai, M. (1965a). On the system of social ranks in a natural troop of Japanese monkeys. In K. Imanishi, & S. Altmann (Eds.), *Japanese monkeys.* Atlanta: Emory University.

Kawai, M. (1965b). On the newly acquired pre-cultural behaviour of the natural troop of Japanese monkeys on Koshima islet. *Primates, 6,* 1–30.

Keeton, W.T. (1969). Orientation by pigeons: is the sun necessary? *Science, 165,* 922–928.

Kellogg, W.N., & Kellogg, L.A. (1933). *The ape and the child.* New York: Whiltlesey House.

Kenyon, K.W., & Rice, D.W. (1958). Homing of Laysan albatrosses. *Condor, 60,* 3–6.

Kinder, E.F. (1927). A study of the nest-building activity of the albino rat. *Journal of Experimental Zoology, 47,* 117–161.

Köhler, W. (1925). *The mentality of apes.* New York: Harcourt Brace.

Konishi, M. (1964). The role of auditory feedback in the control of vocalisation in the white-crowned sparrow. *Zeitschrift für Tierpsychologie, 22,* 770–783.

Krebs, J.R. (1976). The song of the great tit says "Keep Out". In G. Ferry (Ed.), *The understanding of animals* (1984). Oxford: Basil Blackwell.

Krebs, J.R., & Davies, N.B. (Eds.) (1978). *Behavioural ecology: an evolutionary approach.* Oxford: Blackwell.

Kreithen, M.L. (1978). Sensory mechanisms for animal orientation—can any new ones be discovered? In K. Schmidt-Koenig, & W.T. Keeton (Eds.), *Animal migration, navigation and homing.* Berlin: Springer-Verlag.

Kroodsma, D.E. (1979). Vocal dueling among male marsh wrens: evidence for ritualised expressions of dominance/subordinance. *Auk, 98,* 506–515.

Kroodsma, D.E. (1984). Songs of the alder flycatcher *(Empidonax alnorum)* and willow flycatcher *(Empidonax trailli)* are innate. *Auk, 101,* 13–24.

Kuo, Z.Y. (1938). Further study of the behaviour of the cat towards the rat. *Journal of Comparative Psychology, 25,* 1–8.

Lack, D. (1943). *The life of the robin.* London: Penguin.

Laidler, K. (1980). *The talking ape.* London: Collins.

Lamarck, J.B. (1809). *Philosophie zoologique* (H. Elliot, trans.). London: Macmillan.

Lamond, H.G. (1949). Mothering a lamb. *Sheep and Goat Raising, 29*(9), 36–38.

Lea, S.E.G. (1984). *Instinct, environment and behaviour.* London: Methuen.

Lednor, A.J., & Walcott, C. (1983). Homing pigeon navigation: the effects of in-flight exposure to a varying magnetic field. *Comparative Biochemistry and Physiology, 76,* 665–671.

Leuze, C.C.K. (1980). The application of radio tracking and its effect on the behavioural ecology of the water vole. In C.J. Armlaner, & D.W. Macdonald (Eds.), *A handbook of biotelemetry & radio tracking.* Oxford: Pergamon.

Lewin, R. (1978). Rutting on Rhum. In G. Ferry (Ed.), *The understanding of animals* (1984). Oxford: Basil Blackwell.

Leyhausen, P. (1956). Das Verhalten der Katzen *(Felidae). Handbook of Zoology, Berlin, 10*(21), 1–34.

Lieberman, P. (1984). *The biology and evolution of language.* Cambridge, MA: Harvard University Press.

Lilly, J.C. (1962). Vocal behaviour of the bottlenosed dolphin. *Proceedings of the American Philosophical Society, 106,* 520–529.

Lilly, J.C. (1965). Vocal mimicry in *Tursiops:* ability to match numbers and durations of human vocal bursts. *Science, 147,* 520–529.

Lloyd, J.E. (1966). Studies on the flash communication system in *Photinus* fireflies. *Miscellaneous Publications of the Museum of Zoology, University of Michigan, 130,* 1–95.

Lloyd, J.E. (1975). Aggressive mimicry in *Photuris* firelies: signal repertoires by femmes fatales. *Science, 197,* 452–453.

Lorenz, K. (1935). The companion in the bird's world. *Auk, 54,* 245–273.

Lorenz, K. (1950). The comparative method in studying innate behaviour patterns. *Symposium of the Society of Experimental Biology, 4,* 221–268.

Lorenz, K. (1958). The evolution of behaviour. *Scientific American, 199*(6), 67–78.

Lorenz, K. (1966). *On aggression.* New York: Harcourt, Brace & World.

Lorenz, K., & Tinbergen, N. (1938). Taxis und Instinkthandlung in der Eirollbewegung der Graugans. *Zeitschrift für Tierpsychologie, 2,* 1–29.

Mackinnon, J. (1974). *In search of the red ape.* London: Collins.

Maier, S.F., & Seligman, M.E.P. (1976). Learned helplessness: theory and evidence. *Journal of Experimental Psychology, 105,* 3–46.

Marler, P.R. (1956). Studies of proximity in chaffinches (3). Proximity as a cause of aggression. *Animal Behaviour, 31*, 32–44.

Marler, P.R. (1970). A comparative approach to vocal learning: song development in white-crowned sparrows. *Journal of Comparative & Physiological Psychology, 71*, 1–25.

Marler, P.R. (1982). Avian and primate communication: the problem of natural categories. *Neuroscience & Biobehavioural Reviews, 6*, 87–94.

Marler, P.R. (1983). Monkey calls: how are they perceived, what do they mean? In J.F. Eisenberg, & D.G. Kleiman (Eds.), *Advances in the study of mammalian behaviour*. Special publication of the American Society of Mammalogists no. 7.

Marler, P.R. (1984). Defining communication. Cited in M. Bright (Ed.), *Animal language*. London: BBC Publications.

Marler, P.R. (1991). Differences in behavioural development in closely related species: birdsong. In P. Bateson (Ed.), *The development and integration of behaviour: essays in honour of Robert Hinde*. London: Cambridge University Press.

Marler, P.R., & Hobbett, L. (1975). Individuality in the long range vocalisations of wild chimpanzees. *Zeitschrift für Tierpsychologie, 38*, 97–109.

Marler, P.R., & Peters, S. (1980). Birdsong and speech: evidence for special processing. In P. Eimas, & J. Miller (Eds.), *Perspectives on the study of speech*. Hillsdale, NJ: Lawrence Erlbaum Associates Inc.

Marler, P.R., & Tamura, M. (1964). Culturally transmitted patterns of vocal behaviour in sparrows. *Science, 146*, 1483–1486.

Marler, P.R., & Waser, M.S. (1977). The role of auditory feedback in canary song development. *Journal of Comparative and Physiological Psychology, 91*, 8–16.

Masserman, J., Wechkin, S., & Terris, W. (1964). "Altruistic" behaviour in rhesus monkeys. *American Journal of Psychiatry, 121*, 584–585.

Matthews, G.V.T. (1955). *Bird navigation*. London: Cambridge University Press.

Maynard Smith, J. (1972). *On evolution*. Edinburgh: Edinburgh University Press.

Maynard Smith, J. (1974). The theory of games and the evolution of animal conflicts. *Journal of Theoretical Biology, 47*, 209–221.

Maynard Smith, J. (1982). *Evolution and the theory of games*. London: Cambridge University Press.

McCabe, B.J., Horn, G., & Bateson, P.P.G. (1981). Effects of restricted lesions of the chick forebrain on the acquisition of filial preferences during imprinting. *Brain Research, 205*, 29–37.

Melrose, D.R., Reed, H.C.B., & Patterson, R.L.S. (1971). Androgen steroids associated with boar odor as an aid to the detection of oestrus in pig artificial insemination. *British Veterinary Journal, 127*, 497–501.

Mendel, G. (1866). Experiments in plant hybridisation. Trans. in J.A. Peters (Ed.), *Classical papers in genetics*. Englewood Cliffs, NJ: Prentice-Hall.

Menzel, E.W., & Halperin, S. (1975). Purposive behaviour as a basis for objective communication between chimpanzees. *Science, 189*, 652–654.

Menzel, G.W. (1984). Human language—who needs it? In G. Ferry (Ed.), *The understanding of animals*. Oxford: Blackwell.

Menzel, R., & Erber, J. (1978). Learning and memory in bees. *Scientific American, 239*(1), 80–87.

Miles, R.C. (1958). Learning in kittens with manipulatory, exploratory and feed incentives. *Journal of Comparative and Physiological Psychology, 51*, 39–42.

Moltz, H. (1960). Imprinting: empirical basis and theoretical significance. *Psychological Bulletin, 57*, 291–314.

Montgomery, K.C. (1954). The role of exploratory drive in learning. *Journal of Comparative and Physiological Psychology, 47*, 60–64.

Morgan, C.L. (1894). *Introduction to comparative psychology.* New York: Scribner's.

Morgan, E. (1973). *The descent of woman.* New York: Bantam Books.

Morgan, E. (1982). *The aquatic ape.* New York: Stein & Day.

Morris, D. (1967). *The naked ape.* London: Cape.

Morris, D. (1981). *The soccer tribe.* London: Cape.

Morton, E.S. (1975). Ecological sources of selection on avian sounds. *American Naturalist, 109*, 17–34.

Moyer, K.E. (1968). Kinds of aggression and their physiological basis. *Communications in Behavioural Biology, 2*, 65–87.

Müller-Hill, B. (1988). *Murderous science: elimination by the scientific selection of Jews, Gypsies and others.* Oxford: Oxford University Press.

Munn, C.A. (1986). Birds that cry "wolf". *Nature, 319*, 143–145.

Murie, A. (1944). *The wolves of Mount McKinley. US Department Interior Fauna Series No 5.* Washington: US Government Printing Office.

Narins, P.M., & Capranica, R.R. (1980). Neural adaptations for processing the 2-note call of the Puerto-Rican tree frog, *Elentherodactylus-coqui. Brain & Behaviour, 17*(1), 48–66.

Nice, M.M. (1943). Studies in the life-history of the song sparrow II. *Transactions of the Linnaean Society of New York, 6*, 1–328.

Noirot, E. (1972). The onset of maternal behaviour in rats, hamsters and mice. *Advances in the Study of Behaviour, 4.*

Norris, K.S., & Dohl, T.P. (1980). Behaviour of the Hawaian Spinner dolphin, *Stenella longirostris. Fish Bulletin, 77*:4, 821–849.

Nottebohm, F. (1981). A brain for all seasons: cyclical anatomical changes in song control nuclei of the canary brain. *Science, 214*, 1368–1370.

Nottebohm, F., & Goldman, S. (1983). Female canary brains grow new cells for song. *Proceedings of the US National Academy of Sciences, 80*, 2390.

Olton, D.S. (1979). Mazes, maps and memory. *American Psychologist, 34*, 583–596.

Packer, C. (1977). Reciprocal altruism in *Papio anubis. Nature, 265*, 441–443.

Packer, C., & Pusey, A. (1982). Co-operation and competition within coalitions of male lions: kin selection or game theory? *Nature, 296*, 740.

Papi, F., Ioale, P., Fiaschi, V., Benvenuti, S., & Baldaccini, N.E. (1978). Pigeon homing: cues detected during the outward journey influence initial orientation. In K. Schmidt-Koenig & W.T. Keeton (Eds.), *Animal migration, navigation and homing.* Berlin: Springer-Verlag.

Parker, G.A. (1974). Assessment strategy and the evolution of fighting behaviour. *Journal of Theoretical Biology, 47*, 223–243.

Patterson, F.G. (1978). The gestures of a gorilla: language acquisition in another pongid. *Brain and Language, 5*, 72–97.

Patterson, F.G. (1979). Conversations with a gorilla. *National Geographic, 154*(4), 438–465.

Pavlov, I.P. (1927). *Conditioned reflexes: an investigation of the physiological activity of the cerebral cortex.* New York: Dover.

Payne, R.S., & McVay, S. (1971). Songs of humpback whales. *Science, 173*, 585–597.

Pearce, J.M. (1987). *An introduction to animal cognition.* Hove: Lawrence Erlbaum Associates Ltd.

Pepperberg, I.M. (1983). Cognition in the African grey parrot: preliminary evidence for auditory/vocal comprehension of the class concept. *Animal Learning and Behaviour, 11*, 179–185.

Pepperberg, I.M. (1986). Acquisition of anomalous communicatory systems: implications for studies on interspecies communication. In R.J. Schusterman, J.A. Thomas, & F.G. Wood (Eds.), *Dolphin cognition and behaviour: a comparative approach*. Hillsdale, NJ: Lawrence Erlbaum Associates Inc.

Piaget, J. (1952). *The origins of intelligence in children*. New York: International Universities Press.

Portmann, A. (1945). Die Ontogenese des Menchen also Problem der Evolutionsforschung. *Verhandlung der schweizerischen naturforschenden Gesellschaft, 1945*, 44–53.

Prechtl, H.F.R. (1953). Zur Physiologie der angeborenen auslosenden Mechanismen I: Quantitative Untersuchungen über die Sperrbewegung junger Singvögel. *Behaviour, 1*, 32–50.

Premack, A.J., & Premack, D. (1972). Teaching language to an ape. *Scientific American, 227*, 92–99.

Premack, D. (1983). Animal cognition. *Annual Review of Psychology, 34*, 351–362.

Pryor, K.W. (1981). Why porpoise trainers are not dolphin lovers: real and false communication in the operant setting. *Annals of the New York Academy of Science, 304*, 137–143.

Pryor, K.W. (1986). Reinforcement training as interspecies communication. In R.J. Schusterman, J.A. Thomas, & F.G. Wood (Eds.), *Dolphin cognition and behaviour: a comparative approach*. Hillsdale: Lawrence Erlbaum Associates.

Pryor, K.W., Haag, R., & O'Reilly, J. (1969). The creative porpoise: training for novel behaviour. *Journal of the Experimental Analysis of Behaviour, 12*, 653–661.

Pye, D. (1980). Adaptiveness of echolocation signals in bats: flexibility in behaviour and in evolution. *Trends in Neurology, 3*, 232–235.

Pyke, G.H. (1979). The economics of territory size and time budget in the golden-winged sunbird. *American Naturalist, 114*, 131–145.

Räber, H. (1948). Analyse des Balzverhaltens eines domestizierten Truthahns (Meleagris). *Behaviour, 1*, 237–266.

Ramsey, A.O., & Hess, E. (1954). A laboratory approach to the study of imprinting. *Wilson Bulletin, 66*, 196–206.

Rasa, O.A.E. (1984). Dwarf mongoose and hornbill mutualism in the Taru desert, Kenya. *Behavioural Ecology and Sociobiology, 12*, 181–190.

Rensch, B., & Altevogt, R. (1953). Visuelles Lernvermögen eines Indischen Elefanten. *Zeitschrift für Tierpsychologie, 10*, 119–134.

Rescorla, R.A. (1968). Probability of a shock in the presence and absence of the CS in fear conditioning. *Journal of Comparative and Physiological Psychology, 66*, 1–5.

Rescorla, R.A. (1972). Informational variables in Pavlovian conditioning. In G.H. Bower (Ed.), *Psychology of learning and motivation Vol. 6*. New York: Academic Press.

Rescorla, R.A., & Solomon, R.L. (1967). Two-process learning theory: relations between Pavlovian conditioning and instrumental learning. *Psychological Review, 74*, 151–182.

Reynolds, V. (1963). Behaviour and social organisation of forest chimpanzees. *Folia Primatologica, 1*, 95–102.

Richards, D.G. (1986). Dolphin vocal mimicry and vocal object labelling. In R.J. Schusterman, J.A. Thomas, & F.G. Wood (Eds.), *Dolphin cognition and behaviour: a comparative approach*. Hillsdale, NJ: Lawrence Erlbaum Associates Inc.

Richards, D.G., Wolz, J.P., & Herman, L.M. (1984). Vocal mimicry of computer-generated sounds and vocal labelling of objects by a bottlenosed dolphin *Tursiops truncatus*. *Journal of Comparative Psychology, 98*, 10–28.

Riechert, S.E. (1978). Games spiders play: behavioural variability in territorial disputes. *Behavioural Ecology and Sociobiology, 3*, 135–162.

Robinson, S.R. (1980). Antipredator behaviour and predator recognition in Belding's ground squirrel. *Animal Behaviour, 28*, 840–852.

Rosch, E.H. (1973). Natural categories. *Cognitive Psychology, 4*, 328–350.

Rose, S. (1983). *Biology, ideology and human nature.* Address delivered to the Annual General Meeting of the Association of the Teaching of Psychology, London.

Rose, S., Kamin, L.J., & Lewontin, R.C. (1984). *Not in our genes: biology, ideology and human nature.* Harmondsworth: Penguin.

Rosenblatt, J.S., & Lehrman, D.S. (1963). Maternal behaviour of the laboratory rat. In H.L. Rheingold (Ed.), *Maternal behaviour in mammals.* New York: Wiley.

Ross, S., Sawin, P.B., Zarrow, M.X., & Denenberg, V.H. (1963). Maternal behaviour in the rabbit. In H.L. Rheingold (Ed.), *Maternal behaviour in mammals.* New York: Wiley.

Rowell, T. (1972). *The social behaviour of monkeys.* Harmondsworth: Penguin.

Rumbaugh, D.M. (1965). Maternal care in relation to infant behaviour in the squirrel monkey. *Psychological Reports, 16*(1), 171-176.

Rumbaugh, D.M. (1975). The learning and symbolising capacities of apes and monkeys. In R.H. Tuttle (Ed.), *Socioecology and psychology of primates.* The Hague: Mouton.

Rumbaugh, D.M. (1977). *Language learning by a chimpanzee: the Lana project.* New York: Academic Press.

Ruppenthal, G.C., Arling, G.L., Harlow, H.F., Sackett, G.P., & Suomi, S.J. (1976). A 10-year perspective of mother-less monkey behaviour. *Journal of Abnormal Psychology, 85*, 341–349.

Savage-Rumbaugh, E.S., & Hopkins, D. (1986). Awareness, intentionality and acquired communicative behaviours: dimensions of intelligence. In R.J. Schusterman, J.A. Thomas, & F.G. Wood (Eds.), *Dolphin cognition and behaviour: a comparative approach.* Hillsdale, NJ: Lawrence Erlbaum Associates Inc.

Savage-Rumbaugh, E.S., McDonald, K., Sevcik, R.A., Hopkins, W.D., & Rupert, E. (1986). Spontaneous symbol acquisition and communication by pygmy chimpanzees *(Pan paniscus). Journal of Experimental Psychology: General, 115*, 211–235.

Savage-Rumbaugh, E.S., Pate, J.L., Lawson, J., Smith, T., & Rosenbaum, S. (1983). Can a chimpanzee make a statement? *Journal of Experimental Psychology: General, 112*, 457–492.

Savage-Rumbaugh, E.S., Rumbaugh, D.M., & Boysen, S.L. (1978). Symbolic communication between two chimpanzees *(Pan troglodytes). Science, 201*, 641–644.

Savage-Rumbaugh, E.S., Rumbaugh, D.M., Smith, S.T., & Lawson, J. (1980). Reference: the linguistic essential. *Science, 210*, 922–925.

Schaffer, H.R., & Emerson, P.E. (1964). The development of social attachments in infancy. *Monographs of social research in child development, 29*, no. 94.

Schaller, G. (1964). *The year of the gorilla.* Chicago: University of Chicago Press.

Scheich, H., Langer, G., Tidemann, C., Coles, R.B., & Guppy, A. (1986). Electroreception and electrolocation in platypus. *Nature, 319*, 401–402.

Schjelderuppe-Ebbe, T. (1922). Beiträge zur Sozialpsychologie des Haushuhns. *Zeitschrift für Psychologie, 88*, 225–252.

Schleidt, M. (1980). Personal odor and nonverbal communication. *Ethology and Sociobiology, 1*, 225–231.

Schlichte, H.J., & Schmidt-Koenig, K. (1971). Zum Heimfindevermögen der Brieftaube bei erschwerte optischer Wahrnehmung. *Naturwissenschaften, 58*, 329–330.

Schneirla, T.C. (1965). Aspects of stimulation and organisation in approach/withdrawal processes underlying vertebrate behaviour development. In D.S. Lehrman, R.A. Hinde, & E. Shaw (Eds.), *Advances in the study of behaviour 1*. New York: Academic Press.

Schneirla, T.C., Rosenblatt, J.S., & Tobach, E. (1963). Maternal behaviour in the cat. In H.L. Rheingold (Ed.), *Maternal behaviour in mammals*. New York: Wiley.

Schusterman, R., & Krieger, K. (1984). California sea lions are capable of semantic comprehension. *The Psychological Record, 34*, 3–23.

Schwartz, B., & Gamzu, E. (1977). Pavlovian control of operant behaviour. In W.K. Honig, & J.E.R. Staddon (Eds.), *Handbook of operant behaviour*. Englewood Cliffs, NJ: Prentice-Hall.

Scott, J.P., & Fredericson, E. (1951). The causes of fighting in mice and rats. *Physiological Zoology, 24*, 273–309.

Seligman, M.E.P. (1970). On the generality of the laws of learning. *Psychological Review, 77*, 406–418.

Seligman, M.E.P. (1971). Phobias and preparedness. *Behaviour Therapy, 2*, 307–320.

Seligman, M.E.P. (1975). *Helplessness: on depression, development and death*. San Francisco: Freeman.

Seuren, P. (1976). Paper delivered at the VI Congress of the International Primatological Society, Cambridge, UK. Reported in "Monitor". In G. Ferry (Ed.), *The understanding of animals* (1984). Oxford: Basil Blackwell.

Seyfarth, D.M., & Cheyney, D.L. (1980). The ontogeny of vervet monkey alarm calling behaviour: a preliminary report. *Zeitschrift für Tierpsychologie, 54*, 37–56.

Seyfarth, D.M., & Cheyney, D.L. (1982). How monkeys see the world: a review of recent research on East African vervet monkeys. In C.T. Snowdon, G.H. Brown, & M.R. Petersen (Eds.), *Primate communication*. London: CUP.

Seyfarth, D.M., Cheyney, D.L., & Marler, P. (1980). Monkey responses to three different alarms: evidence for predator classification and semantic communication. *Science, 210*, 801–803.

Sherman, P.W. (1981). Kinship, demography and Belding's ground squirrel nepotism. *Behavioural Ecology and Sociobiology, 8*, 251–259.

Sherman, P.W. (1985). Alarm calls of Belding's ground squirrels to aerial predators: nepotism or self-preservation? *Behavioural Ecology and Sociobiology, 17*, 313–323.

Skinner, B.F. (1938). *The behaviour of organisms*. New York: Appleton-Century-Crofts.

Skinner, B.F. (1957). *Verbal behaviour*. New York: Appleton-Century-Crofts.

Skinner, B.F. (1969). *Contingencies of reinforcement*. New York: Appleton-Century-Crofts.

Skinner, B.F. (1972). *Beyond freedom and dignity*. Harmondsworth: Penguin.

Slater, P.J.B. (1981). Chaffinch song repertoires: observations, experiments and a discussion of their significance. *Zeitschrift für Tierpsychologie, 56*, 1–24.

Slater, P.J.B. (1983). The study of communication. In T.R. Halliday, & P.J.B. Slater (Eds.), *Communication*. Oxford: Blackwell.

Sluckin, W., & Salzen, E.A. (1961). Imprinting and perceptual learning. *Quarterly Journal of Experimental Psychology, 13*, 65–77.

Smith, W.J., Smith, S.L., Oppenheimer, E.C., & deVilla, J.G. (1977). Vocalisations of the black-tailed prairie dog *Cynomys ludovicianus*. *Animal Behaviour, 25*, 152–164.

Stratton, P.M. (1983). Biological preprogramming of infant behaviour. *Journal of Child Psychology and Psychiatry, 24*(2), 301–309.

Suarez, D., & Gallup, G.G.Jr. (1981). Self-recognition in chimpanzees and orang-utans, but not gorillas. *Journal of Human Evolution, 10*, 175–188.

Suomi, S.J., Collins, M.L., & Harlow, H.F. (1973). Effects of permanent separation from mother on infant monkeys. *Developmental Psychology, 9,* 376–384.

Teas, J. et al. (1982). Aggressive behaviour in the free-ranging rhesus monkeys of Kathmandu, Nepal. *Aggressive Behaviour, 8,* 63–77.

Terrace, H.S. (1979). *Nim.* New York: Knopf.

Thorndike, E.L. (1911). *Animal intelligence: experimental studies.* New York: Macmillan.

Thorpe, W.H. (1961). *Bird-song.* London: Cambridge University Press.

Thouless, C.R., & Guinness, F.E. (1986). Conflict between red deer hinds: the winner always wins. *Animal Behaviour, 34,* 1166–1171.

Tinbergen, N. (1948). Dierkundeles in het meeuwenduin. *De Levende Natur, 51,* 49–56.

Tinbergen, N. (1951). *The study of instinct.* Oxford: Oxford University Press.

Tinbergen, N. (1959). Comparative studies of the behaviour of gulls (*Laridae*): a progress report. *Behaviour, 15,* 1–70.

Tinbergen, N. (1963). On the aims and methods of ethology. *Zeitschrift für Tierpsychologie, 20,* 410–433.

Tinbergen, N., & Perdeck, A.C. (1950). On the stimulus situation releasing the begging response in the newly-hatched herring-gull chick (*Larus argentatus Pont.*). *Behaviour, 3,* 1–39.

Tolman, E.C. (1932). *Purposive behaviour in animals and man.* New York: Century.

Tolman, E.C. (1948). Cognitive maps in rats and men. *Psychological Review, 55,* 189–208.

Trevor, S. (1992). *Survival Special: Keepers of the Kingdom.* Anglia Productions, first broadcast ITV (UK), 21/8/92.

Trivers, R.L. (1971). The evolution of reciprocal altruism. *Quarterly Review of Biology, 46,* 35–57.

Trivers, R.L., & Hare, H. (1976). Haplodiploidy and the evolution of the social insects. *Science, 191,* 249–263.

Tuttle, M.D., & Ryan, M.J. (1981). Bat predation and the evolution of frog vocalisations in the neotropics. *Science, 214,* 677–678.

Tyack, P. (1981). Interactions between singing Hawaiian humpback whales and conspecifics nearby. *Behavioural Ecology, 8*(2), 105–116.

Tyack, P. (1983). Differential response of humpback whales *Megaptera novaengliae* to playback of song or social sounds. *Behavioural Ecology, 13*(1), 49–55.

Uhrich, J. (1938). The social hierarchy in albino mice. *Journal of Comparative Psychology, 25,* 373–413.

Ulrich, R.E., & Azrin, N.H. (1962). Reflexive fighting in response to aversive stimulation. *Journal of the Experimental Analysis of Behaviour, 5,* 511–520.

von Frisch, K. (1950). *Bees: their chemical senses, vision and language.* Ithaca, NY: Cornell University Press.

Walcott, C. (1978). Anomalies in the Earth's magnetic field increase the scatter of pigeon's vanishing bearings. In K. Schmidt-Koenig, & W.T. Keeton (Eds.), *Animal migration, navigation and homing.* Berlin: Springer-Verlag.

Walcott, C., Gould, J.L., & Kirschvinck, J.L. (1979). Pigeons have magnets. *Science, 205,* 1027–1029.

Walcott, C., & Schmidt-Koenig, K. (1973). The effect of anaesthesia during displacement on the homing performance of pigeons. *Auk, 90,* 281–286.

Walker, M.M., Kirschvinck, J.L., Chang, S.-B.R., & Dizon, A.E. (1984). A candidate magnetic sense organ in the yellowfin tuna *Thunnus albacares. Science, 224,* 751–753.

Washburn, S.L., & deVore, I. (1961). The social life of baboons. *Scientific American, 224*(6), 62–71.

Watson, J.B. (1903). *Animal education.* Chicago: University of Chicago Press.

Watson, J.B. (1913). Psychology from the standpoint of a behaviourist. *Psychological Review, 20,* 158–177.

Wells, R.S., Irvine, A.B., & Scott, M.D. (1980). The social ecology of inshore odontecetes. In L.M. Herman (Ed.), *Cetacean behaviour.* New York: Wiley.

Wenner, A.M. (1964). Sound communication in honeybees. *Scientific American, 210,* 116–124.

White, N.R., & Barfield, J. (1987). Role of the ultrasonic vocalisation of the female rat *(Rattus norvegicus)* in sexual behaviour. *Journal of Comparative Psychology, 101,* 73–81.

Wilson, C., & Weston, E. (1947). *The cats of wildcat hill.* New York: Duell, Sloan & Pearce.

Wilson, E.O. (1975). *Sociobiology: the new synthesis.* Cambridge, MA: Harvard University Press.

Wilson, E.O. (1978). *On human nature.* Cambridge, MA: Harvard University Press.

Wilson, E.O., & Bossert, W.H. (1963). Chemical communication among animals. *Record of Progress in Hormone Research, 19,* 673–716.

Wynne-Edwards, V.C. (1962). *Animal dispersion in relation to social behaviour.* New York: Hafner.

Ydenberg, R.G., & Dill, L.M. (1986). The economics of fleeing from predators. *Advances in the Study of Behaviour, 37,* 305–317.

Yeagley, H.L. (1951). A preliminary study of a physical basis of bird navigation II. *Journal of Applied Physiology, 22,* 746–760.

Yerkes, R. (1925). *Almost human.* New York: Century.

Yodlowski, M.L., Kreithen, M.L., & Keeton, W.T. (1977). Detection of atmospheric infrasound by homing pigeons. *Nature, 265,* 725–726.

Zoloth, S.R., & Green, S. (1979). Monkey vocalisations and human speech: parallels in perception? *Brain, Behaviour and Evolution, 16,* 430–442.

Zuckerman, S. (1932). *The social life of monkeys and apes.* New York: Harcourt.

Glossary

Allele: one of a matching pair of genes, located on a particular chromosome and with its opposite number on the matching chromosome.

Altricial animals: animals that are born helpless, or relatively so, and which need a period of intensive nurturing by their parent before they are able to move around, as opposed to precocial animals.

Anthropocentric: centred around human beings—in other words, a way of looking at life which assumes that human beings are the centre and purpose of all evolution.

Anthropomorphism: inferring human thoughts, motives, emotions or values in animal activity—literally, giving their behaviour a human shape.

Associationism: the school of thought which sees all learning as the result of learned connections, or associations, between a stimulus and a response.

Behaviourism: a reductionist school of thought in psychology which argued that thoughts, motives etc were unmeasurable and unobservable, and that a scientific approach to psychology should concern itself only with manifest behaviour.

Cartesian dualism: this takes two forms, although both ultimately derive from the same philosophical reasoning. The first is the idea that the human mind and the body are qualitatively different, with the former being rational while the latter is entirely mechanistic. In its second form, Cartesian dualism is concerned with the distinction between human beings and

animals, claiming that the latter operate entirely mechanistically, while human beings are rational and can think.

Circular argument: an argument that does not permit refutation, because it assumes that its conclusions are valid, and takes them as its starting point.

Cladistics: a process of tracing the evolutionary development of species based on similarity of forms and structures

Conspecific: attributes possessed by members of the same species, but not by members of other species.

Coriolis force: the directional force caused by the Earth's rotation, which produces a tendency towards circumpolar rotational movement.

Diploid: having a full set of genes and chromosomes—in other words, having pairs of chromosomes rather than just once chromosome from each pair.

Displacement: a form of behaviour pattern in which an animal suddenly breaks off a ritualised display and performs some other, apparently irrelevant, behaviour instead.

Empiricism: an approach to knowledge which emphasises measurement and direct observation as the primary source of all knowledge.

Ethology: the study of human or animal behaviour in its natural environment.

Eusocial species: animal species which live in large, closely-related groups such as ants or bees, which maintain shared responsibility for the raising of the species and have differentiated types with differing tasks, all contributing to the welfare of the colony.

Fixed action pattern: a pattern of inherited behaviour which appears in its entirety when triggered by the appropriate stimulus, and which is genetically determined and conspecific.

Genome: the genetic structure of a species, as manifested in the particular sequence of genes and chromosomes which serve to produce a typical member of that species.

Genotype: the genetic structure or make-up of the individual, which interacts with environmental factors to produce the phenotype

Haploid: possessing only half the requisite number of chromosomes for development—one for each pair of chromosomes. This is the characteristic of reproductive cells, and is required for sexual reproduction

Homeostasis: a physiological "steady state" which is maintained by monitoring and feedback systems within the body.

Homology: physical or physiological comparability—being the same, evolutionarily or structurally.

Infrasound: sound which is so low in pitch as to be undetectable by human hearing.

Kinaesthetic senses: the internal senses of the body which are concerned with detecting bodily movement, balance, and position.

Magnetite: an iron-based substance found in some bacteria within animal cells, which appears to contribute to a sense of direction by orienting itself relative to the Earth's magnetic field.

Meiosis: the process by which cells divide to form haploid reproductive cells

Mitosis: the "normal" process of cell division, in which the resulting cells are diploid, not haploid.

Neoteny: the idea that some animals, notably humans, are born at a premature stage of development, which permits a greater contribution of learning to the development of the organism.

Neuroethology: the study of the neurological basis of animal behaviour in the natural environment.

Ontogeny: the development of the individual, from conception onwards.

Principle of parsimony: the idea that, given a choice between two competing explanations, it is more scientifically appropriate to choose the less complex, and therefore more economical, explanation.

Phenotype: the way that the organism develops, as a result of the interaction between its genetic characteristics and its environment.

Pheromone: a chemical transmitted through the air, which carries signals about an animal's physical condition and which influences the hormonal responses of an animal of the same species receiving it.

Phylogeny: the evolutionary development of a given species.

Polyandry: when a female animal has more than one male mate.

Polygyny: when a male animal has more than one female mate.

Precocial animals: animals which achieve physical competence very rapidly after birth or hatching, such that they are able to move freely about their environment.

Reciprocal altruism: a concept used by sociobiologists to explain why animals sometimes act in ways which do not benefit themselves but do benefit others. The idea is that this is an "investment", and that the other animal is likely to return the favour, and thus the act benefits the survival of the doer's genes. Although such explanations are of course possible, they do eventually become rather tortuous, particularly with respect to inter-species co-operation

Reification: the process of treating an adverb as if it were a noun, so that it seems as if an objective "thing" exists, rather than a way of doing things. The classic examples here are the concepts of intelligence and aggression.

Social Darwinism: a right-wing socio-political theory which took the Darwinian idea of "survival of the fittest" to advocate social organisation in which those who were economically disadvantaged or enfeebled should be ignored or allowed to die out. It was used to oppose supportive social practices such as community medical provision or welfare.

Sociobiology: a version of evolutionary theory based on the principle of kin selection, and the idea that the prime mover in evolution is the survival of the genes, not the individual animal. Its undoubted value for understanding eusocial insects led to some rather more questionable extrapolations to other forms of animal society, notably human social behaviour.

Stotting: a vertical leap made by African antelopes when they perceive a predator, immediately before running away. Thought to be a signal to the predator that it has been seen, so pursuit is unlikely to be successful.

Ultrasound: sounds that are too high-pitched for human ears to detect.

Author index

Subject index

functions, 165–6
mechanisms, 163–5
sparrows, 46, 59, 74–5
and territoriality, 118, 119,
    165–6
blackbirds
mobbing, 182, 183
territoriality, 123
bonobos, reconciliation,
145
"bourgeois" strategy, 128
brain
birds, 164
evolutionary
    development, 215–16
humans, 18, 96, 168, 215,
    219
and imprinting, 103–6
butterflies, territoriality,
128–9

canaries, song, 164
capitalism, and evolution,
28–9
Cartesian dualism, 2–3, 45
cats
curiosity, 186–7
learning, 63
parenting, 91
cerebrum, 215, 216, 219
cetaceans
see also dolphins;
    porpoises; whales
communication, 168–72
chaffinches
gaping, 56–7
song, 161–2, 165, 166
cheetahs, hunting, 133–4
chimpanzees
communication, 173–5
dominance, 138, 140–1
and human language,
    198–9
and humans, 14, 18–19,
    36–7

imitation, 185
learning, 69–70
and mirrors, 194
reconciliation, 143–5
and sign language,
    199–201, 203–10
social organisation, 36–7
and territory, 121–2
threat displays, 51, 173
chromosomes, 17, 41–3
cladistics, 114
classical conditioning, 6,
    59–63
cloning, 43
coevolution, 26–7
cognition, 9, 181–212
and classical
    conditioning, 62
cognitive mapping, 187–92
concept formation, 192–5
imitation, 181–6
and language, 197–212
and motivation, 186–7
novelty, 195–7
cognitive mapping, 187–92
colonies, 122
colour, perception of, 150
communication, 147–8
animals with humans,
    197–212
bees, 158–61
birdsong, 161–7
cetaceans, 168–72
chimpanzees, 173–5
and deception, 148–9
about environment,
    158–61, 174–5
and perception, 150–8
symbolic, 175–9
voluntary and
    involuntary, 149
comparative psychology
American tradition, 5, 6
description and
    explanation, 7–9

European tradition, 6–7,
    80
philosophy, 2–3
research, 10
and the Zeitgeist, 36–8
concept formation, 192–5
conditioning, 6
classical, 59–63
operant, 63–9
consummatory behaviour,
    56, 57–8, 113
control, 69
courtship, 79–88
and appropriate mating,
    83
co-operation, 81–3
displays, 81–2
ducks, 7, 46
as fitness display, 85–6
grebes, 50–1, 79, 86–
    87
and improving the breed,
    84–5
lyrebirds, 85–6
manakins, 81–2
and parenting, 86
red deer, 84–5, 127–8
as reinforcing
    pair-bonding, 86–8
spiders, 83–4
sticklebacks, 47, 80–1, 83
and survival, 83–4
and territoriality, 119
crabs, claws, 51–2
critical periods, 74–5,
    218
for imprinting, 99–100
crystallised song, 163
cuckoos, 50
culture, human, 215,
    218–20
curiosity, 186–7

deception, and
    communication, 148–9